EPHESIANS

Brazos Theological Commentary on the Bible

EPHESIANS

M I C H A E L   A L L E N

Brazos Press

a division of Baker Publishing Group
Grand Rapids, Michigan

© 2020 by Michael Allen

Published by Brazos Press
a division of Baker Publishing Group
PO Box 6287, Grand Rapids, MI 49516-6287
www.brazospress.com

Paperback edition published 2021
ISBN 978-1-58743-550-8

Printed in the United States of America

The Library of Congress has cataloged the hardcover edition as follows:
Names: Allen, Michael, 1981– author.
Title: Ephesians / Michael Allen.
Description: Grand Rapids, Michigan : Brazos Press, a division of Baker Publishing Group, 2020. | Series:
    Brazos theological commentary on the Bible | Includes bibliographical references and index.
Identifiers: LCCN 2020018562 | ISBN 9781587430961 (cloth)
Subjects: LCSH: Bible. Ephesians—Commentaries.
Classification: LCC BS2695.53 .A55 2020 | DDC 227/.507—dc23
LC record available at https://lccn.loc.gov/2020018562

In keeping with biblical principles of creation stewardship, Baker Publishing Group advocates the responsible use of our natural resources. As a member of the Green Press Initiative, our company uses recycled paper when possible. The text paper of this book is composed in part of post-consumer waste.

To Daniel J. Treier

CONTENTS

SERIES PREFACE

Near the beginning of his treatise against gnostic interpretations of the Bible, *Against Heresies*, Irenaeus observes that scripture is like a great mosaic depicting a handsome king. It is as if we were owners of a villa in Gaul who had ordered a mosaic from Rome. It arrives, and the beautifully colored tiles need to be taken out of their packaging and put into proper order according to the plan of the artist. The difficulty, of course, is that scripture provides us with the individual pieces, but the order and sequence of various elements are not obvious. The Bible does not come with instructions that would allow interpreters to simply place verses, episodes, images, and parables in order as a worker might follow a schematic drawing in assembling the pieces to depict the handsome king. The mosaic must be puzzled out. This is precisely the work of scriptural interpretation.

Origen has his own image to express the difficulty of working out the proper approach to reading the Bible. When preparing to offer a commentary on the Psalms he tells of a tradition handed down to him by his Hebrew teacher:

> The Hebrew said that the whole divinely inspired scripture may be likened, because of its obscurity, to many locked rooms in our house. By each room is placed a key, but not the one that corresponds to it, so that the keys are scattered about beside the rooms, none of them matching the room by which it is placed. It is a difficult task to find the keys and match them to the rooms that they can open. We therefore know the scriptures that are obscure only by taking the points of departure for understanding them from another place because they have their interpretive principle scattered among them.[1]

---

1. Fragment from the preface to *Commentary on Psalms 1–25*, preserved in the *Philokalia*, in *Origen*, trans. Joseph W. Trigg (London: Routledge, 1998), 70–71.

As is the case for Irenaeus, scriptural interpretation is not purely local. The key in Genesis may best fit the door of Isaiah, which in turn opens up the meaning of Matthew. The mosaic must be put together with an eye toward the overall plan.

Irenaeus, Origen, and the great cloud of premodern biblical interpreters assumed that puzzling out the mosaic of scripture must be a communal project. The Bible is vast, heterogeneous, full of confusing passages and obscure words, and difficult to understand. Only a fool would imagine that he or she could work out solutions alone. The way forward must rely upon a tradition of reading that Irenaeus reports has been passed on as the rule or canon of truth that functions as a confession of faith. "Anyone," he says, "who keeps unchangeable in himself the rule of truth received through baptism will recognize the names and sayings and parables of the scriptures."[2] Modern scholars debate the content of the rule on which Irenaeus relies and commends, not the least because the terms and formulations Irenaeus himself uses shift and slide. Nonetheless, Irenaeus assumes that there is a body of apostolic doctrine sustained by a tradition of teaching in the church. This doctrine provides the clarifying principles that guide exegetical judgment toward a coherent overall reading of scripture as a unified witness. Doctrine, then, is the schematic drawing that will allow the reader to organize the vast heterogeneity of the words, images, and stories of the Bible into a readable, coherent whole. It is the rule that guides us toward the proper matching of keys to doors.

If self-consciousness about the role of history in shaping human consciousness makes modern historical-critical study actually critical, then what makes modern study of the Bible actually modern is the consensus that classical Christian doctrine distorts interpretive understanding. Benjamin Jowett, the influential nineteenth-century English classical scholar, is representative. In his programmatic essay "On the Interpretation of Scripture," he exhorts the biblical reader to disengage from doctrine and break its hold over the interpretive imagination. "The simple words of that book," writes Jowett of the modern reader, "he tries to preserve absolutely pure from the refinements or distinctions of later times." The modern interpreter wishes to "clear away the remains of dogmas, systems, controversies, which are encrusted upon" the words of scripture. The disciplines of close philological analysis "would enable us to separate the elements of doctrine and tradition with which the meaning of scripture is encumbered in our own

---

2. *Against Heresies* 9.4.

day."[3] The lens of understanding must be wiped clear of the hazy and distorting film of doctrine.

Postmodernity, in turn, has encouraged us to criticize the critics. Jowett imagined that when he wiped away doctrine he would encounter the biblical text in its purity and uncover what he called "the original spirit and intention of the authors."[4] We are not now so sanguine, and the postmodern mind thinks interpretive frameworks inevitable. Nonetheless, we tend to remain modern in at least one sense. We read Athanasius and think of him stage-managing the diversity of scripture to support his positions against the Arians. We read Bernard of Clairvaux and assume that his monastic ideals structure his reading of the Song of Songs. In the wake of the Reformation, we can see how the doctrinal divisions of the time shaped biblical interpretation. Luther famously described the Epistle of James as an "epistle of straw," for, as he said, "it has nothing of the nature of the gospel about it."[5] In these and many other instances, often written in the heat of ecclesiastical controversy or out of the passion of ascetic commitment, we tend to think Jowett correct: doctrine is a distorting film on the lens of understanding.

However, is what we commonly think actually the case? Are readers naturally perceptive? Do we have an unblemished, reliable aptitude for the divine? Have we no need for disciplines of vision? Do our attention and judgment need to be trained, especially as we seek to read scripture as the living word of God? According to Augustine, we all struggle to journey toward God, who is our rest and peace. Yet our vision is darkened and the fetters of worldly habit corrupt our judgment. We need training and instruction in order to cleanse our minds so that we might find our way toward God.[6] To this end, "the whole temporal dispensation was made by divine Providence for our salvation."[7] The covenant with Israel, the coming of Christ, the gathering of the nations into the church—all these things are gathered up into the rule of faith, and they guide the vision and form of the soul toward the end of fellowship with God. In Augustine's view, the reading of scripture both contributes to and benefits from this divine pedagogy. With countless variations in both exegetical conclusions and theological frameworks, the same pedagogy of a doctrinally ruled reading of scripture characterizes the broad sweep of the

3. Benjamin Jowett, "On the Interpretation of Scripture," in *Essays and Reviews* (London: Parker, 1860), 338–39.

4. Jowett, "On the Interpretation of Scripture," 340.

5. *Luther's Works*, vol. 35, ed. E. Theodore Bachmann (Philadelphia: Fortress, 1959), 362.

6. *On Christian Doctrine* 1.10.

7. *On Christian Doctrine* 1.35.

Christian tradition from Gregory the Great through Bernard and Bonaventure, continuing across Reformation differences in both John Calvin and Cornelius à Lapide, Patrick Henry and Bishop Bossuet, and on to more recent figures such as Karl Barth and Hans Urs von Balthasar.

Is doctrine, then, not a moldering scrim of antique prejudice obscuring the Bible, but instead a clarifying agent, an enduring tradition of theological judgments that amplifies the living voice of scripture? And what of the scholarly dispassion advocated by Jowett? Is a noncommitted reading—an interpretation unprejudiced—the way toward objectivity, or does it simply invite the languid intellectual apathy that stands aside to make room for the false truism and easy answers of the age?

This series of biblical commentaries was born out of the conviction that dogma clarifies rather than obscures. The Brazos Theological Commentary on the Bible advances upon the assumption that the Nicene tradition, in all its diversity and controversy, provides the proper basis for the interpretation of the Bible as Christian scripture. God the Father Almighty, who sends his only begotten Son to die for us and for our salvation and who raises the crucified Son in the power of the Holy Spirit so that the baptized may be joined in one body—faith in *this* God with *this* vocation of love for the world is the lens through which to view the heterogeneity and particularity of the biblical texts. Doctrine, then, is not a moldering scrim of antique prejudice obscuring the meaning of the Bible. It is a crucial aspect of the divine pedagogy, a clarifying agent for our minds fogged by self-deceptions, a challenge to our languid intellectual apathy that will too often rest in false truisms and the easy spiritual nostrums of the present age rather than search more deeply and widely for the dispersed keys to the many doors of scripture.

For this reason, the commentators in this series have not been chosen because of their historical or philological expertise. In the main, they are not biblical scholars in the conventional, modern sense of the term. Instead, the commentators were chosen because of their knowledge of and expertise in using the Christian doctrinal tradition. They are qualified by virtue of the doctrinal formation of their mental habits, for it is the conceit of this series of biblical commentaries that theological training in the Nicene tradition prepares one for biblical interpretation, and thus it is to theologians and not biblical scholars that we have turned. "War is too important," it has been said, "to leave to the generals."

We do hope, however, that readers do not draw the wrong impression. The Nicene tradition does not provide a set formula for the solution of exegetical problems. The great tradition of Christian doctrine was not transcribed, bound in folio, and issued in an official, critical edition. We have the Niceno-Constantinopolitan Creed, used for centuries in many traditions of Christian worship. We have ancient baptismal affirmations of faith. The Chalcedonian Definition and the creeds and canons of other church councils have their places in official church documents. Yet the rule of faith cannot be limited to a specific set of words, sentences, and creeds. It is instead a pervasive habit of thought, the animating culture of the church in its intellectual aspect. As Augustine observed, commenting on Jeremiah 31:33, "The creed is learned by listening; it is written, not on stone tablets nor on any material, but on the heart."[8] This is why Irenaeus is able to appeal to the rule of faith more than a century before the first ecumenical council, and this is why we need not itemize the contents of the Nicene tradition in order to appeal to its potency and role in the work of interpretation.

Because doctrine is intrinsically fluid on the margins and most powerful as a habit of mind rather than a list of propositions, this commentary series cannot settle difficult questions of method and content at the outset. The editors of the series impose no particular method of doctrinal interpretation. We cannot say in advance how doctrine helps the Christian reader assemble the mosaic of scripture. We have no clear answer to the question of whether exegesis guided by doctrine is antithetical to or compatible with the now-old modern methods of historical-critical inquiry. Truth—historical, mathematical, or doctrinal—knows no contradiction. But method is a discipline of vision and judgment, and we cannot know in advance what aspects of historical-critical inquiry are functions of modernism that shape the soul to be at odds with Christian discipline. Still further, the editors do not hold the commentators to any particular hermeneutical theory that specifies how to define the plain sense of scripture—or the role this plain sense should play in interpretation. Here the commentary series is tentative and exploratory.

Can we proceed in any other way? European and North American intellectual culture has been de-Christianized. The effect has not been a cessation of Christian activity. Theological work continues. Sermons are preached. Biblical scholars produce monographs. Church leaders have meetings. But each dimension of a formerly unified Christian practice now tends to function independently. It is as if a weakened army has been fragmented, and various corps have retreated to isolated fortresses in order to survive. Theology has lost its competence in exegesis.

---

8. *Sermon* 212.2.

Scripture scholars function with minimal theological training. Each decade finds new theories of preaching to cover the nakedness of seminary training that provides theology without exegesis and exegesis without theology.

Not the least of the causes of the fragmentation of Christian intellectual practice has been the divisions of the church. Since the Reformation, the role of the rule of faith in interpretation has been obscured by polemics and counterpolemics about *sola scriptura* and the necessity of a magisterial teaching authority. The Brazos Theological Commentary on the Bible series is deliberately ecumenical in scope because the editors are convinced that early church fathers were correct: church doctrine does not compete with scripture in a limited economy of epistemic authority. We wish to encourage unashamedly dogmatic interpretation of scripture, confident that the concrete consequences of such a reading will cast far more light on the great divisive questions of the Reformation than either reengaging in old theological polemics or chasing the fantasy of a pure exegesis that will somehow adjudicate between competing theological positions. You shall know the truth of doctrine by its interpretive fruits, and therefore in hopes of contributing to the unity of the church, we have deliberately chosen a wide range of theologians whose commitment to doctrine will allow readers to see real interpretive consequences rather than the shadowboxing of theological concepts.

The Brazos Theological Commentary on the Bible endorses a textual ecumenism that parallels our diversity of ecclesial backgrounds. We do not impose the thankfully modest inclusive-language agenda of the New Revised Standard Version, nor do we insist upon the glories of the Authorized Version, nor do we require our commentators to create a new translation. In our communal worship, in our private devotions, and in our theological scholarship, we use a range of scriptural translations. Precisely as scripture—a living, functioning text in the present life of faith—the Bible is not semantically fixed. Only a modernist, literalist hermeneutic could imagine that this modest fluidity is a liability. Philological precision and stability is a consequence of, not a basis for, exegesis. Judgments about the meaning of a text fix its literal sense, not the other way around. As a result, readers should expect an eclectic use of biblical translations, both across the different volumes of the series and within individual commentaries.

We cannot speak for contemporary biblical scholars, but as theologians we know that we have long been trained to defend our fortresses of theological concepts and formulations. And we have forgotten the skills of interpretation. Like stroke victims, we must rehabilitate our exegetical imaginations, and there are likely to be different strategies of recovery. Readers should expect this reconstructive—not reactionary—series to provide them with experiments in postcritical doctrinal interpretation, not commentaries written according to the settled principles of a well-functioning tradition. Some commentators will follow classical typological and allegorical readings from the premodern tradition; others will draw on contemporary historical study. Some will comment verse by verse; others will highlight passages, even single words, that trigger theological analysis of scripture. No reading strategies are proscribed, no interpretive methods foresworn. The central premise in this commentary series is that doctrine provides structure and cogency to scriptural interpretation. We trust in this premise with the hope that the Nicene tradition can guide us, however imperfectly, diversely, and haltingly, toward a reading of scripture in which the right keys open the right doors.

R. R. Reno

AUTHOR'S PREFACE

When undertaking the task of commenting on Ephesians, one best keeps close to the argument of the epistle itself. Therefore, this volume will begin without any extended introduction and launch right into the exposition of the text. Comments on authorship, provenance, and the like will appear in the volume at apposite moments. Such typically introductory comments will also be rather brief. This brevity flows not from a naïveté about simply reading the text in abstraction but from a sense that the available data governing such decisions is rather smaller than typically acknowledged and that the ability to read Ephesians apart from such hypotheses is notably greater than it is with other New Testament texts (given its function as a circular letter). Interpretive attentiveness is as much about opening our eyes to behold the wondrous things in the text as it is about closing off speculative conjecture (in this text's case, far more present in the historical-critical tradition than in any dogmatic imaginations of centuries past).

That said, perhaps a few words about the governing theological assumptions of biblical commentary are helpful by way of clarifying presuppositions. The following seven principles have shaped my approach to commenting on the text of this epistle.

1. Holy scripture serves as an instrument of God's loving address of his people, wherein the exalted Christ continues to exercise his office as prophet and the Holy Spirit even now serves as our promised teacher.
2. To listen to and read through holy scripture is to sit underneath the living and active word of God (Heb. 4:12–13) in the posture of faith and intellectual dependence, humility, and teachableness.

3. Exegesis seeks to follow the way the words run, attending to their varied contexts: a given sentence, paragraph, chapter, book, testament, the whole Bible, and the wider literary conversation regarding God.

4. Exegesis occurs amidst this wider conversation, which not only considers God but frequently does so with regard to the witness of holy scripture. Therefore, theological exegesis of Ephesians or any other canonical text necessarily participates in a traditioned form of intellectual inquiry and best exists within that context in a self-conscious embrace of that social reality, listening to and engaging with the communion of the saints.

5. The goal of a commentary on holy scripture is to help shape *attentiveness* for more contemplative and faithful reading and *imagination* for fuller and more fitting application of the scriptural text.

6. Commentary serves the text and best functions by remaining transparent to the claims of the text and by regularly staying close to the expression of the text in its attempt to help elucidate the judgments of the text, avoiding extraneous jargon as much as possible (realizing, of course, that sometimes clarifying requires turning to terms and categories elsewhere to illumine just what is said here).

7. Listening and then giving intelligible witness about scripture is difficult but not without hope, because the God of the gospel is powerful and wise and intent on communicating that knowledge to his people (see Eph. 1:17–19; 3:16–19).

Surely this commentary fails to enact these principles consistently. And undoubtedly other things could be said; this is no full sketch of hermeneutical theology. The task of listening and then speaking an intelligible and fitting witness is a journey and a battle from which no interpreters can yet extricate themselves. Nonetheless, the principles did provide a rubric and rhythm to walking the path of interpretation as I composed this commentary. They do not guarantee some sort of result or foreclose the process of actually reading the text—one cannot out-theorize sin, even in its intellectual forms—but they do aim to characterize and guide that interpretive activity.

Writing this commentary has not been an isolated task. Indeed, like the apostle, I do not cease to give thanks, remembering many in my prayers, for their kindness to me in the preparation of this book.

First, colleagues at Reformed Theological Seminary helped in a variety of ways. A sabbatical leave helped bring the commentary to completion; for making that possible, I'm grateful especially to Scott Swain, Bob Cara, and Ligon Duncan. John Muether selflessly bore the administrative brunt of my absence during that season, and Christina Mansfield helped with many other details. Librarians Michael Farrell and Lisa Oharek helped with many needed resources. Teaching assistant Josiah Armes helped with copyediting and proofreading, and his watchful eye saved me from many blunders.

Second, I edited the manuscript while enjoying a visiting fellowship at the Faculty of Divinity at the University of Cambridge. I am grateful to colleagues there, not least to Ian McFarland and Peter Harland. Morning conversations with Jono Linebaugh helped refine my judgments and arguments repeatedly. And my family—Emily, Jackson, and Will—willingly moved across the ocean so I could enjoy that opportunity and research environment.

Third, I am grateful for many opportunities to have preached and taught on Ephesians in various congregations through the years, especially for the chance to teach on it at Coral Ridge Presbyterian Church in Fort Lauderdale and then to preach through the text at New City PCA in Orlando.

Fourth, friends at Brazos Press helped with yet another project. I'm grateful that the series editor, Rusty Reno, entrusted this epistle to me and welcomed me as a contributor to the Brazos Theological Commentary on the Bible series. It's a joy to work with my friend Dave Nelson as my editor. The whole team at Brazos has helped bring the manuscript along to completion.

Fifth, Professor John Webster was contracted to write this commentary until his death in May 2016. He did not leave a draft behind that I could consult, yet he did regularly reference Ephesians throughout his many essays. I have tried to bear witness to his profound impact on the field of Christian theology and on me personally by citing him throughout this volume, when and where he would address various sections of the text. While this volume is surely no substitute for what he would have written, I pray it does gesture gratefully toward his lead.

Sixth, a number of friends and colleagues read the manuscript and provided comments or conversation about Ephesians over recent years. Jono Linebaugh, Wesley Hill, Scott Swain, Fred Sanders, and especially Dan Treier have been of particular help in discussing the text and in some cases reading and giving feedback on the entirety of the commentary.

Seventh, the volume is dedicated to Dan Treier: in remembrance of almost two decades of kindness, encouragement, wisdom, and good cheer; in gratitude for his continued devotion to a friend, evident not least in his help with this specific volume; and in hopes of many years of friendship still ahead.

ABBREVIATIONS

General

→   indicates a cross-reference to within this commentary on passages in Ephesians

Bibliographic

CD   Karl Barth. *Church Dogmatics*. 4 vols. Edinburgh: T&T Clark, 1956–75.

ST   Thomas Aquinas. *Summa Theologiae*. Blackfriars edition. 61 vols. Edited by Thomas Gilby and T. C. O'Brien. New York: McGraw-Hill, 1964–80.

Old Testament

Gen.	Genesis	Esther	Esther
Exod.	Exodus	Job	Job
Lev.	Leviticus	Ps. (Pss.)	Psalm (Psalms)
Num.	Numbers	Prov.	Proverbs
Deut.	Deuteronomy	Eccl.	Ecclesiastes
Josh.	Joshua	Songs	Song of Songs
Judg.	Judges	Isa.	Isaiah
Ruth	Ruth	Jer.	Jeremiah
1–2 Sam.	1–2 Samuel	Lam.	Lamentations
1–2 Kings	1–2 Kings	Ezek.	Ezekiel
1–2 Chron.	1–2 Chronicles	Dan.	Daniel
Ezra	Ezra	Hosea	Hosea
Neh.	Nehemiah	Joel	Joel

Amos	Amos	Hab.	Habakkuk
Obad.	Obadiah	Zeph.	Zephaniah
Jon.	Jonah	Hag.	Haggai
Mic.	Micah	Zech.	Zechariah
Nah.	Nahum	Mal.	Malachi

New Testament

Matt.	Matthew	1–2 Thess.	1–2 Thessalonians
Mark	Mark	1–2 Tim.	1–2 Timothy
Luke	Luke	Titus	Titus
John	John	Phlm.	Philemon
Acts	Acts	Heb.	Hebrews
Rom.	Romans	Jas.	James
1–2 Cor.	1–2 Corinthians	1–2 Pet.	1–2 Peter
Gal.	Galatians	1–3 John	1–3 John
Eph.	Ephesians	Jude	Jude
Phil.	Philippians	Rev.	Revelation
Col.	Colossians		

EPHESIANS 1

1:1 Paul, an apostle of Christ Jesus by the will of God, to the saints who are faithful in Christ Jesus:

These words have roots near and far. They begin with an identification of their near or proximate cause: it is Paul who writes here. Paul the apostle plays a decisive role, displayed across a full half of the New Testament. His upbringing and conversion as well as his ministry and writing appear on display for posterity. When we read that this text comes from Paul, we have an unusual measure of specific familiarity compared to other writings from the first century. There is a deeper cause, however, for Paul is identified only as the author in his apostolic service. That term "apostle" itself points beyond and before to the very one who had sent him: to Jesus Christ. We do well, then, to heed the words of this epistle by attending to its sources near and far.

First, Paul is identified as the author in this first verse. Questions have been raised about whether this is the historical Paul or a literary Paul. While Christians classically took Paul to be the author in every sense of the term, many moderns have suggested a more complex or indirect authorial reference.

Why do many believe Paul incapable or unlikely of penning this text? Several reasons have been offered, and sometimes they are not sufficiently distinguished (especially helpful in laying out the critical arguments are K. Barth 2017: 55–58 and Fowl 2012: 9–28). First, doubters claim that the vocabulary and style differ so significantly from the undisputed Pauline texts as to be written by another. Second, the themes and theology of the letter are noted as being divergent, not least regarding its eschatology. Third, the close relationship to Colossians (itself a disputed letter in modern scholarship) is taken by some to render Pauline authorship impossible. If Ephesians depends on Colossians, and if Colossians is not of

Paul himself, then Ephesians is not either. What would be the effects? Ephesians has been recognized as a canonical text and, from earliest days, received as a Pauline text. While its canonical status is not likely to be jeopardized, reading it as written by another would require a rethinking of what might be meant by the authorship claim in the first verse. Most argue that it would be written by a disciple of Paul, even one authorized by Paul and drawing on and extending Paul's apostolic commitments. It is worth noting, however, that pseudepigraphic literature was not typically viewed in the early Christian era with anything but disdain. Would someone close to Paul dare to write under his name if it was a practice viewed with suspicion? Wouldn't statements from Paul himself condemning false claims of authorship lead any purported "Pauline community" to express hesitation in this regard (2 Thess. 2:1–2; 3:17)? Or would that not be disrespectful? One would either need a more positive valuation of a pseudepigraphic text or need to venture the more radical suggestion that someone unconnected to Paul was doing so.

What sense do we make of these arguments? These three threads need to be examined individually and cumulatively. First, stylistic arguments turn on the nature of distinctive vocabulary. Ephesians has 2,429 words, with 530 distinct words; of these terms, only 84 do not appear in the Pauline writings, and 41 do not appear anywhere else in the New Testament. Such numbers are almost exactly paralleled in the case of Galatians: its 2,200 words involve a vocabulary of 526 words, of which 80 do not appear elsewhere in Paul, and 35 (more if one counts proper names) do not appear anywhere else in the New Testament. Yet Galatians is treated as an undisputed text (Fowl 2010: 20). The style of Ephesians admittedly includes longer, more complex sentences than are typical in Paul's writings (e.g., Eph. 1:3–14). However, stylistic argument and distinct vocabulary do rather little to suggest substantive reasons for suspecting the traditional attestation.

Second, many argue that Ephesians does not operate with the apocalyptic viewpoint typical of Paul's writings. It does not speak always under the looming sense of an imminent end. Instead, it ventures to speak of households and order and rhythms of communal life that point toward long-term formation. The presence of household codes here serves as the most pointed illustration of Ephesians' uniqueness and even jars many moderns to doubt Pauline authorship. But are the household codes really that different from Paul's teaching on social relations in the undisputed texts? Some argue that they conflict with Gal. 3:26–28, though that is questionable (→5:22–6:9). They surely do not conflict with principles of authority and submission latent in Rom. 12:3–8 and 13:1–7. Ephesians does add eschatological elements that are less obvious in texts such as 1 Corinthians or Galatians, but we have to ask if that is a reason to doubt Ephesians' authorship claims. For instance, Romans and Galatians are frequently viewed as speaking rather differently about the law; even if they are read coherently, as they should, each still highlights different elements in its own distinct way. Why in modern critical study do differences on Torah not manifest an insurmountable rupture prompting doubt about authorship but different eschatological emphases do? All in all, there are good internal and external reasons not to take theological distinctiveness as a reason for doubting authorship claims (K. Barth 2017: 58; Fowl 2010: 22–25).

Third, Ephesians does speak in ways that parallel Colossians. If one surveyed recent commentators, one would likely get a sense that Colossian priority is favored, though many differ or hesitate to speak confidently one way or another. Indeed, making such judgments is speculative at best, remarkably tendentious at worst (for the complications, see charts and analyses in Talbert 2007: 4–6). Yet all would agree that the texts run parallel in terms of vocabulary, themes, and style. Of course, these parallels might help augment a case that neither text is as *alter*-Pauline as modern critical readers suppose (though they may differ from undisputed Paulines, they have notable commonalities as a Pauline subcorpus). In a real sense, this third line of argument serves to countermand the previous two: the parallels here show that whatever distinctiveness is present in Ephesians is present not only there but, to some extent and in sometimes diverging ways, in Ephesians *and* Colossians. Therefore, the parallels with Colossians offer no prompt to judge Ephesians as less likely Pauline and may well help augment the case that the style and substance of Ephesians is even less idiosyncratic than often judged (given that it is shared also by Colossians in so many cases). For a similar argument, see especially Karl Barth (2017: 56–57).

What about early interpreters? What was the church's judgment prior to the modern era? The earliest attestation of the text is indisputably Pauline: see *1 Clement* 46.6; Ignatius, *To the Ephesians* 1.1–2; Polycarp, *To the Philippians* 12.1; Irenaeus, *Against Heresies* 5.2.3, 5.8.1; and Clement of Alexandria, *Stromateis* 4.8. At least two early texts evidence awareness of the category of pseudepigraphic texts and yet speak distinctly of Ephesians as being Pauline: Tertullian's *Prescription against Heretics* 36 and the Muratorian Fragment. Presumably these figures and communities would have had a broader sense of Greek style and vocabulary, of thematic and generational change regarding theology, and of the expanding Pauline corpus (not least Colossians and its relationship to Ephesians). That some of them overtly talk about texts in the primitive Christian milieu that are pseudepigraphic and yet specifically judge that Ephesians is authentic is no small thing. Given the flimsy nature of critical arguments, each of which is weak on its own and only further weakened when viewed together, over against this global affirmation of early witnesses, we have every reason to take the text's claim to Pauline authorship at face value. It may be that we have reason to take purportedly historical-critical objections as being in this particular case neither historical nor critical.

The epistle itself suggests that Paul is frankly the least interesting of the causes of this scripture. Paul does not flourish his own experience with a congregation, nor does he allude to his own future plans herein. Whereas other epistles penned by this apostle to the Gentiles trace back their testimony to deep familiarity or tease out the hopes for ministry yet to come, Ephesians does not bear such marks. In its finale, we will hear a brief and blunt word: "So that you also may know how I am and what I am doing, Tychicus the beloved brother and faithful minister in the Lord will tell you everything. I have sent him to you for this very purpose, that you may know how we are, and that he may encourage your hearts" (6:21–22). One name (Tychicus), one action (sending him to report), one goal (that they might be encouraged by this update). Clearly Paul's pastoral pedigree, much less his present struggle (→3:1), do not factor heavily into this writing.

Paul's personal reserve does not suggest some kind of unmooring of his identity. He is not going the route of abject self-immolation. His biographical brevity takes the form of captivation. Someone more significant must be attested. Someone else's action must be confessed and communicated. That someone finds reference in two ways. First, Paul labels himself in such a way that is externally rooted by calling himself an "apostle." This term connotes genuine authority and vital responsibility, to be sure, but it is wholly derived from another. Karl Barth comments, "There is something exceptional and impossible about him, but it is not his genius, his experience, his unmediated knowledge, or anything that can be accounted for psychologically as greatness or character." There is a mortification of his own meaningfulness, yet Barth follows with a vivification of his place: "What makes him an apostle is his mission, his instructions, and the service he is to offer, which are not, from a psychological point of view, even *his own matter* but the matter that *has him* and sends him" (K. Barth 2017: 60). To be an apostle is, at its root, to be sent by another. Paul names himself as one sent by Christ Jesus, the exalted Son (→3:7–10). The risen Christ addressed Paul, stunning him and in so doing saving him from a mangled posture toward his lordship (see further Acts 9). Elsewhere Paul will insist that, though he was a persecutor of the church, God "was pleased to reveal his Son to me, in order that I might preach him among the Gentiles" (Gal. 1:16). That statement prompts us to note the second way in which Paul points to someone behind himself: his apostleship comes "by the will of God."

Ephesians will point time and again beyond the surface affairs and the obvious perceptions we might take in. A key purpose of the letter, explicitly so (→1:17–19; 3:16–19), is to reshape the spiritual sense or sensitivity of the reader. Paul intends to stretch the dimensional constraints of our sight, lest our myopia incline us to miss the most interesting activity. This expansion of imagination comes even in the naming of the author, for Paul will not let us go a hair's breadth without characterizing himself as sent by another and, ultimately, as an apostle whose ministry is rooted in the eternal purposes of the God who wills. To qualify Paul's role in this way does not denigrate the benefits of reading his text like other texts. We can bring the tools of literary criticism to bear in reading Ephesians, alert to its scope, shape, and sequence. And yet there is more that we dare not miss. These words and this testimony to the nations have mysterious roots all the way back in God's eternity (→3:1–3), and thus we expect more here than we would from other texts (be they ancient or contemporary). While we might read this text with much profit against its background in the Greco-Roman world, the history of Jewish literature, and the development of early Christian instruction, we nonetheless must—absolutely must—attend to these words with a commitment to perceive them as another instance of divine gift.

These words also have a target that is both specific and suggestive. The specific target has been debated as to whether a particular locale comes in for address here: "who are in Ephesus." The more suggestive address ranges more widely: "to the saints who are faithful in Christ Jesus." We do well to consider the possible local reference, to reflect on the text-critical issues present here as well as the title appended to the epistle ("The Letter of Paul to the Ephesians"). As with the authorship question, so here many make a large deal of this question; yet the interpretative payoff is markedly less significant (whereas the authorship question at least has potential ramifications for how one interprets 3:1–13; 4:1; 6:20).

Brevard Childs (2008) reminds us that Ephesians comes to us amidst a collection of letters and that its placement therein bears significance. The relationship to Colossians is no doubt the most intriguing, given the verbal and thematic parallels. But we read Ephesians as part of a larger corpus that circulated together and has been received by Christians as a whole. Indeed, we might say that Ephesians plays a distinctive and hermeneutical role in the church's reception of that

Pauline collection, for it alone bears the marks of a letter unmoored from local crises and particular anachronisms. While the other letters all commend Christ in relation to various flare-ups, Ephesians alone does not manifest a concern to address a significant controversy. Given this, it provides something of a Pauline melody against which we might read the other letters, noting where they fall in step and where they introduce new movements for pastoral reasons. All this has to be related to the admittedly complex documentary evidence, which may tilt toward omitting the phrase "who are in Ephesus" and the title "to the Ephesians" (on which see Thielman 2010: 12–16). Omission is the harder reading (the key question being: why would it ever be omitted once included?), and thus slightly more promising on text-critical grounds. We have reasons, admittedly tentative, to read the text minus the reference to Ephesus (though, of course, it likely circulated—even intentionally—to Ephesus among other cities in Asia Minor).

Returning to the words of 1:1, then, we must attend to Paul's address to "the saints who are faithful in Christ Jesus." Three things are worthy of attention. First, Paul writes to "the saints." Other items will be attested regarding their experience, history, and character, ranging from their moral, ethnic, cultural, and contextual description. Yet Paul fixes on their holiness at the inception of the letter. He distinguishes them as set apart, for that is what it means to be a saint. He views them in another dimension, we might say, from those who share so many other demographic commonalities with these men and women. In many ways, Ephesians provides a set of lenses or spectacles through which we see the church as what we confess to be "the communion of saints."

Second, the saintliness of these addressees is bound up with their being "faithful." The term employed here, *pistois*, marks them apart by means of that uniquely Christian virtue. Christians do well to remember that faith is not a universal honorific. Saints are those defined and set apart by their life of trust. There is something remarkably self-effacing in the terminology here, reminding us that saintliness is shaped by a life of appropriate dependence. The elites of Asia Minor, like the well-to-dos of the modern world today, ran in cultures marked by their pompous bravado. The gospel summons us to a notably different posture: trust. The apostle does name the moral virtue of the church, but it is a moral transformation that itself points away from control and composure to deeper roots in the divine character, in the one in whom we place trust.

Third, these saints are "faithful *in Christ Jesus*." Here we have allusion to what will quickly become overt in the epistle—namely, that the most significant realities about its audience are bound up with their union with Jesus Christ. Ephesians opens up a new dimension of life in the Christian community, illumining the personal and social tie held in union with Jesus Christ. Even the letter's addressees cannot be stated without casting an eye to the deeper realities amidst them. Just as saintliness ought not be thought of apart from the uniquely Christian dignity received from God above, so we dare not attend to the value of that faith apart from its roots in its object—that is, "in Christ Jesus." Reformational theology was so moved by this reality—that faith's significance lies in its object—as to address the matter regularly in catechisms. "Q. Why do you say that you are righteous by faith alone? A. Not because I please God by virtue of the worthiness of my faith, but because the satisfaction, righteousness, and holiness of Christ alone are my righteousness before God, and because I can accept it and make it mine in no other way than by faith alone" (Heidelberg Catechism 61; see also Westminster Larger Catechism 73). Ephesians characterizes saintly faith ultimately by its object, fundamentally by its union with Jesus himself.

1:2 Grace to you and peace from God our Father and the Lord Jesus Christ.

These words can easily be passed over and treated as mere rhetorical flourish, yet they deserve a careful and attendant gloss, for we find that they are an invitation to the depths of what the letter itself addresses. Paul wishes grace and peace for them, and we will see that these are the elements of his argument. He will describe God's kind gift and will sketch its harmonious effects. He will be satisfied neither to praise God's largesse without tracing out its impact into real lives, nor with any attempt to consider the practical contours of Christian life apart from seeing their source in God's agency. He highlights this twinned relationship—grace and peace—by locating both personally in the action that comes "from God our Father and the Lord Jesus Christ."

Similar greetings mark the beginning of many Pauline letters (Rom. 1:7; 1 Cor. 1:3; 2 Cor. 1:2; Gal. 1:3; Phil. 1:2; 2 Thess. 1:2; Phlm. 3). Indeed, the greeting can be found also in non-Pauline writings of the New Testament (1 Pet. 1:2; 2 Pet. 1:2; Rev. 1:4), so that it likely represents a fundamental and widespread Christian greeting (M. Barth 1974a: 71). We ought not be surprised, for Paul's corpus addresses contingent circumstances with a consistent eye to the singular gift of God in Christ and its many ripple effects in renewing human life and community. No crisis marks this letter, and that makes this phrase's presence all the more telling. Paul's interventions into strife and his missive into the ecclesiological calm are attended by the same desire: whether in good times or bad, grace is needed, and peace is meant to follow, and this comes only "from God our Father and the Lord Jesus Christ."

What precisely can we say about this grace and the peace that the apostle wishes for these readers? Grace refers to the kindness and mercy of the Lord toward his people. Other terms—justice and righteousness most notably—would address the kind of reciprocity and equity that mark this relationship, but grace marks out the way in which God is the giver of gifts. *Charis* can and does "perfect" gifts in various ways in Jewish and Greco-Roman literature; Paul will characterize the gift of God in a number of notable ways that can only be discerned by reading on (Barclay 2015). And this incremental revelation is the point, for this invocation of blessing and this desired effect are meant to gesture toward the broader argument of the epistle. As we read, we look for grace and the way in which it will be defined, shaped by the unfolding witness of the text. Too easily, discussions of Paul's presentation of the gospel tend toward assuming that grace is a known reality and only its opposite—"works" in many contexts, sin in others—requires specification. Too often, recent New Testament scholarship has suggested that grace was an idea permeating the Jewish mindset (Sanders 1977), pointing to the presence of the term in texts from that and previous eras. Yet those comparative arguments frequently fail to see that notable texts such as Wisdom of Solomon speak often of grace, to be sure, albeit in ways from which Paul diverged notably (Barclay 2015; Linebaugh 2013a). Whereas Wisdom would define grace as a gift given to one who would put it to optimal use, Paul understands grace as the favor shown to the ungodly, the enemy, the dead. The epistle will have to train us to hear "gift" well—that is, in a way that befits the Christian.

Peace speaks of the social character of the community marked by this grace (see especially the repeated reference in 2:14, 15, 17). Whereas "maturity" is the common term for wholeness of the Christian self (see Matt. 5:48; Heb. 5:14; cf. Eph. 4:13), peace characterizes the Christian society in terms of wholeness. Jonathan Pennington (2017: 71–72) highlights a number of texts in the Old Testament (Gen. 26:29; 34:21; Ps. 122:6; Zech. 6:13) that employ the term *shalom* to convey this notion of wholeness. Ephesians later characterizes the gospel of our Lord as "the gospel of peace" (Eph. 6:15). This epistle conveys the notion of wholeness in terms of persons (ch. 2) and gifts (ch. 4), so that again a desired effect of reading this letter serves as a benchmark or guide for our further meditation (see M. Barth 1974a: 74). We dare not presume to know intuitively what peace would be. It is far too easy for malformed hopes of what we name as harmony actually to be problems, in which case the gospel is but a disrupting and transforming answer. But Paul reminds us frequently that Christ not only answers deep human questions but also grants us still greater questions. Like the psalmist, we find here that God not only answers our prayers but calls us toward a more penetrating sense of reality and of our real need. Peace given by this God is not the mere absence of our distastes nor the presence of our wants, but a wholeness to which our present yearnings must be transfigured.

So the message involves grace and peace, a twofold blessing that is addressed again at the letter's conclusion: "Peace be to the brothers, and love with faith, from God the Father and the Lord Jesus Christ. Grace be with all who love our Lord Jesus Christ with love incorruptible" (6:23–24). Note that the order of grace and peace is reversed here: it forms a chiasm of sorts with the opening. At the end the letter sums up how we live together in love (peace) and reminds the reader of how we are rooted (grace).

These easily overlooked realities are not only significant as abstract or universal realities; they are "to you." The promise of the text does not simply offer proverbial pontification about the ways of the world but attests to what God has given "to you." The personal and intimate—that which is deeply formative of one's self—is addressed by this.

Neither the cause (of God's grace) nor the call (to societal peace) can be presumed upon, so Paul goes on to define and particularize. These aspired hopes are "from God our Father and the Lord Jesus Christ." Paul does not hesitate to use causal language with regard to God (*apo*, "from") when speaking of this gift and the wholeness that it brings to our common life, but we must see that the causal language pushes deeper underneath the seemingly material or immanent conditions of human life. "God our Father" and the "Lord Jesus Christ" cannot be restricted to monikers for a tribal deity and a mere Jewish man. These terms *theou* and *kyriou* bespeak divine identity; as with its other occurrences in apostolic scripture, the appellation of *kyrios* to the person of Jesus identifies this one as the God of Israel, the great I AM (see Exod. 3:14). David Yeago (1994) and Kavin Rowe (2009) have helped sketch the ways in which the apostle Paul, like the later evangelists, applies this transcendent name (the name used to mark out the God of Exod. 3:14) to Jesus himself.

The God named here is the one who bears perfection, then, as God and Lord, but he is also the one whose perfection expresses itself in drawing near to his people. So this one is not only Father to the eternal Son, but out of that eternal generation of the Son he willfully pursues adopted children so that we too might address him as "our Father." This Lord can be named with a terribly common

Jewish name, Jesus (or Joshua), yet he uniquely bears a title and an office that was long anticipated by his people, the Messiah or Anointed One (*Christou*, "Christ"). We will see throughout the coming verses that the God of eternity shows no embarrassment or aloofness but takes up this world and even the blood found therein. His glory can and does extend into the seemingly messy and minute. C. S. Lewis once commented that the modern British are skittish toward believing that partaking of common elements such as bread and wine has any genuine religious benefit; but the creator and sustainer of the world does not share this view.[1] He delights to condescend in such a way. As he does not remain aloof but makes himself near through the sacraments, so here he makes himself known in this Jesus.

1:3 Blessed be the God and Father of our Lord Jesus Christ, who has blessed us in Christ with every spiritual blessing in the heavenly places,

God may be blessed. God has blessed us. Understanding the relationship of these two statements proves remarkably significant. Here eternity and history seem to face each other. In this verse the mutable and the immutable are drawn together. But can they stand together, or will they collapse on one another?

Modern theologians have suggested increasingly that God's capacity to bless us hangs on his own involvement within and openness to our history. Ronald Goetz speaks of the "new orthodoxy" of the "suffering God," seeking to explain what has been a groundswell in Christian theology since the Holocaust, owing to the pathbreaking work of figures like Jürgen Moltmann and revisionary texts like his *Crucified God*.[2] The vulnerable God can bless us in Christ—that is, in the cross and the sorrow of this redeemer. Blessing can resound on this God as well. Indeed, theologians such as Robert Jenson have argued that involvement in history can be an ontological perfection.[3] This sort of sketch, what Jenson might call an effort at evangelizing our metaphysics, seems on the surface to accord with the reciprocal blessings mentioned here.

Will the broader context allow for such a rendering? Will the way the words run here in 1:3 even support this tendency? Context seems to complicate matters, first, for there is a notably jarring set of phrases appearing throughout this long sentence that will run through 1:14. We do not avoid anything approaching

1. C. S. Lewis, *Mere Christianity* (New York: Macmillan, 1978), 65.
2. Ronald Goetz, "The Suffering God: The Rise of a New Orthodoxy," *Christian Century* (April 16, 1986): 385–89; Jürgen Moltmann, *The Crucified God: The Cross of Christ as the Foundation and Criticism of Christian Theology*, trans. R. A. Wilson and John Bowden (New York: Harper & Row, 1974).
3. Robert Jenson, *Systematic Theology*, vol. 1, *The Triune God* (Oxford: Oxford University Press, 1997).

reciprocity out of adherence to a perfect-being theology that draws on abstract or ideal speculation. That would be the way of assumption and premonition, which we might methodologically call speculation and spiritually diagnose as idolatry. But we do listen to Ephesians itself and hear a bracing call that God stands alone, not isolated but singular nonetheless. John Webster has argued that "the passage is scattered with gestures toward God's wholly realized life":

> The blessings with which God has blessed us in Christ are "in the heavenly places" (1:3)—in the "highest heavens," that is, the place where God and his Christ are ineffably exalted, "far above" (4:10), from where Christ exercises his universal and supreme lordship over "things in heaven and things on earth" (1:10).
>
> These divine blessings flow, moreover, from the eternal relations of Father and Son: God the Father chose us in Christ "before the foundation of the world" (1:4); created circumstance follows and does not cause or shape divine election.
>
> And so God the Father is "the Father of glory" (1:17), the inextinguishable source of light and radiant presence; God the Son is one who is again "far above" (1:21)—not a mere competing power or name, not circumscribed by spatial or temporal locale, but the universal and self-authored presence that can emerge only from the infinite recesses of God's own life.
>
> What is manifest, therefore, in the mission of Christ is God's mysterious will (1:9): Christ's work flows from and makes apprehensible the antecedent divine purpose, which is not reactive but which comprehends and forms created history.
>
> He "who fills all in all" (1:23) is in himself replete, filling all things but filled by none; and so there is a creation and a redemptive history and a church. (Webster 2011: 390–91)

In light of these hints of perfect transcendence, then, we might be inclined to say that the Blessed One who blesses is not himself blessed because he blesses but was already blessed, is already blessed, and shall evermore be blessed. Return of blessing there may be, but we dare not render this in terms of easy reciprocity or a tit-for-tat and quid pro quo sketch of life with God.

Substantively, this is compelling. But the syntax actually proffers a more straightforward path when read in its Old Testament context. The opening call that God is blessed (*berakhah*) regularly occurs throughout the Psalter: "'Blessed be God . . .' (Ps. 66:20); 'Blessed be the LORD, the God of Israel' (Ps. 41:13, etc.)" (Bruce 1984: 253). The language of blessing—that God may be blessed and the one who blesses—employs the same verbal term to connote God's enlivening of us and our praising or magnifying his name.

What is 1:3 commending if not a straightforward reciprocity of constitutive blessings? The God who blessed us is the one who shall still be himself blessed. God blesses in ways that seem costly, sacrificing his Son for the sins of the world. Yet redemption does not mark the course of God's giving himself away. The God who blesses us does so without thereby giving up his own blessedness. Ephesians 1:3 prompts us for what will be repeated in various prepositional phrases—namely, the participatory shape of our salvation and the mystery of life in union with God in Christ (see "in him" in 1:4, 7, 10, 11, 13; "in the Beloved" in 1:6; "in Christ" in 1:3, 9). The mediating work of the Son enfolds others into his own blessedness rather than passing off that blessedness like a possession whose ownership is always and only a zero-sum matter.

Yet we must go further: not only is this God not giving himself away in giving his only Son, but he is all the more blessed in that he is now also enthroned on the praises of his people (Ps. 22:3). While it is not constitutively reciprocal, there is a mysteriously responsive *berakhah* offered back to the Lord. Not only has God gone up with a shout (Ps. 47:5), but God's grace has now gone up with a shout. "Blessed be the name of the Lord"—this is the refrain of the people who have themselves been blessed. That metaphysical distinction between God's blessing them into life and their creaturely blessing offered as praise and acclaim to the God of all life implicitly states the great matter of Christian theology—namely, the perfect God's presence with his people for their blessing and his glory.

So this "God and Father of our Lord Jesus Christ" is blessed now and forevermore. And this in spite of his blessing us—nay, *even as* he "has blessed us in Christ with every spiritual blessing in the heavenly places." He has not withheld his highest glory from us but has shared "every spiritual blessing," yet this largesse has not thereby stripped him of his resources. God's glory is not a capital fund of fully private property but, in the gospel, becomes a social good for those "in Christ." And his generosity has not overwhelmed our finite frame either, for this capital glory exists "in the heavenly places."

Ephesians will repeatedly seek to draw our attention to things heavenward. In many ways, chapters 1–3 especially, as well as the epistle as a whole, explode what Charles Taylor calls the "immanent frame."[4] Like looking afresh through 3-D glasses, we are now able to see reality in its depth dimension. While we may be overwhelmed and waylaid by what is mundane or worse, in Christ we have all spiritual or godly goodness in the heavenly places. Paul will shortly turn to label

4. Charles Taylor, *A Secular Age* (Cambridge, MA: Belknap, 2007), 539.

this rich blessing as the inheritance of an adopted people, sons and daughters of the most high King (→1:5).

1:4 even as he chose us in him before the foundation of the world, that we should be holy and blameless before him.

Ephesians 1:4 points backward and forward. Its connections seek to show the deep source and the high purpose of God's rich, heavenly blessings given through Jesus Christ. Ephesians offers a vivid portrait of the present, obliterating the reductively immanent frame by taking in the heavenly spectrum but also by sketching the present as part of a deeper narrative. The text resituates us within a broader metaphysics of heaven and earth and a wider narrative that runs no shorter than Alpha to Omega.

First, this verse points backward by taking up the language of choice and election. The term used here, *exelexato*, appears infrequently in Paul (cf. 1 Cor. 1:27–28) but more commonly in the Gospels and Acts. This choice occurred "before the foundation of the world," suggesting its precedence and eternal depth. The term connotes choice and selection, alluding to the exercise of the divine will in designating these persons as objects of God's own election.

Second, this verse also gestures forward to the intended aims of Christ's heavenly blessings—namely, "that we should be holy and blameless before him." Note that holiness and blamelessness are not completely synonymous. We see this distinction even in Leviticus: "You are to distinguish between the holy and the common, and between the unclean and the clean" (10:10). Cleanliness or blamelessness is preferable to being unclean and blameworthy. Yet purity is not itself holiness. Holiness demands a still further devotion to the Lord. The holy is clean rather than unclean, but also holy as opposed to common. Christ blesses us not only that we might be purified from sin but that we might be alive to God (*coram Deo*, "before God").

1:5–6 In love he predestined us for adoption as sons through Jesus Christ, according to the purpose of his will, to the praise of his glorious grace, with which he has blessed us in the Beloved.

Ephesians 1:5–14 now runs through the three tenses of Christian salvation with greater attentiveness to details. Verses 5–6 specifically return to that eternal past, wherein God's electing will was upon these saints "before the foundation of the world."

This previous choice is now termed "predestination," and Paul clarifies that it occurs "in love." We have to read Eph. 1:5 in light of the rest of the epistle. In this case Eph. 2:1–3 proves pertinent, for God's gracious love creates the beauty in which God delights, rather than delights in a beauty that already exists. Indeed, Paul will soon speak of not only an absent beauty but a deranged death and grotesque existence that we possess apart from Jesus Christ. So predestination occurs "in love," but we do well to remember that remarkable claim from Luther's 1518 Heidelberg Disputation: "The love of God does not find, but creates, that which is pleasing to it. The love of man comes into being through that which is pleasing to it" (Luther 1957: 57).

Three further statements qualify or characterize this loving predestination. First, God's adoption of sons through Jesus Christ occurs "according to the purpose of his will," reminding us that the intended aim or "purpose" (*eudokian*) for our well-being is God's own. History is not wayward and rambling but bears out this deeply rooted purposiveness. Second, God's own direction leads "to the praise of his glorious grace," for his pursuits refract on him in blessedness (→1:3). Third, predestination to adoption cannot be drawn the slightest bit away from the way "with which he has blessed us in the Beloved."

Some have feared that predestination really connotes a hidden god, perhaps a god with a shadow side different from the manifestation of God's glory in the face of Jesus Christ. But Paul will have none of it. Predestination speaks to divine resolve of precisely that blessing that characterizes the work of Jesus Christ. Yet we dare not tame Jesus or shave off the rough edges of his blessing, for he comes to bring a sword (Matt. 10:34), he speaks in parables to confound the doomed (Matt. 13:13), and he attests a future judgment to eternal perdition (Matt. 25:31–46). Predestination roots the blessing in Jesus rather than pointing away to some other face or mask of the divine being, but Jesus also pronounces woes and curses, and we would be remiss if we trimmed down predestination to be any less significant there.

Not only can predestination not be severed from Jesus, but it also cannot stop short of leading to praise. The God who wills this history and these events—in the particular story of Jesus's sojourn and now in these Christian lives—is to be acclaimed. A bit more specifically, Paul believes that his eternal election prompts praise of his "glorious grace" (see similar phrasing in 1:12, 14). Does this grace bestow his glory? Or does his glory overflow into and prompt the giving of this grace? The genitive relationship could be rendered in either direction grammatically, though the wider context of chapters 1–3 may well prompt us to avoid

any separation here. Not only in 1:7–8 but also later in 1:23 and 3:19 the glory
of God will be bound up with the grace of God: not only standing behind it as
source and before it as goal but also bearing it as gift (for the God who is full fills
us all with that which is his own). We not only acclaim the way that his gravitas
leads to his generosity, but we accord him glory, laud, and honor for the way in
which he gives us nothing less than his own self. Glory, like blessing, exists in
God—marking out his singular all-sufficiency—and shall be ascribed to God by
the echoing praise of his children.

1:7–9 In him we have redemption through his blood, the forgiveness of our trespasses,
according to the riches of his grace, which he lavished upon us, in all wisdom and insight
making known to us the mystery of his will,

Paul now returns to the affairs at hand in the story of the gospel, having contem-
plated their eternal depths in God's own predestining love. The earlier reference
to "adoption . . . *through* Jesus Christ" (1:5) now takes an even more particular
bent: "redemption *through* his blood." The instrument of our being enfolded
into the divine family by adoption and redemption from sin cannot simply be
identified by the name of Jesus but is identified even more specifically by reference to his shed blood.

This blood is defined or clarified as "the forgiveness of our trespasses." The
seventeenth-century theologian John Owen spoke of how the death of death
occurred in the death of Christ, wherein his shed blood atoned for sins. The
first time Owen addressed the matter, he argued that God might have simply
forgiven sin by fiat but willingly chose to put forward his incarnate Son as a
sacrifice for human sin. A few years later, in his "Dissertation on Divine Justice,"
Owen argued that divine justice demands satisfaction and not merely abeyance
of human sin.[5] The argument hinges on biblical teaching and on the doctrine of
divine simplicity. First, biblical teaching frequently attests the way in which both
justice and mercy mark the atoning work of God. "Steadfast love and faithfulness meet; righteousness and peace kiss each other" (Ps. 85:10). In that most
famous of psalms, the conclusion comes with acclamation that "surely goodness
and mercy shall follow me" (Ps. 23:6). The gratuity of God fulfills rather than
repudiates the good justice of God. When we are victims of mistreatment, this
promise can serve as a salve to our pains. But we must be equally willing to stand

5. See Carl R. Trueman, *The Claims of Truth: John Owen's Trinitarian Theology* (Carlisle: Paternoster,
1998).

under the same sign when acknowledging the only pathway by which our own injustice may be forgiven.

Yet the necessity of redemption through blood and forgiveness by means of atonement does not bespeak divine weakness or lack. Critics of such atonement theology—whether in its Anselmian form, its earlier Jewish sacrificial mode, or its later Protestant penal manifestation—regularly lodge the complaint that only a weak God would be unwilling or incapable of forgiveness apart from a seeming bloodlust. Does this turn from eternity and blessing to blood and forgiveness signal a divine insufficiency? Quite the opposite, for language of excess appears here: "according to the riches of his grace" points to the fullness that is his own, while "which he lavished upon us" alerts us that those depths of the divine storehouse are poured out for us (→3:16). Paul will return to this pairing in concluding this chapter with the acclamation that the church is "the fullness of him who fills all in all" (1:23) and later in praying that "you may be filled with all the fullness of God" (3:19). We dare not race past this earlier mention, however, for the benefits of Christ's grace are here tied to the depths of God's own triune fullness.

Fullness cannot be caught, however, like any other object of knowledge. So it is not for nothing that this is depicted as a "mystery" and must be revealed "in all wisdom and insight." This will not be the only mystery in Ephesians (cf. 3:3, 4, 9; 5:32). Later Paul will herald boldly the proclamation of "the mystery of the gospel" (6:19) as one of the more all-encompassing descriptions of his apostolic work (similar to Rom. 16:25–26). These mysteries of the faith bear careful pedagogical delivery, and Paul says that the God and Father of our Lord Jesus Christ makes them known with insightful wisdom. As in Gal. 3:24, there is a divine prudence shown in manifesting the truth to sinners bent to falsehood in a patient, persistent manner that leads to righteousness. We tend to think of pastoral wisdom in exercising thoughtful pedagogy with any given person or congregation, but this verse speaks of God's pedagogical insight in dealing with all his people not merely on a personal register but at a redemptive-historical level.

1:9–10 according to his purpose, which he set forth in Christ as a plan for the fullness of time, to unite all things in him, things in heaven and things on earth.

This prudence in divine pedagogy leads to a goal: the "purpose" (*oikonomian*) that is "set forth in Christ." Indeed, the patience of the divine pedagogy attested here in 1:9 is meant to accent the purposive mystery of Christ. It is surely not for nothing that "Christ" is mentioned here, rather than "Jesus," as this title manifests the kind of patient pedagogical preparation under discussion. Jesus was to be received as the Anointed One or Messiah, as the prophet, priest, and king of Israel.

Christ is made manifest at the "fullness of time." Time cannot be treated as the plodding of years after months after days after seconds of chronological sequence. We may experience time as a succession of instants, one atop another, and yet there is a "fullness of time," and it expresses a divine "purpose" and "plan." Time is teleological and purposive. Time bears the very fullness of the one who is himself full.

Now, this fullness is not some extraneous solution to the vagaries of time, and it is not thereby ambiguous or unknown. He "set [it] forth in Christ," so the emphasis here is on its manifest character. In fact, the previous verses must not be forgotten—namely, that the "riches of his grace" are "lavished upon us" inasmuch as this manifestation of the divine plan appears. God's grace is displayed not only in redeeming but also in revealing; God's riches are shared not merely in becoming incarnate amidst history but also in summing up history in an eternal plan.

This passage illustrates a nexus point for recent debates regarding Paul's theology, whether it is salvation-historical or apocalyptic in form. The language of "mystery made known" connects with the intrusive imagery of apocalyptic theology, while the notion of a purpose and plan (indeed an *oikonomian*) speaks of the historical and narratival character of God's agency. While scholarly trends may veer or tilt from one direction to another (whether toward J. L. Martyn or others' apocalyptic register or again toward N. T. Wright's salvation-historical approach), Paul's language includes both registers. God does sum up time and history, to be sure, and so we must speak not only of redemptive history but of God actually working on history itself: it's not quite right to say "redeeming history"—because history has not sinned—but we might say "transfiguring history" or "filling history." And yet the character of this summing up that is "set forth in Christ" intrudes on the plod of human history and cuts against the grain of any notion of immanent progress. Even its logic has to be graciously "set forth" and revealed and can't be assumed to be obvious or available for observation and analysis apart from divine action.

God unites "all things in him," and we must deal with the universalism and particularism in this claim. God acts on all. God does so in Jesus Christ. Two questions emerge. First, what does it mean that things are united in Jesus Christ? Is this language of redemption or of some creational, metaphysical reality that falls short of Christian salvation? Second, what does it mean that "all things . . .

things in heaven and things on earth" are drawn together in Christ? Does this really have significance for every element of created reality, or does it have some other significance? Might it be construed representatively or hyperbolically? Kevin Vanhoozer suggests a way to think about both questions: "We therefore have to distinguish two kinds of 'being in' or participation in Christ: a general cosmological participation in the Son through whom all things were made (Col. 1:16) and a more particular Christological abiding in the Son in whom there is reconciliation (2 Cor. 5:17). . . . Salvation involves more than relating to God generically as a creature; it involves relating to God covenantally 'in Christ'" (2010: 281–82). Vanhoozer suggests that some participate in salvific union with Christ, while all share in his mediation of existence. In so doing Vanhoozer finds a way to thread the needle of Manichaeanism on the one hand and universalism on the other hand. But of which kind of participation does Eph. 1:10 speak?

Here we see one instance where Ephesians and Colossians do follow the same pathway. Colossians 1 speaks of Christ's significance for "all" in its hymn:

> He is the image of the invisible God, the firstborn of all creation. For by him all things were created, in heaven and on earth, visible and invisible, whether thrones or dominions or rulers or authorities—all things were created through him and for him. And he is before all things, and in him all things hold together. And he is the head of the body, the church. He is the beginning, the firstborn from the dead, that in everything he might be preeminent. For in him all the fullness of God was pleased to dwell, and through him to reconcile to himself all things, whether on earth or in heaven, making peace by the blood of his cross. (Col. 1:15–20)

Paul there repeats the language of "all" (which appears five times in one form or another), and he not only also employs the terms "in heaven and on earth" but appends other pairings (e.g., "visible and invisible").

Back to Eph. 1:10: God unites "things in heaven and things on earth." This literary merism takes in all reality, and it means to help us picture reality in the most basic of terms. Genesis 1 introduces us to created reality as composed of heaven and earth (Gen. 1:1) and then speaks of the filling of these realms with things or occupants. Here all these things, whether in the heavens or on the earth, are united "in him."

Is not all this analysis something of an ontological diversion from dealing with the coming of the Christ? Does metaphysical analysis actually pull us closer to hear the textures of Paul's teaching, or does it not distance and occlude such intimate and patient listening to the tones of scripture? John Webster says something pertinent in asking why grasping Paul's ethical teaching can't be pursued apart from metaphysical inquiry: "Why must Christian ethics contemplate being? In order that our moral lives can be conducted away from idols toward reality. The metaphysical impulse in Christian theology is not a flight from history—far from it: it is an element in the ascesis imposed upon sinners by the gospel, part of the needful dispossession and re-engagement with the truth in which the baptismal form of Christian existence is impressed upon the subjects of God's redemptive goodness" (2015b: 15).

Perhaps speculative or metaphysical theology falls foul of some Reformational worries about thereby tilting away from God's self-revelation toward the hunches of human hypotheses. There surely are traditions of inquiry within the Lutheran and later Reformed churches that have decried metaphysics for just those reasons. And yet it is precisely the scriptural assault on our proclivity toward idolatry that prompts more than a surface reading of the biblical text and goads us toward the material substance—the metaphysical reality—of which it gives witness, either directly or indirectly. To see Jesus here as the one in whom all is summed up serves like a kidney punch to stall our own projected self-direction and to puncture any sense of self-sufficiency.

More must be said of this specific action: *anakephalaiōsasthai*. Irenaeus of Lyons takes the term and runs with it, reading scripture through this lens of recapitulation and tracing ways in which Jesus fills up earlier scriptural elements. The term used here sums something up, drawing together disparate or disconnected parts and moving them onto some sort of resolution and climax. Frequently it is a term employed to sum up an argument, rhetorically speaking, and highlight its consequence. Here, however, Christ sums up or recapitulates all things, things in heaven and things on earth. As Paul will elsewhere say, "All the promises of God find their Yes in him [Christ]" (2 Cor. 1:20). The Son provides both the fulfillment and the final clarification of promises, indeed of all things. So-called apocalyptic readings rightly accent the way in which the action of Christ is total and seismic in its agential power. Yet we do well to attend to the way in which Christ's transcendental and invasive works fill up and tease out categories that the Son gave to his people Israel in prior epochs of covenant history.

1:11 In him we have obtained an inheritance, having been predestined according to the purpose of him who works all things according to the counsel of his will,

The union enjoyed in Christ brings not merely pacification but an inheritance. God owns us as his sons or daughters so that the work of salvation brings not merely survival but an estate. Throughout the epistle more will be said about these riches (1:7, 18; 2:7; 3:8, 16), and the divine storehouse is shared with many sons and daughters.

Of course, we are not natural-born sons and daughters but those adopted (→1:5), which is why the prepositional phrase "in him" continues to recur. Christians possess and partake of riches in Christ—not in themselves, nor in anything native to them. By grace, not by nature, is the watchword here. And, therefore, we must see that this inheritance does not simply come obviously or naturally. Thus, Paul returns to the language of divine intention or will; here he takes up the term "purpose" to speak of God's working out by "the counsel of his will." All things, all history come from his counsel or judgment—that is, his will.

Predestination is language of sovereignty. However much history and its vagaries may appear to drift from anything spiritual or divine, the claim here suggests that history still operates according to God's decretive will. Further, Paul draws a wider and a closer circle: in the closer circle, he charts God's predestining will that we obtain this inheritance in Christ; in the wider circle, he will go further to speak of all things working by God's will. But "the purpose of him" connects these two realities—his predestining love of his own and his global governance of all things. The text does not reduce the global to the salvific, as if the only purpose for the former is the latter. Still further, the text does not purport to say how the global tacks toward the salvific, as if seeking to read the tea leaves of providence. But the text does confess—by faith, not sight—the providential and global direction that has salvific consequence.

1:12 so that we who were the first to hope in Christ might be to the praise of his glory.

Speaking of purpose, Paul not only says that global governance by almighty God serves a purpose in graciously granting an inheritance to those adopted in Christ. He also speaks further of a purpose behind the disbursement of that estate—namely, that it might be to "the praise of [God's] glory." The language of "hope in Christ" serves as a crucial connection point in this regard: because this inheritance comes to those who hope in Christ, the delivery of the promised riches eventually proves his trustworthiness and thereby magnifies his name. Not merely hope itself as an act but those persons ("we") who do hope in Christ are themselves the praise of his glory. The hope placed in Christ grants a quality to the very being of the Christian by turning outward to find fullness in another (much like Heb. 11:13–16 speaks of faith doing so). Christians find their meaning and hope outside their own lives and fully in this Messiah; their very being exalts his goodness and grace.

"We" may refer to the first generation or wave of Christians, though perhaps it is more likely that Paul alludes here to Jewish believers in distinction from Gentile believers. Two reasons suggest such a focus. First, 1:10 has already spoken of the "fullness of time," wherein all has been brought together (see also Gal. 4:4–5). Second, 1:11 then declares the inheritance given, which makes one think on the fact that such an estate must have been promised previously, and where else but to Israel? Third, the following verses contrast the "we" with a "you also": that "you" is marked by belief and the Spirit but also refers to Gentile believers who were formerly "the uncircumcision" (2:11). Most Jews of Paul's own day had spurned the Messiah, and Paul elsewhere lamented with sorrow that reality (Rom. 9:1–5). His words here echo the latter portion of that passage, however, where he argued that the failure of individual Israelites—even of a sizable aggregate of them—did not negate the word of God or the glory of the Lord (see also Rom. 9:5; 11:36).

1:13–14 In him you also, when you heard the word of truth, the gospel of your salvation, and believed in him, were sealed with the promised Holy Spirit, who is the guarantee of our inheritance until we acquire possession of it, to the praise of his glory.

Paul continues describing the present experience of the congregation before pressing on to the future inheritance yet to be possessed. He peers backward to consider what has been accomplished in and for them here, and he does so by speaking alertly of the action of Christ and his Holy Spirit.

First, the Holy Spirit was promised, has been given as a guarantee, and now seals them. The Spirit was foretold and promised, in both Old and New Testament revelation (Joel 2:28–32; Luke 24:49; Acts 1:8). The glory of the Lord indwelt the temple of the Lord in the ancient economy (1 Kings 8); now the glory of God inhabits the Christian man, woman, and child.

Second, this sealing with the Spirit occurred for "you also" and comes only "in him"—that is, in Christ Jesus. The Spirit is no supplement to Christ, and he is no discrete gift. The Spirit is an aspect of Christ's own gift. Sealing with the Spirit comes precisely when one believes in Jesus; thus the empowerment of the presence of the Spirit does not mitigate but crowns one's dependence on the incarnate Son. The notion of being united with or located within Christ has been recurring here (see 1:3, 4, 6, 7, 10, 11; contra many commentators, other "in Christ" references relate that phrase to action and not to our union or location, as in 1:9, 12). These actions of Son and Spirit involve divine action in our very being, not merely on our behaviors or actions. The God of predestination and election deigns to act lovingly in our midst and in our very selves. This heavenly work comes prompted, in this case by one "hear[ing] the word of truth, the gospel of your salvation, and believ[ing] in him." Ephesians 1:13 actually offers parallel statements marked out by the adverbial clause "in whom you also" (*en hō kai hymeis*), highlighting the reality that both hearing and believing Christ are essential to being sealed by his Spirit. The Spirit may be related to an inheritance but is no estate passed pell-mell from one generation to another apart from personal trust.

All this is from God—the Son and Spirit—and returns to God: "to the praise of his glory" (cf. 1:6, 12). God's heavenly work amidst us shows that he provides not merely the atoning sacrifice of the servant king nor even just the heavenly foothold of the exalted Son but also the applicatory indwelling of his only begotten Son. From him is truth, salvation, and the Spirit. Through him is the word, the sealing, and guarantee. Therefore, to him is all glory.

1:15–19a For this reason, because I have heard of your faith in the Lord Jesus and your love toward all the saints, I do not cease to give thanks for you, remembering you in my prayers, that the God of our Lord Jesus Christ, the Father of glory, may give you the Spirit of wisdom and of revelation in the knowledge of him, having the eyes of your hearts enlightened, that you may know what is the hope to which he has called you, what are the riches of his glorious inheritance in the saints, and what is the immeasurable greatness of his power toward us who believe . . .

Paul regularly turns to prayer for his audience (see especially Phil. 1:3–6 and Col. 1:3–14). He is an apostle, a sent one, an emissary whose action finds its power and validity only in the warrant of another. In a vivid sense, his speech comes from him hearing Jesus. Yet here we see that this relationship runs the other way also: he hears of their faith and love, and he turns intuitively to God in his prayers.

Paul first remembers them in his prayers, having "heard of [their] faith in the Lord Jesus and [their] love toward all the saints." These words shape our understanding of his audience in this epistle. Again, his hearing may relate to a broader region and the church therein, as opposed to the particular congregation or church in Ephesus itself. Indeed, his comments on their witness do remain theologically broad and avoid any particular illustration, at the least manifesting the kind of comment compatible with the circulating letter hypothesis. The conclusion of the epistle similarly avoids any terribly specific comment, beyond the reference to Tychicus's coming update (6:21–24).

This detail-less audience is defined as faithful in Christ and loving to all the saints. Any later exhortation comes not to an illegitimate heir; every summons yet to be given shall be heard by those who bear the rule of faith and rule of love. As noted earlier (→1:1), the audience here must be defined as "the holy ones" or "the saints"—that is, those who "are faithful in Christ Jesus." Indeed, grasping this set of theological observations about the audience deepens Paul's call; to those who already bear faith, he will lift their eyes heavenward still more, and to those whose love is shown to all the saints, he will widen yet further their grasp of neighbors—brothers and sisters even—to whom they are sent in love.

Second, Paul gives thanks (*eucharistōn*) for them. Paul's epistle begins with a burst of blessing and exclamation. Ephesians 1:3–14 really does flow with an almost uncontrollable energy as Paul regales the majesty and mighty acts of the triune God. He has repeatedly interjected with the phrase "to the praise of his glory" or its close approximation (→1:6, 12, 14). His praise and his sense that all human history flows to the praise of this God find roots, however, in very earthy realities. He gives thanks for these saints. He renders gratitude because of these sisters and brothers. He offers a sacrifice of thanksgiving tethered directly to an alert awareness that God has worked goodness and mercy in bringing about faith and love in Christ Jesus. It is not too much to speak of Paul as starry-eyed; indeed, it may be too small a quip, better extended by saying that he looks heaven-eyed at the congregations of the region, their resilient faith, their sacrificial love for each other.

Cynicism can be tempting, and Paul's example forces us to avoid falling prey to an ecclesiastical suspicion. We may hear the various descriptions of and summons to the church in Ephesians and find that the empirical data is not overwhelming; for instance, Peter Leithart (2016) suggests that the church is simply not united this side of the Protestant Reformation. But Eph. 1:16 reminds us to perceive, to remember, and to show thanks for what is the case in the life of God's people. It does not summon forth a Pollyannaish naïveté regarding ecclesial morality, but it does beckon us to a heaven-eyed perception of God's presence. So, for instance, whereas denominational and ethnic divisions mar the church in all sorts of ways, we remember with thanks that "there is one body and one Spirit" (→4:4). Only hope grounded in heaven buoys a noncynical posture toward the saints.

Third, Paul does pray for God's giving or grace to continue in and to them. His hearing, his remembrance, and his thanks do not constitute a basis for satisfaction or a contentment with the status quo. Rather, they prompt further supplication before God. It is a normal reality that observing the generosity of God does not remove one's sense of want but rather deepens one's expectant desire for still greater provision from on high. In Exod. 32–34, Moses first asks that God would not destroy the Israelites because of the sin of the golden calf (32:11–13). Having received an affirmative answer, he presses further to ask not only that God allow them to live but also that the Lord continue to accompany them on their journey (33:14–16). Finally, having received a word of reprieve and a promise of divine presence, he goes still further and asks for God to show him his glory (33:18). Because God is a mysterious fount from whom all human joy is derived, deliverance on an anticipated need does not shrink one's prayers and supplications; far from it, every divine deliverance only expands the prayerful imagination for still greater glories that such a God might provide.

Paul does not merely ask for more; he entreats God for specific kindnesses. He asks for three things to be given to these saints who manifest faith and love. First, Paul prays that "the God of our Lord Jesus Christ, the Father of glory, may give you the Spirit of wisdom and of revelation in the knowledge of him, having the eyes of your hearts enlightened" (1:17–18). We must remember that the heart (*kardias*) depicts in biblical imagery something other than our contemporary identification of the heart with affection or emotion. Heart speaks to the intellectual life when construed more narrowly and addresses the self as an acting whole when rendered more broadly. The Christian heart demands enlightenment just as eyes—real, physical, bodily eyes—demand illumination to be able to register contrasts and movement and the spectrum of color.

We must ask whether this "spirit" given refers to the Holy Spirit rendered as a gift in some fresh way or to a human spirit provided anew. The latter might point to a desired transformation of the self, whereas the former accents the inhabitation or personal relation to the very Spirit of the Godhead. The phrase "spirit of wisdom and of understanding" may point us beyond a partitive reading here inasmuch as it seems to draw on and develop the teaching of Isa. 11:2. In that prophetic passage the seven gifts of the Holy Spirit are regaled:

> And the Spirit of the LORD shall rest upon him,
>   the Spirit of wisdom and understanding,

the Spirit of counsel and might,
the Spirit of knowledge and the fear of the LORD.

Paul here takes up the second gift, wisdom, and explicitly quotes Isa. 11:2b. But two contextual observations should be borne in mind. First, Paul tweaks the paired terms; whereas Isaiah speaks of "wisdom and understanding [*syneseōs* in the Septuagint]," Paul prays for "wisdom and revelation in the knowledge of him [*apokelypseōs en epignōsei autou*]." The insertion of the word "revelation" speaks to the invasive and self-revelatory work of God, but this revelation terminates or culminates in "knowledge of him." Paul does join Isaiah in praying for understanding or (his preferred term) knowledge, but the self-revealed and singular character of this knowledge must be qualified by the phrase "of him." The term "him" refers to the Father, not the Son, though it is through the self-manifesting revelation of the Son that the Father is himself known by his children. As Calvin says specifically of this verse, "the gifts of the Spirit are not the endowments of nature" here (1965b: 134). While Calvin and we must elsewhere relate the Spirit's grace to the provision of nature and of its own powers, here Paul looks toward a still greater gift of the Spirit's grace in transfiguring human knowledge by the self-revelatory and enlightening provision of Christ in whom we truly have knowledge of God the "Father of glory" (see also John 1:14–18; 2 Cor. 4:5–6). Second, the seven gifts of the Holy Spirit in Isa. 11:2 begin with the gift of the Spirit himself, the very Spirit who is said to "rest upon him." So the gift of the Spirit cannot be separated from the gifts from that Spirit. Paul prays to the "Father of glory" for God's own glory to be given in the person of the Spirit. Nothing less than the Spirit himself is to be given, yet the Spirit promised by the prophet brings creaturely gifts upon his arrival.

Paul then asks for a second thing to be given to these saints. He prays that "you may know what is the hope to which he has called you, what are the riches of his glorious inheritance in the saints" (1:18). A prayer directed to the "Father of glory" now speaks of its invocation as aiming at a "glorious inheritance in the saints." God's attributes and characteristics are communicable, wherein the goods and glories of God's own life are communicated in creaturely appropriate ways to his earthly children. The hope of God's saints is an inheritance—that is, a rightful claim of God as adopted sons and daughters, those called away from their darkness and called into God's own family. That hope is rich or excessive inasmuch as it is marked by glory. Stephen Fowl (2012: 58) reminds us that 1:18 speaks of God's inheritance, whereas 1:14 addressed the inheritance of the saints.

Third, Paul finally prays that "you may know . . . what is the immeasurable greatness of his power toward us who believe" (1:18–19). Too often the prayers of Paul are treated as ornamental, the theological equivalent of a garnish that serves merely decorative and thus tangential purposes. But Eph. 1–3 is marked front and back by Paul's reports of his prayers for his audience. Both here and in 3:14–21 we see that he catches us up on what he says to God about his readers, regarding both the past for which he gives thanks and the future for which he begs God's help. Ephesians 1:1–18 identifies the blessing and the prayer for what has been and will be given to believers, while 1:19–3:21 speaks of the power that may provide the surety of that future tense and coming blessing. Calvin says, "Either we never think highly enough of the treasure offered to us in the Gospel, or, if we do, we cannot persuade ourselves that we are capable of it, because we perceive nothing in us that corresponds to it, but everything adverse" (1965b: 135). Calvin lands on the divine power, gracious and immeasurable as it is, as the thread that ties together that lofty treasure and our deep need.

Is there a logic to this trifold prayer? While there is a danger of over-reading the grammar, which does not provide a smooth structure, it nonetheless has an integrated shape that deserves attention. Especially helpful in this regard is a paired reading with 3:14–21, whereby the invocation of God here can be read alongside that later recounting of Paul's prayers for his audience (→3:16–19). Paul prays here for the kind of knowledge that pertains to real, life-giving hope, the kind of hope that exceeds the next market swing or political season. Because he longs for them to grasp that radical kind of hope wisely, he knows that they must also understand God's power. Power becomes a major theme for Eph. 1–3, then, because it uniquely manifests the triune God as one who can deliver on such hopes.

1:19b–21 . . . according to the working of his great might that he worked in Christ when he raised him from the dead and seated him at his right hand in the heavenly places, far above all rule and authority and power and dominion, and above every name that is named, not only in this age but also in the one to come.

Paul offers the first of four manifestations of God's great might in 1:19–23. While later manifestations address the audience (individually and communally) and the author, here he begins with the power seen in the resurrection and exaltation of the heavenly Christ. Resurrection comes first, as Paul says that "great might" is shown in that "he raised him from the dead."

Exaltation comes next, and here the Psalms provide imagery for Paul's witness. Psalm 110, the most cited of Old Testament passages in the New Testament, speaks of the right hand of YHWH being shared with a figure who is also, in Paul's language, "far above all rule and authority and power and dominion." The image of being seated hearkens toward the throne room and the position of authority. The psalm depicts this reign, however, in eternal terms; God has sworn, "You are a priest forever after the order of Melchizedek" (Ps. 110:4). Readings of the passage seem to move frequently enough toward the messianic, so much so that Jesus seems to assume an audience will hear it in such a manner (Mark 12:37).

The term *dynameōs* is used to describe God's work in Eph. 1:19, and it reappears in 1:21. The ESV renders it "might" in one verse and "power" in the other verse so as to differentiate them. The NRSV and NIV render both uses with the term "power," showing that there is a verbal recurrence. Differentiation comes via the adjectives in 1:19, which identifies this power as "immeasurably great" (*hyperballon megethos*). The prophets and apostles do not flinch at speaking of powers and principalities, of gods and of lords, but they find subtle ways to polemically herald God's all-surpassing nature: in this case there are powers and dominions that loom large, and yet God's power is greater. The translation "power" also helps highlight the ways in which 1:15–19 and 3:14–21 frame a larger section of the epistle, with 1:20–3:13 illustrating manifestations of God's power.

The Father of glory has "worked in Christ" so as to exalt him "above." The term "above" recurs here: "far above all . . ." and "above every name." Each phrase, in its own way, speaks of global categories. Christ is "far above all rule and authority and power and dominion," a smattering of synonymous and overlapping terms that each gesture toward political or civil authority. Still further, Christ is "above every name that is named," and lest one reduce this comparative statement to some primitive epoch, Paul qualifies it in a global and still future fashion: "not only in this age but also in the one to come." Whereas Paul elsewhere speaks of God granting or giving that name (Phil. 2:9–11), here Christ is exalted to a seat or throne that brings with it a status or being whose name supersedes all others— indeed, supersedes naming itself in a strict sense.

1:22–23 And he put all things under his feet and gave him as head over all things to the church, which is his body, the fullness of him who fills all in all.

Again a psalm appears, this time Ps. 8:6, as Paul turns to the image of the Lord speaking to David's lord and pledging to "put all things under his feet." The use of spatial categories makes an ontological point: all is under him, while he is head over all. Under and over connote ways of relating God and creation, but more specifically of relating the exalted Christ and creation.

Christ is given to the church. His being "head over all things" qualifies the way in which he is given to his own. So close is his tie to his church that Paul says this people "is his body." The head/body pairing suggests that headship or rule in the church is a gift of God (→4:7–11), which reminds us that it is not good for us to be bereft of authority structures (Austin 2010). While we live in a day and age that looks with suspicion on those who hold positions of power—often rightly, sometimes cynically—1:22 depends on an understanding of authority in itself as a gift. Hearing this word aright depends on suspending common assumptions that the ruling class or ruling elite serve their own interests. This head does possess all and govern all, but to the end of filling all.

Christ not only serves as head to the body, but his headship is said to be "over all things." Paul has gestured earlier toward such a global view: "according to his purpose, which he set forth in Christ as a plan for the fullness of time, to unite all things in him, things in heaven and things on earth" (1:9–10); "him who works all things according to the counsel of his will" (1:11). And, of course, 1:22–23 follows 1:21, which relates his rule to "all rule and authority and power and dominion and above every name that is named." Extolling the global rule of the ecclesiastical Lord is not a new idea either; Gerhard von Rad (1966) argues that Israel's reflection on the doctrine of creation was always tethered to its attention given to God's redemption of the Israelites as a people. We need not sit tight on all von Rad's historiographic judgments to grasp this link that does mark the Old Testament witness and also surfaces here in Ephesians—namely, showing that the God who pledges to bless the church is the God whose agency is that of the almighty Lord of all. Whether one's threat takes the form of Egypt, the grave, or the weight of sin, the universal reign of Christ buoys one's confidence in this Redeemer to work the miracle of his grace with efficacious might.

The church is not only Christ's body but is attested as being his fullness too. The apostle describes this fullness as that of "him who fills all in all." Here those who share in the blessing of God (→1:3) are differentiated from God even in their inclusion in God's own life, glory, blessing, and fullness. Perhaps the thought of the filling of all things by the one who is himself full might be furthered by reflecting on a specific episode wherein the economy of grace manifests something remarkable about the abiding significance of God's metaphysical fullness. Gregory of Nazianzus says of Jesus's baptism in the Jordan River:

Yet as John is baptizing, Jesus approaches, perhaps also to sanctify the baptizer, and certainly to bury the old Adam (1 Cor. 15:45) in the water, but before these and for the sake of these things to sanctify the Jordan. As indeed he was spirit and flesh, so he initiates by the Spirit and the water. The baptizer does not accept it; Jesus debates. "I need to be baptized by you" (Matt. 3:14), the lamp (John 5:35) says to the sun (Mal. 4:2), the voice (Matt. 3:3 and par.) to the Word, the friend (John 3:29; Matt. 9:15) to the bridegroom, the one above all born of women (Matt. 11:11 and par.) to the first born of all creation (Col. 1:15), the one who leaped in the womb (Luke 1:41) to the one worshipped in the womb, the one who was and will be the Forerunner (Matt. 11:10 and par.) to the one who has and will be made manifest. . . .

But Jesus comes up again out of the water. For he carries up with himself the world and "sees the heavens opened" (Mark 1:10) which Adam closed for himself and for those after him as he also closed paradise by the flaming sword (Gen. 3:24). And the Spirit testifies to [Christ's] divinity (Matt. 3:16 and par.), for he ran toward one like himself, as does the voice from heaven (Matt. 3:17 and par.), for from there comes the one to whom testimony is given. And the Spirit comes as a dove (Matt. 3:16 and par.), for he honors the body, being seen "corporeally" (Luke 3:22), since it also is God by divinization. (2008: 91–92, 93)

The baptized Jesus has not only borne water as a human, but he has given new birth to water as God. The Jordan flows with waters from on high. Such is the grace of Jesus, who fills all with that which he alone, as the Second Person of the triune Godhead, possesses. Like the prayers of 1:15–19 and 3:14–19, so the more pointed emphasis on the full one filling others begins and ends this first half of Ephesians (1:23 and 3:19). Hence Augustine confesses, "This is what blessing is: to glory in God, and to be indwelt by God" (2000a: 101 [5.17]).

EPHESIANS 2

2:1–3 And you were dead in the trespasses and sins in which you once walked, following the course of this world, following the prince of the power of the air, the spirit that is now at work in the sons of disobedience—among whom we all once lived in the passions of our flesh, carrying out the desires of the body and the mind, and were by nature children of wrath, like the rest of mankind.

"You" is invoked yet again (see also 1:2, 13, 15–18; mention of "we" and "us" is found more broadly in 1:3–9, 11–12, 14, 17, 19). Here the audience—those "saints" and the "faithful in Christ Jesus" (1:1)—are described with regard to their past life in death, their traffic in trespass, and their state of sin.

Why address their sin here? Ephesians 2:1–10 offers the second of four examples demonstrating the power of God. Those signs are significant, for power plays a crucial role in the prayers offered by Paul in 1:19 and 3:16, 18. Indeed the benediction concluding these first three chapters also explicitly highlights the significance of divine power: "Now to him who is able to do far more abundantly than all that we ask or think, according to the power at work within us, to him be glory in the church and in Christ Jesus throughout all generations, forever and ever. Amen" (3:20–21). The promise of abundance from God—that "you may be filled with all the fullness of God" (3:19; →1:23, 4:10)—holds good insofar as God has the power to enact his beneficent promises. Often overlooked in major glossaries of Pauline theology, power dominates the front half of Ephesians.

Paul has already highlighted the resurrection and exaltation of the Son as the first great sign of God's life-giving power (1:20–23). He will later address power deployed to reconcile Jew and Gentile (→2:11–22) as well as to commission the apostolic service of Paul himself (→3:1–13), the third and fourth signs of that divine might. Here, however, Paul reflects on the way in which each and every

Christian man and woman has been the recipient or object of God's life-giving power inasmuch as God has acted to bring them from death to life. We dare not reduce the gospel to the personal, but we also must not lose the personal application of saving divine power among the christological, the social, and the vocational exercise of that same transcendent might.

What is said of their sin? Sin is described in what might be called a thick and nonreductive manner. The primary claim here is that "you were dead in the trespasses and sins in which you once walked" (2:1–2). Grammatically speaking, every other nuance explicates this basic claim. Other terms will be employed that speak of malformation, evil cultural influence, demonic oppression, and the like, yet we dare not miss that these existentially, sociologically, and spiritually active terms do not negate the ultimate issue—death.

What nuances are offered? First, this sinful walk is "following the course of this world" (2:2). The term "world" speaks of the realm beyond the church, a term that may or may not bear or carry explicit mention of sinfulness. Here the world has a particular course or pathway. The Bible has regularly spoken of two ways, a way of life and a way of death. Psalm 1 is most explicit in this regard, but other passages convey this sense as well (e.g., Deut. 30:19). In their past sin and transgression, this audience had fallen in lockstep with the ways of the sinful world. Thus, sociological analyses of what we might deem moral and spiritual malformation are onto something—namely, that systemic and affinity-based socialization is a real cause in the matrix of sin and death. The language of "the world" here speaks predominantly of what we might call "systems" or "systemic" malformation, ways in which particular cultural structures incentivize or nudge us toward particular behaviors. In this case, they foster selfishness or insatiable lust (as in consumerism) or racism and misogyny (as in supremacist hierarchies); other such examples play out in larger and smaller settings, oftentimes even in overlapping and complex manners.

Second, this sinful walk is "following the prince of the power of the air, the spirit that is now at work in the sons of disobedience" (2:2). Mangled socialization will not explain every moral malformation. Even if it does contribute to many facets or even every facet of the sinful walk, it does not provide a sufficient sketch of that malformation. Ephesians 2:2 turns from human socialization to pick out the demonic oppression. There is a "prince of the power of the air." This one is a "spirit"—that is, a being working beyond the bounds of material life—and yet this spirit is "now at work in" human lives. This power's spiritual character, then, does not involve aloofness from human society; far from it, its spiritual capacity enables its proximity to human individuality and systematic shaping. Paul identifies that our stories occur in a spiritual economy that cannot be reduced to the divine economy of God's good purposes but also takes place in the oppressive tyranny of the demonic prince. Sisters and brothers in the Majority World may have held on to this kind of spiritual perception in a way that is now less vibrant in the modern Western world, but Ephesians calls us back to this sort of spiritual alertness.

Third, this sinful walk happens alongside the "sons of disobedience—among whom we all once lived" (2:2–3). If the first nuance addressed systemic methods of socialization, then this third angle highlights the more personal influence of what might be deemed peer pressure. We "once lived" among the "sons of disobedience"; that is, we had interpersonal and relational influence from our peers. Here affinity and proximity play out in more personal forms. The Psalms begin with a warning against such peers:

> Blessed is the man
> > who walks not in the counsel of the wicked,
> nor stands in the way of sinners,
> > nor sits in the seat of scoffers. (Ps. 1:1)

Unfortunately the former walk of the audience was among the wicked; indeed, they did not merely walk among them but they "all once lived" among them, suggesting a more permanent and global sense of exposure.

Fourth, how did this life among the disobedient play out? We "lived in the passions of our flesh." We were "carrying out the desires of the body and the mind" (2:3). Paul has identified systemic or institutional nudges, demonic assault, and even social peer pressure to sin, but he refuses to locate the highways and byways of a sinful walk wholly outside the sinner. Here he looks within: the passions and desires, the body and the mind. Sin does not come unwillingly, even if it may be prompted by seemingly insurmountable external influence or remarkably tragic situations of purported necessity. Sin is prompted by fleshly passion. But even here the internal roots of wayward living cannot be restricted to the lower passions or the appetitive nature, for Paul goes on to point to desires of both "the body and the mind."

"Total depravity" is language employed by many in the Reformed tradition to speak of the effects of original sin. Its global or extensive character has seemed misanthropic, even absurd in its extremism, to many critics. Understandably so, we might say, if it is taken to mean that one is nothing but sinful or, otherwise put, that one is as sinful as one might possibly be. Such claims would negate the ongoing possession of the image of God (Gen. 5:1) and would undercut the affirmation of human dignity this side of the fall (Gen. 9:6). However, total depravity speaks to something that is radical in a different manner. To say that sinful depravity is total is to say that it has marred every nook and cranny of our existence, both in terms of the cosmos as a whole and in terms of the self in all its facets. Ephesians 2:3 disallows us from restricting sin to the body or the flesh and the passionate appetites identified with that physiological existence; no, the mind also and its desires are implicated in that depraved existence.

Fifth and finally, Paul turns to speak of how we "were by nature children of wrath, like the rest of mankind" (2:3). Those who are now "saints" and "faithful in Christ Jesus" were once "like the rest of mankind." They were not cut from another cloth. They were not made with greater potential. They were "children of wrath"; that is, they were rightly due God's wrath. That divine anger—the sort of disciplinary response that jealously guards God's own glory from its unfaithful theft or misallotment—was theirs "by nature." God did not misjudge their character, and they did not merely suffer from secondhand spiritual malaise. They themselves merited that wrath. They in their very being or nature deserved that jealousy from the one true and living God.

When was this pertinent? While other portions of Pauline scripture speak to the ongoing struggle with sin, this portion of Ephesians speaks to a past reality. They "were dead," "once walked" in that way, "once lived" in a heinous manner, and "were by nature" sons and daughters of divine wrath. We can and should discuss in what ways sin continues to mar and mangle the lives of Christians in this overlap of the ages, but these verses do not address that particular question. Here Paul speaks of a state of death to which God shall respond with life-giving power (→2:4–5).

It is possible that our exposition of what is said concerning sin here is somewhat misleading. It is quite possible to itemize seven distinct statements: (1) "you were dead in the trespasses and sins in which you once walked"; (2) "following the course of this world"; (3) "following the prince of the power of the air"; (4) "the spirit that is now at work in the sons of disobedience"; (5) "among whom we all once lived in the passions of our flesh"; (6) "carrying out the desires of the body and the mind"; and (7) "and were by nature children of wrath." If so, then Paul may be artfully mimicking or parodying the sevenfold perfection of creational order in Genesis 1 and in so doing may be paralleling a more explicit sevenfold degeneration described later in the chapter (→2:11–12). Yet this allusive possibility is not nearly as clear as the presence of sin in all its social disorder leading those outside to be "without God in the world" (2:12). A sevenfold schema, while less obvious, would only add further specificity to the exposition followed above.

Before moving ahead to the transitional statement in 2:4, we do well to return to introductory comments on 2:1–3. The divine power that made them alive will sit vividly in the foreground of 2:1–10, but it is highlighted not least by contrast with the background setting of their former death. The lush language used to describe the spiritual blessings and divine works that mark their present reality is matched by equally nuanced and concrete markers for their wayward walk in days past. While it is necessary to speak of a transition from sin to grace, it is never sufficient to do so in a way that remains generic or abstract. Sin, death, and devil always take the form of various pathologies that require specific diagnosis (indeed, typically overlapping diagnoses are not just possible but actual). Similarly, we shall see that the grace of Christ cannot sit like a cliché or mantra but must be connected to the particularities of Christ's work in bringing life where none might be expected.

2:4–7 But God, being rich in mercy, because of the great love with which he loved us, even when we were dead in our trespasses, made us alive together with Christ—by grace you have been saved—and raised us up with him and seated us with him in the heavenly places in Christ Jesus, so that in the coming ages he might show the immeasurable riches of his grace in kindness toward us in Christ Jesus.

The powerful adversative turns the reader's attention from their death-ridden past to God's life-giving action. For all the thick and varied description of human depravity in 2:1–3, verses 4–7 turn entirely to fix on another's being and work— that of the triune God.

"God . . . made us alive together with Christ" (2:4–5). Ephesians 2:1–10 attests the mighty power of God in a second manner, and it matches the first illustration in 1:19–23. Just as the resurrection of Jesus from the dead shows God's almighty strength, so here the Christian's being made alive manifests God's commitment and competence as well. "And [God] raised us up with him and seated us with him in the heavenly places in Christ Jesus" (2:6). The parallel continues: Christ was not only raised but also exalted on high (1:20–21), and here the Christian is also "seated" there "in the heavenly places." The language of heaven as it is found here evokes both a general and a specific connotation. Generally, heaven speaks of the most palpable presence of the living and true God. Specifically, however, the language here is not merely of heaven but of the heavenly throne room, as seen in the pairing of the metaphor of being seated and the context of the heavens. In drawing the reader's mind to the throne room of the heavens, the significance of authority is conveyed.

Paul does not conclude with resurrection and exaltation but continues toward the still-to-come future: "so that in the coming ages he might show the immeasurable riches of his grace" (2:7). God's "kindness toward us in Christ Jesus" takes the form also of an anticipated largesse, which Paul deems "immeasurable riches." In the previous chapter, Paul says that "in love he predestined us for adoption . . . as sons through Jesus Christ" (1:4–5). He goes on to speak of the implications of adoption: "In him we have obtained an inheritance, having been predestined" (1:11); however, any sense that the inheritance has already been disbursed is dissuaded by his following word regarding the Holy Spirit, "who is the guarantee of our inheritance until we acquire possession of it" (1:14). Ephesians will return again and again to the end of adoption—namely, the riches and fullness that God shares with his own. That God may show such favor speaks to its permissibility, not by some external standard, but owing to God's own intrinsic canons of propriety.

So the gospel word speaks to three divine actions here: God resurrects the dead sinner, God seats the newly born Christian in the heavenly throne room, and God will thenceforth be able to show immeasurable riches of grace to that adopted son or daughter. These actions are specific, and they have a particular scope and sequence to them such that Christian spirituality always takes at least this settled shape. And yet their end is one that begs imagination of excessive and varied kindness: in the ages yet to come, God will be in the business of manifesting "the immeasurable riches of his grace." The glory to come cannot be enumerated, though its goodness can be pegged to the fact that God has already accomplished these very narratable and proclamatory works. God acts powerfully in the economy such that God may give excessively in that state of glory.

But Paul does not only describe divine action. He also contemplates its occasion and circumstance, its context and motivations. Three particular claims are made in this regard, summed up by one abiding principle (which will be picked up again in 2:8). First, the God who does these gracious things is "rich in mercy" (2:4). The terminology of mercy speaks of generosity shown particularly to one who has wronged the very giver of that beneficence (see also Rom. 5:6, 8, 10). While Christians are called to love enemies (Matt. 5:43–47; Rom. 12:14–21), we do so because we have been loved by a God who is himself "rich" or plentifully excessive in this very trait. Second, the God performing these gospel acts does so "because of the great love with which he loved us" (Eph. 2:4). While God's action for us must be construed as mercy—as favor to which we are not entitled—that does not equate to kindness haphazardly or arbitrarily disbursed. God's great love falls on us specifically. Paul's earlier language of election speaks to this particularity as well (1:4, 5, 9, 11). Third, the divine love that motivates heavenly action took effect on us "even when we were dead in our trespasses" (2:5). We might say this is the anthropological counterpart to saying theologically that God acts here out of mercy, so this third point really returns to that first qualification and states it inversely.

What sums up these actions and such motivations? "By grace you have been saved" (2:5). This interjection slows the narration of God's action. While it applies to all three actions (resurrection, exaltation, future showing of riches), it is stated on the occasion of the first action being named as a principle underlying all these gospel workings.[1] The language of salvation and the character of grace, by which one is apparently saved, both deserve comment (→2:8–10).

2:8–10 For by grace you have been saved through faith. And this is not your own doing; it is the gift of God, not a result of works, so that no one may boast. For we are his workmanship, created in Christ Jesus for good works, which God prepared beforehand, that we should walk in them.

Paul rehearses and expands on his interjection from 2:5, saying now that "by grace you have been saved through faith." Unlike the earlier statement, here Paul will profess and even parse his meaning at a much more patient clip. Before reflecting on four analytic moves that he pauses to offer, we must give our attention to two key terms, "salvation" and "grace."

Salvation appears here for the first time in verbal form (*sesōsmenoi*), though the nominal form appeared earlier and will reemerge much later in the epistle: "the gospel of your salvation [*sōtērias*]" (→1:13); and "the helmet of salvation" (→6:17). The related language of an agent of salvation or "savior" arises in the epistle also: "Christ is the head of the church, his body, and is himself its Savior" (→5:23).

Interestingly, Colossians never employs the language of salvation, for all the parallels between the two texts. Interpreters might hypothesize about ways in which salvation language was not the most helpful given Colossians' attention to

---

1. In this regard, the interjection functions similarly to Heb. 11:6, which intervenes in the narration of faithful action in Heb. 11:4–38. The principle of 11:6 surely applies to all the characters, not just to Abel and Enoch, who are already mentioned by that point (in 11:4 and 11:5). Similarly here in Ephesians, "by grace you have been saved" describes not merely resurrection but also exaltation and all future beneficence shown to God's adopted children.

a particular heresy or error, perhaps with quasi-gnostic inflections. In such readings, salvation might be too inherently spiritual or personal/individual to be of use in opposing a mystery religion or gnostic alternative; hence Colossians sticks to metaphors of redemption and reconciliation and to more concrete actions such as making alive. Such analysis is not entirely without merit and may well be plausible. Salvation language does narrow or focus on the personal application of Christ's saving work. It does not negate or nullify cosmic activity, about which not only Col. 1 but also Eph. 1 and 3 have much to say, and yet it does accentuate the individual pertinence of salvation (given its pairing with language of personal faith).

Personal and individual faith or piety demands our attention, and yet we do well to remember the two most immediate contexts for these verses. Ephesians 2:1–3 has diagnosed the precondition of sinful need, locating the person among a range of overlapping contexts (social, spiritual/demonic, physiological, and natural/moral) in such a way that the individual's moral standing does not arise for consideration apart from its web of connections with other material and immaterial factors. Then 2:4–7 locates the remedy in the sweeping cosmic, redemptive action of the Christ who has risen and been exalted to the heavens. Any individual salvation, then, cannot be construed in an individualist manner. The need for salvation is personal but not removed from public links of all sorts, and the material basis for salvation has individual effects but is rooted in the one living and true Redeemer, in his being and works. We do well also to remember the wider setting of these verses in the epistle as a whole. The cosmic breadth of redemption has already been attested in chapter 1, and its ecclesiastical context will be sketched further in chapters 4–5.

Grace also demands discussion. It has spread far and wide in Christianity, which sometimes fosters a false sense of transparency, presuming that it is a straightforward or uncontested term. Historians of religion such as E. P. Sanders have offered comparative readings of Paul (or the New Testament more broadly) and Second Temple Jewish texts, observing the presence of grace language in both textual worlds and thus claiming that grace cannot be a dividing line among them (Sanders 1977). This comparative approach led many to assert that Christianity—or the New Testament documents more specifically—did not offer a new concept or reality of grace, for that was well attested already in other sources. In so doing, they argued that earlier Protestant exegesis was overly individualist and frankly eisegetical, reading the existential foibles of an Augustine or a Luther into the writings of Paul.[2]

2. N. T. Wright, *Paul and the Faithfulness of God* (Minneapolis: Fortress, 2013), 113–14 et passim.

Recent years have seen a more textured analysis of grace in its Jewish, Greco-Roman, and Christian contexts. A number of studies have offered reflections on texts that really do debate or converse about the definition of grace—that is, what manner of gift it involves (see esp. Barclay 2015). The major studies have not focused on Ephesians, because it is a disputed Pauline text, yet they have ranged broadly over the major writings of Paul. While acknowledging the presence of grace language across the wider intellectual milieu of Paul, they identify ways in which he is battling to redefine a common concept. Wisdom of Solomon may speak of grace in terms of a gift given to one likely to make good use of it, whereas it is for Paul a gift given to the weak, the ungodly, the sinners, and the enemies, as in Rom. 5:6–10 (Linebaugh 2013a). For this reason Barclay and Linebaugh speak of Paul perfecting the concept of grace in certain ways, accenting its counterintuitive nature as a gift in that world (and, we might argue, in our own as well). We will see that what Paul says here to expand on this phrase "by grace you have been saved" fits hand in glove with this newer comparative reading of grace, far more so than it does with the readings of Sanders and his interpretive generation (which have often been termed the "new perspective on Paul," which is more accurately a perspectival shift on how Paul relates to the Judaism of his day).

The phrasing in 2:8, "for by grace you have been saved through faith," is virtually identical to 2:5, "by grace you have been saved," though two additions are found here. First, this restatement provides the explanation or basis for what has preceded (as suggested by the conjunction "for" [*gar*], which might otherwise be rendered "because"). This gracious salvation undergirds the reality of "kindness toward us in Christ Jesus" (2:7). A god might exalt a creature for lots of reasons, whether due to entitlement or merit or fitting potential. But those motivations would not prompt us to call that exaltation "kind." In fact, it is crucial to remember that the language of kindness in 2:7 actually defines or constrains our understanding of grace ("his grace in kindness").

Second, Paul now appends a prepositional phrase that this gracious salvation comes to you "through faith" (*dia pisteōs*). This is not the first mention of faith in the epistle; Paul has already rooted his prayers for them in his having heard not merely of their love but also of their "faith in the Lord Jesus" (→1:15–16). Indeed, he had described narratively their coming to faith immediately prior to that verse when he said, "In him you also, when you heard the word of truth, the gospel of your salvation, and believed in him, were sealed with the promised Holy Spirit" (1:13). There belief is defined not least by its connecting or uniting us to Christ

("In him you also") but then also by its fit in a period marked by anticipation, a time in which we await the glory of the eschaton (1:14).

Four statements elaborate on this gracious salvation by faith. First, "this is not your own doing" (2:8). Paul excludes human agency in a sense here. We need to read this line alongside that of Gal. 2:20 ("It is no longer I who live"), as each line offers a rebuke to a sense of autonomy or utter independence. Paul's statement here demands an implicit metaphysics of creation lest it be heard as utter nonsense. But we must acknowledge that our modern world has traversed toward judgments regarding metaphysics that render such judgments implausible.[3] Cognizant of that cultural malformation and seeking to hear Eph. 2:8a accurately, we must ask what "this" refers to. The gender of the pronoun does not match that of any antecedent in the immediately prior clause, and, therefore, it likely takes in the totality of that sentence. What do we not do? "By grace you have been saved by faith"—the blunt principle suggests that this whole nexus is not ultimately our doing.

Second, "it is the gift of God" (2:8). Again the language of grace appears (→2:5). This phrase relates directly and inversely to what has just been said in the preceding clause; in other words, "this" that you have not done is the same "it" that God gives. The gift is related to God (*theou* is in the genitive). The most common interpretation here may well be a relation of source or material causality—namely, that God has acted to bring about this salvation by grace and by faith. God does so, ordinarily or typically, through various means and with regard to human volition, but God does so nonetheless. The Heidelberg Catechism alerts us to this reality: "Q. 65. Since, then, faith alone makes us share in Christ and all his benefits, where does such faith originate? The Holy Spirit creates it in our hearts by the preaching of the holy gospel, and confirms it by the use of the holy Sacraments." The typical pathway of this gift—as will be outlined in Eph. 4—is found in the means of grace. Not surprisingly, then, the "General Thanksgiving" in Morning Prayer (ever since 1662) in the *Book of Common Prayer* attests thankfulness "above all for your immeasurable love in the redemption of the world by our Lord Jesus Christ; for the means of grace, and for the hope of glory." God not only redeems and eventually glorifies, but God gives the faith (and grows that faith) through these means of grace, which are a divine gift.

---

3. See J. B. Schneewind, *The Invention of Autonomy: A History of Modern Moral Philosophy* (Cambridge: Cambridge University Press, 1998); William C. Placher, *The Domestication of Transcendence: How Modern Thinking about God Went Wrong* (Louisville: Westminster John Knox, 1996); Christopher J. Insole, *Kant and the Creation of Freedom: A Theological Problem*, Changing Paradigms in Systematic and Historical Theology (Oxford: Oxford University Press, 2013).

It may be well to consider a less heightened occasion wherein we can observe God's action internal to the human and then the attendant human moral agency. Turning from salvation and faith to something else is helpful because those categories can seem fraught with weightiness. Psalm 51 famously describes David's cry for grace. Among his pleas is this request that has found its way into various penitential liturgies: "O Lord, open my lips, and my mouth will declare your praise" (Ps. 51:15). God's opening of the psalmist's lips does not undercut but actually prompts and ensures the mouth's declaration. The sovereignty of divine action leading to human praise is expressed in no less tight a manner than is the divine prevenience stated here in Eph. 2:7–8, and the metaphysical context for understanding both venues is the same. Just as we would have no hesitation in joining with David in praying for God to open our mouths that we might praise God, so we ought not pause in speaking of God bringing us to express saving faith.

Some have turned to the language of irresistible grace to express this divine gift. They are rightly alert to parallel passages such as "Work out your own salvation with fear and trembling, for it is God who works in you, both to will and to work for his good pleasure" (Phil. 2:12–13). That second clause speaks of God working in Christians not only toward their good intent ("to will") but also to actually enact or perform that intention ("to work"). Perhaps we should call that divine assistance and enablement irresistible given that it is patently said to have its intended effect. But Lutheran theologian Robert Jenson demurs: "Grace is neither resistible nor irresistible, since we are never in a position to resist or want to resist, successfully or unsuccessfully. The one who pours out on us the liberating Spirit, does so from his heavenly throne hidden within us. The Spirit indeed opens the gate of our hearts, to the Father and to one another—from inside" (2002: 291). Jenson does not suggest that the language of irresistible grace is too strong. Rather, he argues that it makes too small a matter of God's enacting presence, for God is not an agent like other agents and not a factor that may or may not be resisted. God's work in this respect occurs subvolitionally, we might say, in a parallel to the language of subconsciousness. Paul employs language of creational agency by God in his conclusion to this section (→2:10), highlighting that unconstrained power put to work in making us anew by grace.

Third, this gracious salvation by faith is "not a result of works" (2:9). The contrast of grace and works and the contrast of faith and works may appear more frequently in contexts where justification appears (e.g., Gal. 2; Rom. 4), but here Paul does repudiate a works principle. He reinstitutes works as a necessity for which we have been created anew (→2:10), but here he utterly rejects any suggestion that salvation is a result of works (*ex ergōn*). There have been debates about the related phrase "works of the law" that seek to specify far more tightly their referent to particular Jewish practices such as diet, circumcision, and so on. Good reasons can be given as to why that limitation may not even hold in those other passages, but this passage (like Titus 3:4–7, where the idiom of salvation [v. 5] happens to be paired with that of justification [v. 7]) has no such focus. Rather, it is excluding works qua works. That is not to say that one manifestation, perhaps even a leading manifestation in certain situations in the first century, would not be a Jewish ethnocentrism, but Paul is excluding any and every human form of self-construction (whether by means of social class, racial and ethnic identity, physical beauty, religious praxis, financial or political power, or moral progress).

It is worth pausing to note that the sixteenth-century Protestant Reformers were aware that works could very well manifest in a range of ways in different times. We may assume that Luther saw the late medieval Roman priests behind every target of Paul's polemic, and yet the Wittenberger was alert to the distinctions and degrees involved in such comparison. Luther and Calvin alike regularly inveighed against their opponents, noting how strongly Paul would react to better versions of works—*better* because, for example, the Galatian heresy involved supplementing the sufficient work of Christ with law-keeping that had been taught earlier *as opposed to* late medieval struggles that involved merely ecclesial tradition that had not ever been delivered from Sinai on high (Luther 1979: 23, 34, 36–37, 42–43, 46, 144–45, 285, 289; Calvin 1965: 170). This is not merely a historiographic tour, because many of the more pressing manifestations of works today might be even more marked by pure human-social constructivism: we tend to look at sociological or ephemeral markers as bearing greater significance than did first-century Jews or even late-medieval Christians. But no human work serves as the lodestar from which saving results. All this is ultimately from God.

We do well to probe further lest our pondering over grace and works remain at the level of anthropology and human agency (either affirmed or denied). We must ask, to what divine reality must we trace back this gracious kindness shown in salvation by faith, not by works? Underneath the moral order lies a metaphysical reality. John Webster says, "God is beyond—not constituted by—all relations; nevertheless, he sets himself before creatures and brings them into relation to himself" (2017: 45). God's replete fullness lies beneath any engagement with his creatures, for God does not need or employ them to fill any gap or insufficiency in God's own life and work. Therefore, God can be said to act by grace—that is, by his own freedom exercised for their good. The gracious character of the divine economy and the moral character of salvation received by faith, not as a result of works, ultimately derive from the self-sufficiency of the triune God.

Soteriology must be rooted in one's doctrine of God. The economy manifests a life internal to the Godhead. In an essay speaking of the root principle of what he called "Calvinism" (a term that I would greatly prefer to be replaced by the category "Reformed"), Herman Bavinck describes a theological tendency in these terms:

> The root principle of this Calvinism is the confession of God's absolute sovereignty. Not one special attribute of God, for instance His love or justice, His holiness or equity, but God Himself as such in the unity of all His attributes and perfection of His entire Being is the point of departure for the thinking and acting of the Calvinist. From this root principle everything that is specifically Reformed may be derived and explained. It was this that led to the sharp distinction between what is God's and creature's, to belief in the sole authority of the Holy Scriptures, in the all-sufficiency of Christ and His word, in the omnipotence of the work of grace. (Bavinck 1894: 3–4)

The root principle here, which Bavinck calls "God's absolute sovereignty," can be misinterpreted given that he does not speak primarily of *gubernatio* or providence specifically, nor of any "one special attribute of God, . . . but God Himself as such in the unity of all His attributes and perfection of His entire Being." Others might speak of God's self-sufficiency, aseity, independence, or his fullness within the triune life of God. I would personally take those terms to better convey the concept that Bavinck means to highlight and to do so in a way that has wider catholic purchase. His basic premise, then, is that God's absolute aseity or fullness in and of himself, quite apart from us and without any need, grounds his every action.

If that is so for all God's actions, what we call his economy, then his salvific work described here in Eph. 2:4–10 is one such (admittedly complex) instance. Bavinck goes further in speaking of how this connection between the economy of grace and the very being of God dictates our theological responsibility—namely, that we trace back or reduce (in the medieval sense of the word *reductio*) all spiritual or salvific phenomena to the very being of God from whom they come:

> For this reason the Calvinist in all things recurs upon God, and does not rest satisfied before he has traced back everything to the sovereign good-pleasure of God as its ultimate and deepest cause. He never loses himself in the appearance of things, but penetrates to their realities. Behind the phenomena he searches for the noumena, the things that are not seen, from which the things visible have been

born. He does not take his stand in the midst of history, but out of time ascends into the heights of eternity. History is naught but the gradual unfolding of what to God is an eternal present. For his heart, his thinking, his life, the Calvinist cannot find rest in these terrestrial things, the sphere of what is becoming, changing, forever passing by. From the process of salvation he therefore recurs upon the decree of salvation, from history to the idea. He does not remain in the outer court of the temple, but seeks to enter into the innermost sanctuary. (Bavinck 1894: 4–5)

The kind of soteriology affirmed herein demands the kind of divine blessedness affirmed earlier (→1:3, 21–23). In our reading of the plain sense of Eph. 2:1–10, we must always hear the word of God contemplatively, asking what it reveals not merely of sinful women and men redeemed graciously by faith in Christ but also, still deeper, what this gospel reveals of the living and true God (Webster 2015a: 143–58).

Fourth, Paul says that this salvation by grace and by faith takes place "so that no one may boast" (2:9). Paul dissuades boasting and implicitly prepares us to return again to the praise of God's gracious glory (see also 1:6, 12, 14). Calvin is observant here in drawing an image from Bernard of Clairvaux: "They wrongfully retain the credit for grace that passes through them, as if a wall should say that it gave birth to a sunbeam that it received through a window" (Calvin 2006: 762 [3.12.8]). It is not for nothing that we quote Calvin here, for this passage offers still more evidence that Paul really does concern himself with defining grace and salvation in ways that accent God's agency, that rebuff an intuitive human impulse toward self-boasting, and that fix our attention ever on God's redemptive presence. As a range of arguments have shown in recent years, we can see that texts such as this one do impel the kind of readings offered by the Protestant Reformers. Luther and the others may well be debated on their material claims, but it simply will not do to consign their very questions to the dustbin of existential eisegesis or to demur that they are not provoked by real claims of the text. As has been shown through more patient attention given to them in their interpretative acts, they really do manifest an interest in thinking with the text (Allen 2013a; Allen and Linebaugh 2015; Chester 2017; Linebaugh 2013b).

Again, Paul seeks to offer something of a global explanation for all the varied testimonies he has offered of God's sovereign action. To that end he concludes with a logical explanation (as indicated by "for" [*gar*]): "For we are his workmanship, created in Christ Jesus for good works, which God prepared beforehand, that we should walk in them" (2:10). The master maker has worked out his goodness in fashioning us; Paul turns explicitly to the language of creation here to speak of the radicality of this new saving action. Elsewhere Paul will relate the power of redemption by linking these realities: "God, who said, 'Let light shine out of darkness,' has shone in our hearts to give the light of the knowledge of the glory of God in the face of Jesus Christ" (2 Cor. 4:6). Paul there speaks of how the illuming work in Jesus is like the creative agency of God in calling forth light in the beginning. Here in Eph. 2:10, Paul relates salvation by faith through grace to being "created in Christ Jesus."

What is involved in that creational language? And why would it pop up here, somewhat idiosyncratically it may seem, amidst this summary of 2:1–10? Perhaps the words of Kathryn Tanner can helpfully orient us to the matter:

> If our lives can still be turned around through God's help, this presumes no optimism about sin's consequences, as if something good remained of us to be the basis for simple modification. Instead, the grace that changes us has its analogue in the divine acts that created us—from nothing. The movement from our sinful state to the life we lead in Christ is like the rebirth of the dead. The starkest possible disjunction distinguishes the states between which we move from sin to grace—from death, on the one hand, to life, on the other—and therefore this movement is something like our literal recreation. Only God can help us cross from death to life, from nothing to something; we are no more responsible for this recreation through our own powers than we are for our creation. (2010: 64–65)

Thus described, it makes sense that Paul sums up Eph. 2:4–9 with this image in 2:10. Re-creative language highlights the need for divine action. As Tanner notes, this thought world accents the "starkest possible disjunction" between sinful nature and graced nature.

Paul speaks not merely of the power latent in this loving action but also of its purpose: "for good works . . . that we should walk in them." The terminology of "good works" (*ergois agathois*) appears rather infrequently in the New Testament; in the Pauline corpus it occurs only here and in the letters to Timothy and Titus (1 Tim. 2:10; 5:10, 25; 6:18; Titus 2:7, 14; 3:8, 14); even beyond the Pauline corpus, it is minimally present (Matt. 5:16; John 10:32; Acts 9:36; Heb. 10:24). The metaphor of walking is remarkably common, by contrast, in the scriptures of both the Old and New Testaments; Acts is illustrative in using the term "walking" (*peripateō*) to speak of practicing or conducting one's whole life in a certain manner (for good or for ill): "Walking in the fear of the Lord and in the comfort of the Holy Spirit, it [the church] multiplied" (Acts 9:31) and "In past generations he allowed all the nations to walk in their own ways" (Acts 14:16). The psalms regularly recount the challenge of life as a way in which we walk, again either to life or to death (i.e., Pss. 1:1; 119:1, 3). In both New Testament and Psalms contexts, then, language of walking is paired with that of "the way," a term that becomes emblematic of Christianity (i.e., Pss. 1:1, 6; 101:6; 119:1; 128:1; Acts 9:2; 19:23; 22:4; 24:14, 22; cf. Prov. 1:15 for a call to avoid walking in false ways). Here we read that the purpose of divine preparation is our walking in these good works—that is, actively engaging in them and conducting our whole life according to their pattern. It does also highlight the reality that this moral agency takes the form of an eschatological journey of pilgrimage: no longer in Egypt, we are not yet in Canaan, and so we are called to keep walking in God's way.

While this new creation is a gift or grace of God that is unmerited, it nonetheless does provoke and even involve moral action, as John Barclay says: "This obedience is not instrumental (it does not acquire the gift of Christ, nor any additional gift from God), but it is integral to the gift itself" (2015: 519). This purposed human agency, however, is defined still further, yet again, by locating it within the divine economy. These good works to which we are created in Christ are those "which God prepared beforehand." What does it mean that God "prepared" them? How does this term "beforehand" actually function? The verb employed here (*proētoimasen*) appears elsewhere in Paul: "What if God, desiring to show his wrath and to make known his power, has endured with much patience vessels of wrath prepared for destruction, in order to make known the riches of his glory for vessels of mercy, which he has *prepared beforehand* for glory . . . ?" (Rom. 9:22–23). Both instances fit within broader contexts that speak of the mystery of divine election: Rom. 9 explores that mystery analytically and exegetically (turning to stories of the Old Testament and repeatedly exploring potential objections), while Eph. 1 has already pressed the mystery toward God in praise and delight (1:4–5, 12–14).

The language of "preparing beforehand" pretty well paraphrases the theological term "predestination"—that is, that God destines or fits us ahead of time. Predestination presumes a particular metaphysic that is participatory, lest it place God and creatures in a posture of competitiveness. Thomas Aquinas grasped this notion by pointing to the way in which we are given life and being so as to act participatively:

> Anything that has a nature or form or a virtue perfectly, can of itself work according to them; not, however, excluding the operation of God who works inwardly

in every nature and in every will [by giving such things to it]. [But] that which has a nature, or form, or virtue imperfectly, cannot of itself work, unless it be moved by another. Thus the sun that possesses light perfectly can shine by itself; whereas the moon which has the nature of light imperfectly, sheds only a borrowed light. Again, a physician, who knows the medical art perfectly, can work by himself; but his pupil, who is not yet fully instructed, cannot work by himself, but needs to receive instructions from him. (*ST* I-II.68.2, reply)

We might imagine a world and beings wherein any such divine operation would be external and thus would be oppositional at its core. But the biblical teaching regarding the way in which the God of Israel acts is not oppositional. In winning the battle for his people, the Lord does not render their swords or shields moot, only effective (1 Sam. 17:47; 2 Chron. 20:15). Because the triune God of the gospel exists in a categorically different metaphysical realm, this one may work sovereignly without thereby undercutting our creaturely freedom.

Augustine proclaims this derivative, contingent existence as capable of true glory: "This is my glory, Lord my God, that for ever I may confess to you that nothing I have derives from myself, but that all good things are from you, who are God, all in all" (2000a: 299). We may chafe at this sort of suggestion, for modern culture frequently exalts the image of the self-made man or woman. It may seem counterintuitive to confess that glory and dependence are bound up together, but this is just to express the insight of that earlier concept employed in this verse—namely, creatureliness. To say that we are "created in Christ Jesus" is to say that we have doubled down on creatureliness, living not only on borrowed breath but also now on graced glory.

2:11–12 Therefore remember that at one time you Gentiles in the flesh, called "the uncircumcision" by what is called the circumcision, which is made in the flesh by hands—remember that you were at that time separated from Christ, alienated from the commonwealth of Israel and strangers to the covenants of promise, having no hope and without God in the world.

In 2:11 we enter a new realm, wherein the language of sin and grace and being made alive and faith will have been left behind and a new set of terms will enter the foreground: Jew and Gentile, circumcision and uncircumcision, flesh and peace, body and temple. If the preceding ten verses (2:1–10) fixate on God's power made manifest in personal salvation, then these twelve verses (2:11–22) turn our attention to corporate reconciliation wrought by that same power of the almighty God. In moving to a new realm, however, we are not leaving behind the notion of the new creation—that is, that the triune God has "created us in Christ Jesus" (2:10). In this section, we will see more of how the grace of new creation relates to the pangs of our sinful nature, socially speaking.

Though we enter a new realm, the section begins with the word "therefore" (*dio*), and we must ask what prompts this logical call to remembrance. Is the antecedent statement that of 2:10 alone? Perhaps the language of new creation is meant to be explicated by these verses; indeed, the conclusion of this section seems to pick up the building imagery, as 2:10 had spoken of Christians as God's "workmanship" (→2:20–22). Or is the antecedent the entirety of 2:8–10? It may be that we ought to read the remainder of chapter 2 as unpacking consequences of salvation by grace. Or is the whole of 2:1–10 the backdrop for this "therefore" in 2:11? The structure of 2:11–22 maps onto that of 2:1–10, each starting with a reminder of the death from which we have come (2:11–12 paralleling 2:1–3) and the new life (following the adversative "but" [*de*] in 2:13 and 2:4). It may well be that this broader answer best satisfies, as 2:1–10 and 2:11–22 do serve as parallel explications of God's powerful grace in response to sin (first personally, second socially). Nonetheless, we are not prevented from also seeing the terminology of God's workmanship picked up in the climactic section of 2:11–22 and developed via building terminology; in fact, the broader parallel makes exposition at just that point, rather than immediately in 2:11–12, especially appropriate.

What shall we then remember? In fact, "remember . . . remember" is the repeated exhortation: Gentile believers in the cities of Asia Minor are to remember from whence they have come. They are to remember seven realities that made them who they were. Almost like a reverse creation sequence, these seven statements identify them in their previous existence.[4] Only after dwelling on their malformation in these varied ways can we hear the good news: "But now" (2:13).

They are, first, to remember that they were "Gentiles in the flesh." Socially speaking, the most significant divide of the early Christian world was that of Jew and Gentile. Now, "Gentile" was not a self-appellation, but these hearers have learned to apply to themselves a term that Jews used to describe all non-Jews. In many ways this first description is emblematic of all those that follow, for they all tease out its significance in various ways. And this first remembrance regards

---

4. The book of Numbers also includes a sevenfold de-creation account in picking out seven of the ten grumblings of Israel and elaborating on them in chiastic form (11:1–3; 11:4–34; 11:35–12:16; 13:1–14:45; 16:1–17:11; 20:2–13; 21:4–9), on which see David L. Stubbs, *Numbers*, Brazos Theological Commentary on the Bible (Grand Rapids: Brazos, 2009), 113–14.

a beginning that they, in and of themselves, were incapable of acknowledging. Thus, it is a reminder that the sinner or sinful community does not merely lack the power to effect a needed change, but also suffers from an inability to perceive the needed change. The Bible teaches us graciously how to acknowledge and name our problems, whether in the lament psalms or here in the witness of a group of people who have learned to name their past as Gentiles beyond the range of God's generous rule.

They are, second, to remember being called "the uncircumcision." The Jews, those known as "the circumcision," referred to or "called" them Gentiles. We see that Jews spoke of them and named them. And at least one significant naming was a naming of privation: these ones lacked circumcision. Christians have frequently spoken of sin as privation, a concept developed with special vividness in the writings of Augustine. In his writings, reality is good inasmuch as it is created and sustained and thereby participating in God, and yet sin leads reality to wilt in its loss or deprivation of some element of that good, a suffering we can term a privation. Here we see that these persons were formerly good creations of God, though lacking the sign of circumcision.

What was the significance of this sign that they lacked? Circumcision was commanded of Abraham and Isaac in Gen. 17: "Every male among you shall be circumcised. You shall be circumcised in the flesh of your foreskins, and it shall be a sign of the covenant between me and you" (17:10–11). What covenant? Genesis 17:1–8 has described a covenant order between "God Almighty" and ninety-nine-year-old Abram (17:1). God promises descendants (17:2, 6) and land (17:8) and that Abram will be a blessing to diverse nations (17:4–5). In these three ways 17:1–8 expands on what was originally promised in Gen. 12:1–3. But here it is expanded by highlighting the center of the covenant: "to be God to you ... and I will be their God" (17:7–8).

So Paul's Gentile hearers were uncircumcised and lacked that covenant promise. Yet Eph. 2:11 does not merely call them "the uncircumcision" and juxtapose them with the circumcised. It qualifies that description of this sign, saying they are "called 'the uncircumcision' by what is called the circumcision, which is made in the flesh by hands." Stephen Fowl says, "This indicates that coming to understand one's past outside of Christ as a Gentile past is a contested matter. At the very least it will involve learning to see Gentileness in a very particular way, which many Jews might not accept" (2012: 86).[5] As Fowl notes, Paul does

5. For a sense of the variety of ways with which circumcision was taken by Jews, see Thiessen (2011).

not seem to be undermining the claim that they were uncircumcised, and yet he does relativize that claim. He highlights here the way in which Jews viewed them as excluded, but that social exclusion was not the most definitive facet of their Gentile past (even if some Jews might be bewildered by that claim). Hence he calls them to remembrance again, looking past this surface-level sign to deeper realities in the next verse.

They are, third, to remember "that you were at that time separated from Christ." After a pause of sorts, Paul launches into a further call to remembrance (signified by the term *hoti*). An in-depth analysis of their Gentile life must begin with their relationship to Christ, and that relationship has to be defined by "separation" or being "apart from" Christ. This segregation must be understood in juxtaposition to the many instances of inclusivity found earlier in the epistle, where repeatedly Christians are said to be in Christ in some way (e.g., 1:1, 3, 4, 5, 6, 7, 9, 10).

They are, fourth, to remember being "alienated from the commonwealth of Israel." We need to interpret this alienation as not reducible to the social exclusion mentioned in the preceding verse. In other words, this alienation is more fundamental than mere social exclusion by and from those who call themselves "the circumcision." It is surely significant that "the commonwealth of Israel" (*tēs politeias tou Israēl*) is the object of this alienation, for it highlights the kingdom of God and the reign of his own justice that were not the sphere of Gentile civility. The term *politeias* appears only here and in Acts 22:28 in the New Testament; it seems to connote citizenship. The more notable term here is the name Israel, for the sort of citizenship that these former Gentiles lacked is that of the people who have striven with God (*tou Israēl*). Other cities or polities struggle with majority and minority, native-born and immigrant, landowners and journeymen, but this entity struggles with God. In the past, these Gentiles had lived a secular political life; they had been alienated from a politics that strove with God.

They are, fifth, to remember being "strangers to the covenants of promise." How one interprets the language of covenants here should relate to some extent to the way in which one will interpret 2:15—that is, what it means to "abolish the law of commandments expressed in ordinances." Some take a stark approach, suggesting that the author here completely relativizes or even repudiates the law of Moses. In such a reading, Gentiles have been brought in because the Mosaic code as such has been decimated (replaced or fulfilled by the law of Christ). Yet 2:12 points in just the other direction. The problem named here is not the covenant of law or commandments but the fact that Gentiles were alien to the "covenants of promise." They had no divine word guaranteeing them divine fealty or provision.

They are, sixth, to remember "having no hope." Inasmuch as they lacked a divine promise, they had no hope. But we must inquire about what that hope regarded. Is Paul addressing a civic hope, a spiritual hope, a moral hope, a material hope? Reading contextually suggests that this hope would be defined by theological language: reading backward, a hope defined by promise, Israel, and Christ; reading forward, a hope of being with God in the world.

Seventh and finally, they were "without God in the world." If the original creation account of Gen. 1 concluded with the seventh day wherein God rested or made his dwelling place to be with his people in that Edenic paradise, then here we learn that these hearers were not merely politically marginal but spiritually isolated from God. And Paul here manifests what he has prayed for—namely, the power to see further into the spiritual reality than might otherwise be the case. Underneath real fraying of a social fabric, Paul can perceive a genuine godlessness. Eventually, of course, he will wrap up the epistle by reminding his hearers that their battle is not against earthly powers, not against mere flesh and blood (→6:12).

2:13–17 But now in Christ Jesus you who once were far off have been brought near by the blood of Christ. For he himself is our peace, who has made us both one and has broken down in his flesh the dividing wall of hostility by abolishing the law of commandments expressed in ordinances, that he might create in himself one new man in place of the two, so making peace, and might reconcile us both to God in one body through the cross, thereby killing the hostility. And he came and preached peace to you who were far off and peace to those who were near.

"But now" (*nyni de*) Paul speaks a word of divine power. Just as 1:20 spoke of divine power raising Jesus from death and 2:4 testified to God giving new birth to those children of wrath, so here triune power brings the estranged into the presence of God. For all the role these verses have played in civil rights sermons, we do well to remember that their mood is not hortatory (which will come by implication here and by explicit exhortation later: →4:1–3) but declarative.

Christ is the goal and the pathway, Augustine would say (see Byassee 2007: 54–58). Here we see that Christ is the end of peace as well as the conduit of enjoying that peace. "He himself is our peace," we read here. First, Christ is definitive of that peace, wherein he fulfilled the law (Matt. 5:17–21) but also knew that the law served humanity, not vice versa (Mark 2:27). He honors the law, offering his flesh and blood to bring its cultic demands to full maturation once and for all. But he also shows this process of legal provision to have a goal—namely, that blood, being given through the cross, need not be demanded anymore. Second, Christ is the pathway or way to that peace. We have peace "in Christ Jesus" alone.

Ephesians 2:14–15 does speak destructively as a means to reconstruction. God breaks down and abolishes before God creates and makes. There are earlier scriptural examples of this sort of language, perhaps none so significant as the way in which these terms are taken up in the call to Jeremiah: "See, I have set you this day over nations and over kingdoms, to pluck up and to break down, to destroy and to overthrow, to build and to plant" (Jer. 1:10). Those six infinitives define the purpose of the prophetic task, and they do so in two distinct ways: plucking up, breaking down, destroying, overthrowing (here we have the imagery of deconstruction), building, and planting (there we hear of God's reconstructive or restorative work). Similarly, Eph. 2:14 speaks of a wall coming down just before 2:15 speaks of a new creation.

What do the verbs convey regarding God's action? Deconstruction can and should be described first. We learn first in 2:14 that "he has broken down in his flesh the dividing wall of hostility," and 2:16 will go further in speaking of him "killing the hostility." Reconstruction comes second, and Paul says in 2:15 that "he might create in himself one new man in place of the two." The language parallels 2:10, where creational imagery also appears. The language of deconstruction accents the way in which the gospel is no salve or band-aid but has to bring the promise of God's word to the totality of our sin-riddled existence. Indeed, the word has to kill before it makes alive, to mortify prior to vivifying. The "new creation" language again (as in 2:10) speaks of the way in which grace transfigures our existence, so that nature is restored and moved toward perfection. In this case, perfection for us, socially speaking, means that the distinction of God's own people, the Jews, was ultimately meant to be for the Gentiles and not at the cost of the Gentiles (as rooted in texts such as Gen. 12:3a; Exod. 19:6–7).[6]

What do the nouns and adjectives say concerning our final state and ultimate reality? The "far off have been brought near," and he "has made us both one." So the gracious reality defined here is one wherein these Gentiles are near, and in being brought close to God they also are unified with the Jews. The new reality involves the presence of God, yes, but also the public consequence of that intimacy. Presence makes for a new polity in the kingdom of God; the Abrahamic promise is finding mysterious and wider eschatological fulfillment.

6. Jo Bailey Wells, *God's Holy People: A Theme in Biblical Theology*, Journal for the Study of the Old Testament Supplement Series 305 (Sheffield: Sheffield Academic Press, 2000).

More specifically, God in Christ has abolished "the law of commandments expressed in ordinances"—but what does this mean? And how does this relate to the plain fact that Paul—even in Ephesians (→6:2)—will continue to employ the Israelite torah/law as moral instruction? The term translated "abolished" (*katargēsas*) by the ESV appears elsewhere in Paul, translated in all sorts of ways, as can be illustrated simply in how the ESV renders it within Romans: "nullify" (3:3), "overthrow" (3:31), "is void" (4:14), "brought to nothing" (6:6), "released" (7:2, 6). The passage where it plays a repeated, central role is 2 Cor. 3, for *katargeō* appears four times in seven verses (3:7, 11, 13, 14; see also 1 Cor. 13:8–11, where it appears three times). To get a handle on its likely semantic meaning, we are wise to look at that passage briefly and see if it sheds light on what is going on here in Eph. 2.

In 2 Cor. 3, Paul considers the story of Exod. 32–34 and argues that Moses's face had to be covered because the glory of the Lord shone on his face in Exod. 34. The ESV translates *katargeō* in 2 Cor. 3:7, 11, and 13 as "being brought to an end" and in 3:14 as "taken away," though it has been shown elsewhere that a more helpful rendering might be "rendered inoperative" (Hafemann 1995: 310). There the sinfulness of the Israelites rendered inoperative the witness to glory that was Moses's face and demanded a veil, lest they be judged and condemned. How might this cast light on the use of the term in Eph. 2? Perhaps we should read Eph. 2:15 as speaking not of nullification but of limitation.

The "law of commandments" is not cast out, though it is limited in its efficacy and intent: it no longer defines those in and out. But what law is being limited? Not merely the law as such, but a law "expressed in ordinances," which has a very Deuteronomic flavor to it.[7] Whereas Eph. 2:8–9 speaks much more broadly of works (*ergōn*), here the law fixes more narrowly on the civic and cultic demands given Israel in its ordinances (paralleling Gal. 2:11–21 more specifically). One illustration of a broader works principle is a fixation on specific social mores and religious rites as a differentiating factor in marking out the people of God. While the soteriological principle cannot be reduced to that ecclesiological one (herein lies one error of the so-called new perspectives on Paul), that ecclesiological consequence must needs follow from the more nascent soteriological point. Paul does not oppose any ritual specification of the people of God (even Gal. 3:26–28 identifies the sign of baptism), though he does limit the present-day role of the "law of commandments" in such fashion. This side of Pentecost, the ceremonial

7. Parallels to Col. 2:13–23 are also notable.

code of Moses will not function in terms of differentiating God's own from the people outside the fold, for Gentiles are now by faith in Christ made one with Jewish believers.

Ephesians 2:16 speaks of "killing the hostility," which only comes at a cost. Hostility, in other words, does not go away cheaply. Miroslav Volf has reflected on this costly peacemaking: "Without entrusting oneself to the God who judges justly, it will hardly be possible to follow the crucified Messiah and refuse to retaliate when abused. The certainty of God's just judgment at the end of history is the presupposition for the renunciation of violence in the middle of it."[8] Here in Eph. 2:16, judgment has been brought forward, highlighted by the reference to this peace coming "through the cross." Earlier allusions to this event only highlight its reality: "by the blood of Christ" (2:13) and "in his flesh" (2:14). At and through the cross, we see God's resolve to work reconciliation, with the Father delivering up the Son (Acts 2:23) and the Son sacrificing himself (John 10:18).

Christ dies and proclaims. We need to be alert to the full sweep of Paul's christological claims here, lest we truncate our sense of the peacemaking Son and his gift of peace to his fellow heirs. He does a work of reconciliation and this task involves a bloody death attested here. We also read herein of his preaching ministry not merely to those Gentiles who were crosswise from God's purposes but also to "those who were near." We need then to attend to Christ as both sacrifice and shepherd. Paul preached to the people of God who were already "near" and who were "far off"; indeed, his preaching to the "far off" was one means whereby they were brought near.

2:18–22 For through him we both have access in one Spirit to the Father. So then you are no longer strangers and aliens, but you are fellow citizens with the saints and members of the household of God, built on the foundation of the apostles and prophets, Christ Jesus himself being the cornerstone, in whom the whole structure, being joined together, grows into a holy temple in the Lord. In him you also are being built together into a dwelling place for God by the Spirit.

The section concludes by turning to temple imagery, through which it conveys the priority of "access . . . to the Father" (2:18). Access to the Father is the basis for the peace described in 2:13–17. A similar notion recurs at the conclusion of the letter, where the blessing says, "Peace be to the brothers, and love with faith,

8. Volf, *Exclusion and Embrace: A Theological Exploration of Identity, Otherness, and Reconciliation* (Nashville: Abingdon, 1996), 302.

from God the Father" (6:23). Rightful presence in the Father's household brings peace in its wake. Here the syntax quickly turns somewhat haphazard and clunky, though this too is instructive. Whereas 2:18 introduces the notion of access, 2:19 turns to speak of citizenship and household membership before returning in the next verse to "dwelling place" language (which continues from 2:20 to 2:22). Indeed, the jolting incision of 2:19 likely seeks to relativize polity language to that of "presence" categories; political and familial identification will be framed by one's place within the "holy temple in the Lord" (2:21).

What can be said about this temple? First, it is "built on the foundation of the apostles and the prophets" (2:20). Why accent apostles with the first mention? Apostles herald the newness of the Christ's coming and passion, and therefore they are privileged here. That being said, the prophets of old also merit mention and are in no way expunged as structural elements of this churchly scaffolding. "Prophets" likely refers to those Israelite heralds inasmuch as the letter has not addressed present-day prophetic activity (though that will come later: →4:11), and the immediate context has been ruminating on the ongoing implications of God's former revelation. In both cases—apostolic and prior prophetic testimony—authorized speech of those emissaries of the Son serves a fundamental role in his upbuilding of this new community (→4:7–12).

Second, Paul goes to say of the temple, "Christ Jesus himself [is] the cornerstone" (2:20). There is some debate regarding the precise translation of the term *akrogōniaiou*: Is it a headstone or a cornerstone? Expounding Ps. 87:1–3 and its reference to the city's "foundations upon the mountains" in light of Christ as cornerstone in Eph. 2:20, Augustine wrestles with the question: "How then can both be true—that the prophets and apostles are the foundations, and that Christ Jesus is the foundation, beside whom there can be no other?" Considering that psalm, he says, "How are we to think of it, except that as he is properly said to be the Holy One of all holy ones, so he is figuratively called the foundation of foundations?" (Augustine 2002: 248). While "cornerstone" tends to be preferred, the fundamental image is just the same. Both stones serve an abiding significance and an ongoing active role. It is this insistent activity that is highlighted here, for the text goes on to say, "in whom the whole structure, being joined together, grows into a holy temple in the Lord" (2:21). Christ's central role does not get reduced to antiquity and yesteryear but finds expression in ongoing terms. Oriented around him, the church grows up.

Third, the Holy Spirit plays a highlighted role here. Ephesians 2:18 said that our access to the Father was through Christ and "in one Spirit." Verse 22 recurs to this claim, saying, "In him you also are being built together into a dwelling place for God by the Spirit." Actually, the repetition is even tighter than the English suggests, because the phrasing repeats (*en pneumati*, "in the Spirit" albeit with and without *heni*, "one"). The language of "the Spirit" (2:18, 22) echoes that of 1:3 ("every spiritual blessing," *en pasē eulogia pneumatikē*).

Fourth, the language beginning 2:22 echoes that of 1:13: "In him you also." The christological point also introduces this whole section, for 2:18 says that "through him" access to the Father can be enjoyed. We rightly come to the conclusion of this section by attending to this christological focus, for that reminds us that 2:11–22, like 2:1–10 before it, exemplifies the same divine power (1:18–19) that was initially manifest in action directed toward (though not terminating on) Jesus Christ (1:20–22). His resurrection, the sinner's salvation by grace, and the building together of one new temple in the Lord are not mere products of power. We must read 1:19 alongside 1:18, for there were three things to be known: our hope, our glorious inheritance, and the triune God's might toward believers.

While the resurrection of Jesus obviously unites hope, the Son's inheritance, and God's own power, we must confess that these next two manifestations of divine power in 2:1–10 and 2:11–22 flow no less from that nexus. John Webster speaks of this christological inclusion: "We are because he is. We are only because he is. That is what is meant by faith in the gospel's God: living trustfully from the work and communicative presence of creator, redeemer and perfector, and so being free to lay aside the wretched responsibility for securing ourselves, which is one of the bitterest fruits of the fall. But because he is, we really are. His exaltation is the sure ground of creaturely being and the promise of proper creaturely glory" (Webster 2007).

Sinners and societies that need divine intervention experience it "in him," so this notion of christological inclusion or union is no small matter. In a vivid sense, we see here how the epistle can begin by addressing its audience as "saints" and "faithful ones," to be sure, but only "in Christ Jesus." Still further, we must remember that those in Christ receive the blessing of that greeting, "grace to you and peace." Perhaps more explicitly and directly than any other portions of this epistle, Eph. 2:1–10 illustrates that grace and 2:11–22 manifests that peace.

EPHESIANS 3

3:1–3 For this reason I, Paul, a prisoner of Christ Jesus on behalf of you Gentiles—assuming that you have heard of the stewardship of God's grace that was given to me for you, how the mystery was made known to me by revelation, as I have written briefly.

In entering this new chapter, we traverse another episode of God's powerful might that is shown to his adopted children, and in so doing we remain still within the lengthy analysis of Paul's confidence for praying as and what he does in 1:15–19. In fact, Paul will return to those prayers regarding power and knowledge in 3:14–19. As with 1:21–23, 2:1–10, and 2:11–22, so here a demonstration of gracious power is meant to solidify our confidence in the powerful God of the gospel. Knowing these life-giving acts of might in the past, we are to be confident and bold in joining Paul to ask now for God's power to be displayed in deepening our knowledge and love.

With this example, Paul turns autobiographical. Paul introduced himself in 1:1 as "an apostle of Christ Jesus by the will of God" and here identifies himself further as "a prisoner of Christ Jesus on behalf of you Gentiles" (3:1). That Paul alerts them to his status as a prisoner is not surprising, as he is not hesitant to do so elsewhere (explicitly in Phil. 1:7, implicitly in Col. 1:24). It is perhaps slightly more jarring to observe the two ways in which Paul qualifies or characterizes his imprisonment. First, he is a prisoner not of Rome but "of Christ Jesus." In saying this, he minimizes or relativizes the role and status of the Roman bureaucratic machinery and he implicitly reduces the pomp and power of the state. There are all sorts of reasons to avoid viewing Rome as a foregrounded concern of Paul (on which see Kim 2008: 3–73; Barclay 2011: 363–88), but he does implicitly undermine any inflated claims of imperial or political significance. Second, Paul appends the phrase "on behalf of you Gentiles" (*hyper hymōn tōn ethnōn*) in 3:1. In so doing, Paul uses the second person ("you"), which after 3:4 he will drop until 3:13. We ought not miss the personal link, however: Paul relates his imprisonment to his audience in some way. Precisely how he makes that link comes in his calling them "you Gentiles." And so we do well to pause and reflect on how the Gentile mission shaped Paul's imprisonment.

We should not jump to assumptions that this letter has any direct literary relationship to the Acts of the Apostles, but we do well to tend to its thematic and historical parallels. In Acts, Paul's devotion to the Christian community in Ephesus merits lengthy attention (chs. 19–20). Paul found and baptized disciples (19:1–7) and labored for roughly two years in the synagogue and Tyrannus Hall to speak the word of the Lord to both Jews and Greeks (19:8–10), leading to miracles and public repentance by converts (19:11–20). Soon enough a riot ensued from worry that Paul's proclamation and its results were undercutting the economy, tied as it was to commerce in silver for the shrines of Artemis (19:21–41). While Paul left to journey into Macedonia and Greece (20:1–2) and intended to journey on to Jerusalem (20:16), he nonetheless sent for elders from Ephesus (20:17). He addressed them by reminding them that he taught them the "whole counsel of God" (20:27) and did not use them for financial gain (20:33–35). He offered a parting blessing: "And now I commend you to God and to the word of his grace, which is able to build you up and to give you the inheritance among all those who are sanctified" (20:32).

Even if Ephesians isn't actually written directly to Ephesus, or at least not exclusively to Ephesus (→1:1), the letter was quickly identified with the church at Ephesus such that the name was appended to the epistle. Interestingly, Paul's blessing in Acts 20:32 accents major themes in Ephesians—that is, that the saints would be built up and given their inheritance. So there are notable parallels. And yet Acts does not identify Paul being imprisoned in Ephesus; he journeyed on and was imprisoned eventually when he went to Jerusalem (Acts 21:33). Why then would Paul speak of imprisonment for the sake of Gentiles? He clearly does not mean that Gentiles imprisoned him; while Roman authorities served as the instruments of power in this regard, his imprisonment was motivated by Jewish leaders (such is Paul's understanding at least, according to Acts 28:19). Paul is speaking not of the human reasons for his imprisonment but of the divine design of his servitude. His imprisonment was a tool in the Lord's hands to bring Paul eventually to Rome itself (Acts 28:16). Thus, Paul could say—among the concluding words of the Acts of the Apostles—that "this salvation of God has been sent to the Gentiles" (28:28). What had been promised long before by the risen Christ in Acts 1:8—namely, that the apostles would "be my witnesses in Jerusalem and in all Judea and Samaria, and to the end of the earth"—came true in Rome (symbolic of the "end of the earth") through Paul's imprisonment.

Paul is imprisoned not because of these Gentiles but "on behalf of" them. Even here, amidst what would be a gruesome and difficult situation, he discerns purpose. In seeing such design, he demonstrates his own discipleship, for Jesus himself modeled a self-consciousness about divine necessity (e.g., Mark 8:31 and its use of "must"). And Jesus was the perfect instantiation of a model that went back all the way to another—to Joseph, whose abandonment to Egypt and imprisonment served as tools for redeeming his people from famine (Gen. 37–50, esp. 50:20). Like Joseph and Jesus, then, Paul can look through the vagaries of history and discern a divine intent, or at least a spiritual blessing (which may well not take in all the varied divine aims of that providential pathway, much of which remains opaque even to saints). In many ways the very kind of perception—spiritual attentiveness—for which Paul prays that God will empower his audience (→1:17–19; 3:18–19) is put on display here, for Paul shares the fruits of what one sees when the eyes of one's heart are enlightened. The dispersal of the divine estate is perceptible even through a probate process that is painful and politically complicated.

There is memoir, and there is memoir. Paul identifies himself still further, but in so doing he displaces his own agency and delineates his credentials as flowing from God's action rather than any achievement of his own. In 3:2 he identifies himself as a steward, which locates his responsibility as administrative rather than executive. The steward serves at the pleasure of the master, administering according to the master's desires. In the time of the Reformation, the distinction between magisterial and ministerial authority was employed to bring out this facet of pastoral (or apostolic) service.

Even Paul the apostle serves as a minister, one authorized by and thus reporting to another. Only the risen Christ serves as magister or Lord. For this reason, even Paul is beholden to follow the gospel: "But even if we or an angel from heaven should preach to you a gospel contrary to the one we preached to you, let him be accursed" (Gal. 1:8). Perhaps not surprisingly, Paul there identified himself as a "servant of Christ" (Gal. 1:10; the term here, *doulos*, "slave" or "servant," is not the same as *oikonomian*, "stewardship," in Eph. 3:2, though both identify Paul as a man under orders using language of the household economy).

This "stewardship of God's grace" was "given to me for you" (Eph. 3:2). Again, "grace" ranges more widely than we might be prone to assume. While later chapters will describe so-called means of grace in greater detail, here Paul identifies his own apostolic role as one who serves grace to his audience. Protestants may feel quite comfortable with the language of stewardship, and they may just as likely intuitively sense discomfort with the notion of stewarding or serving grace as a description of ministerial office. Yet we do well to probe whether any such hesitation doesn't flow more from pietism or revivalism—each with its own craven turn inward—than from the mainstream Reformation and its ecclesiology. The late John Webster was especially keen to the danger of flattening ministerial or ecclesial action and that of God Almighty. In an early doctrinal essay he put it this way:

> I suggest that the Christological ἐφάπαξ [ephapax] and its drastic curtailment of the *soteriological* significance of human ecclesial activity may best be safeguarded by a theology of mediation which is more apophatic in character. . . . An *apophatic* account of mediation draws attention, not so much to creaturely incapacity as to the utter capacity of God's self-communicative presence in Christ and Spirit, thereby entirely reorienting the task of creaturely witness. Apophatic mediation is at heart *indicative*, the mediating reality—object, activity, person, word—does not replace or embody or even "represent" that which is mediated, but is as it were an empty space in which that which is mediated is left free to be and act. . . . And the ontology of such mediation is therefore to be spelled out—over against the Western Catholic tradition—not in terms of an ontology of presence, but in terms of what might be called an ontology of indication. Mediating realities have their being in the action of indicating that whose utter plentitude lies wholly beyond them. (Webster 2001: 226–27)

Webster's instinct rightly serves to highlight the singularity of Christ's work (in his passion, yes, but also in his exalted status and heavenly session: he continues to function as Lord and Redeemer now); further, the divine agency of the incarnate Son cannot be identified directly with any ecclesial or pastoral practices (he is never simply identified with his body but also addresses and confronts his body as a prophet). And yet Webster's concern to hedge us away from an exuberant clericalism must be paired with a word about divine promise and divine covenant—namely, that God deigns to be present in the act of ministerial indication: ecclesial space does enjoy the presence of God. Now, one likely cannot juxtapose an "ontology of presence" and an "ontology of indication" in such a stark manner, whether conceptually or historically. Paul locates the way in which his authority and agency participates in God's economy, of which alone he is a steward, and yet describes how his pastoral and apostolic practice really does serve as a conduit of God's grace. With Webster, we can and must read Eph. 3:2–3, however, in light of 1:3–14, wherein the doctrine of election shapes our appreciation of ecclesial and clerical practice. In this case, God's grace flows through the conduit of apostolic indication according to the living will of the triune God.

If this is an odd method of manifesting his own authority (comparable perhaps to 2 Cor. 10–12), then Paul uses language that directly addresses this oddity. Ephesians 3:3 speaks of God's gifting and equipping him along the lines of "the mystery . . . made known to me by revelation." A key word has been introduced here, "mystery" (*mystērion*), which explicitly dominates the next several verses of 3:4–6 and implicitly marks 3:7–13 as well. The nature of that mystery will be discussed below (→3:6); here it suffices to note that this mystery "was made known to [Paul] by revelation." Paul not only eschews any claim to creativity or *poiesis*, but he speaks of how his knowledge came by way of revelation. In so doing, he uses a term that he has already used in 1:9 to speak of how God "mak[es] known to us the mystery of his will," so it is a term that yokes the apostle with the audience as a whole rather than some charismatic exception or clerical singularity that serves as a wedge to exalt or differentiate Paul.

What do we make of the allusive statement "as I have written briefly?" Is Paul somehow suggesting that we be aware of earlier accounts of his illumination by God? If so, then the likely referent is found in Gal. 1: "The gospel that was preached by me is not man's gospel. For I did not receive it from any man, nor was I taught it, but I received it through a revelation of Jesus Christ" (1:11–12). The compressed statement "what I also received" in 1 Cor. 15:3 serves as a potential, though less likely, referent. Another option surfaces, however, if we consider the immediate literary context: Paul has not yet given any narrative-style description of his calling, and yet he has identified his credentials as "an apostle of Christ Jesus" (Eph. 1:1). It is quite possible that Paul's allusion here is to his prior self-identification as an apostle or authorized emissary of Jesus Christ. Given that the language of revelation appears so patently in Gal. 1:11–12 as in Eph. 3:3, however, it may be that this first option is the more likely explanation.

3:4–10 When you read this, you can perceive my insight into the mystery of Christ, which was not made known to the sons of men in other generations as it has now been revealed to his holy apostles and prophets by the Spirit. This mystery is that the Gentiles are fellow heirs, members of the same body, and partakers of the promise in Christ Jesus through the gospel.

Of this gospel I was made a minister according to the gift of God's grace, which was given me by the working of his power. To me, though I am the very least of all the saints, this grace was given, to preach to the Gentiles the unsearchable riches of Christ, and to bring to light for everyone what is the plan of the mystery hidden for ages in God, who created all things, so that through the church the manifold wisdom of God might now be made known to the rulers and authorities in the heavenly places.

Paul continues this thread regarding the mystery and his own experience of God making it known to him. Paul's perception does not take the form of a private possession over against the knowledge of others; rather, he says, "When you read this, you can perceive my insight into the mystery of Christ" (3:4). There is no flourishing a curriculum vitae, no listing of his religious accomplishments. In fact, the closest Paul gets to doing so subverts such protocols. He reminds his readers in Philippi that he was "circumcised on the eighth day, of the people of Israel, of the tribe of Benjamin, a Hebrew of Hebrews; as to the law, a Pharisee; as to zeal, a persecutor of the church; as to righteousness under the law, blameless," and yet these marks he counts as "loss" (Phil. 3:5–7). He recounts his "far greater labors, far more imprisonments, with countless beatings, and often near death. Five times I received at the hands of the Jews the forty lashes less one. Three time I was beaten with rods. Once I was stoned. Three times I was shipwrecked; a night and a day I was adrift at sea; on frequent journeys, in danger," and so forth. Again, though, he deflects by saying that in such recounting "I am talking like a madman." Indeed, "if I must boast, I will boast of the things that show my weakness" (2 Cor. 11:23–26, 30).

No, Paul's insight and perception are not to be taken on faith, nor are they demonstrated by means of his power and accomplishment. In reading his letter, his audience too can see the character and the truth of his claims. Mysterious though it may be, his christological proclamation can be appreciated as true. The way in which this verse calls for lay discernment echoes Acts 17: "Now these Jews were more noble than those in Thessalonica; they received the word with all eagerness, examining the Scriptures daily to see if these things were so. Many of them therefore believed" (17:11–12). The Bereans are commended for exegetical alertness, hearing Paul and Silas preach in the synagogue and returning to the Law to see if their proclamation can be trusted. In so doing, they do not exercise a hermeneutic of suspicion or a measure of intellectual distance; rather, we read that in so doing "many of them therefore believed." Trust takes the form of believing it to be demonstrably true, true in the way that can be appreciated by the catechized child of the covenant. So here, Paul invites his readers to examine his claims and expects them to discern the appropriateness of his theological judgments.

Nonetheless, Paul's perception does mark a progression beyond that which was known beforehand, for this mystery "was not made known to the sons of men in other generations as it has now been revealed to his holy apostles and prophets by the Spirit" (3:5). Paul speaks of something novel and fresh in the apostolic age: this mystery regarding the Gentiles (→3:6). The Spirit has revealed this truth now, which most likely refers to the giving of the Spirit to representatives of the nations on the day of Pentecost (Acts 2:1–11). But this giving occurs not only on the day of Pentecost, for later instances of gospel proclamation also see the Gentiles receive the Holy Spirit: "And the believers from among the circumcised who had come with Peter were amazed, because the gift of the Holy Spirit was poured out even on the Gentiles" (Acts 10:45; see also 11:15–18; 15:8).

How can Paul expect his audience to grasp the truth of his claims on the basis of returning to earlier scripture when he purports to teach new things? It is crucial to catch the way he describes the novelty. He does not suggest that the inclusion of Gentiles was not revealed as such; rather, he says that "as it has now been revealed," it "was not made known" then and there. Augustine reminds us that "the New Testament lies concealed in the Old, the Old lies revealed in the New."[1] And patristic exegetes such as Irenaeus (1997: 66–67, 92–101) make much of the Old Testament's revelation of salvation and blessing extending to the nations. Acts tells of Paul and Barnabas giving an account for their Gentile mission, even before the Jerusalem Council, and turning to words from the prophet Isaiah in so doing: "We are turning to the Gentiles. For so the Lord has commanded us, saying, 'I have made you a light for the Gentiles, that you may bring salvation to the ends of the earth'" (Acts 13:46–47).

Some serious scholars claim that the Jerusalem Council renders a judgment with the Spirit against the scriptures (Johnson 1996: 61–134; Fowl 1998: 97–127). I have elsewhere offered an extended argument regarding the issue (Allen and Swain 2015: 74–78, 112–13); suffice it to observe for now that the council's judgment was exegetical. It was prompted by the discernment of the Spirit being given to the Gentiles (per Peter's witness in Acts 15:8), and thus the council discusses what has been a narrative theme from Acts 10 onward. But "judgment" follows

---

1. Augustine, *Questions on the Heptateuch* 2.73, in *Quaestionum in Heptateuchum libri VII. Locutionum in Heptateuchum libri VII. De octo quaestionibus ex veteri testamento*, ed. J. Fraipont and D. De Bruyne, Corpus Christianorum Series Latina 33 (Turnhout, Belgium: Brepols, 1958).

not merely discernment but also scriptural examination, for James turns attention to prophetic precursors:

> Simeon has related how God first visited the Gentiles, to take from them a people for his name. And with this the words of the prophets agree, just as it is written,
>
> > "'After this I will return,
> > and I will rebuild the tent of David that has fallen;
> > I will rebuild its ruins,
> >   and I will restore it,
> > that the remnant of mankind may seek the Lord,
> >   and all the Gentiles who are called by my name,
> >   says the Lord, who makes these things known from of old.'"
> >   (Acts 15:14–18)

James concludes that exegetical argument by saying the Lord "makes these things known from of old," language that adds to what we find here in Eph. 3:5.

Most bluntly, then, Paul identifies the mystery: "This mystery is that the Gentiles are fellow heirs, members of the same body, and partakers of the promise in Christ Jesus through the gospel" (3:6). Three things are said of these Gentiles. They are "fellow heirs," drawing on the language of adoption and family, of inheritance and riches (see also 1:5, 7–8, 14, 18; 2:7, 19).[2] They are "members of the same body," imagery that finds expression most fully in 1 Cor. 12:12–31. Finally, "they are partakers of the promise," though the text does not specify the character of this pledge. An interpretative decision arises regarding the prepositional phrases "in Christ Jesus" and "through the gospel." They might modify the final statement about partaking of the promise or, perhaps more likely, they characterize all three gifts to the nations. The strongest argument for limiting the referent to the third and final blessing is that, otherwise, the promise goes completely unspecified. But there is a reasonable case to be made that the term "promise" (*tēs epangelias*) in 3:6 hearkens back to 1:13 where the Spirit is identified as "the promised Holy Spirit" (*tō pneumati tēs epangelias tō hagiō*). So the third gift is likely the giving of the Holy Spirit (conceptually and narratively not surprising given the role the coming of the Spirit played in early Christian discernment of the inclusion of the

---

2. Augustine reminds us that "the inheritance we look to, as coheirs with Christ, is not diminished by the crowd of people who are to inherit, nor does it dwindle because they have become so numerous; there is as much when the heirs are many as when they are few, and as much for each individually as for all" (2000b: 381).

Gentiles by faith, on which see above). And all three gifts—the inheritance by adoption, inclusion in the reciprocities of the body, and the pledged Spirit—are given "in Christ" and "through the good news."

Lest we think that Paul pushes a narrative of forward human development here, he attributes all progress to the agency of the triune God. "Of this gospel I was made a minister according to the gift of God's grace, which was given me by the working of his power" (3:7). First, the repetition is jarring: "the gift" (*tēn dōrean*), "grace" (*tēs charitos*), and "given" (*tēs dotheisēs*) all commend this notion of God's provision in overlapping and emphatic ways. Second, divine power serves as the connecting thread from 1:15–3:19, with this serving as the fourth and final example whereby God has shown his power: the raising of Christ from the dead, the saving of the sinner by grace, the stitching together of the Jews and Gentiles into one body, and now the calling of Paul the apostle in this final section (→1:21–23; 2:1–10; 2:11–22).

Why was it given to Paul? Aptitude? Promise? "To me, though I am the very least of all the saints, this grace was given" (3:8). Here we see another instance of grace in Paul's lexicon running right against the grain of its semantic function in other Jewish texts of that time. Jonathan Linebaugh traces the way in which Wisdom of Solomon employs the language of grace/gift, wherein favor is directed to one who may not have merited or earned it but who does show promise or aptitude such that they will put it to good use (Linebaugh 2013a). Ephesians 3:7 repeated this terminology, as noted above, but here we see it given texture by linking it with descriptions of those to whom this grace is given, not for zeal like Phineas or any such religious qualification. Paul charts a distinctively Christian course in defining grace, gift, and giving by Christ as no longer directed by judgments of aptitude and potential (as, e.g., in Wisdom of Solomon or other Jewish texts).

There remains a legitimate question about whether the first phrase should be construed concessively ("though I am the very least of all the saints") or otherwise ("as I am the very least of all the saints"); might it be that it is precisely inasmuch as Paul was least that God chose to show grace? Such a construal would not make grace a reward for any behavior or status that can be termed "least," but it would speak to God's choosing an unlikely vessel. Interestingly, Paul says, "I am the very least," not in the past but in the present tense (see also 2 Cor. 12:9). It seems that as in the days of Gideon (Judg. 6–8), so even now, God is in the business of showing his strength through the weakness of his instruments.

So the whence of this calling is God's grace, not Paul's promise. What of its whither? To where and what does this gracious calling lead? Paul employs two infinitives to lay out a schematic of his calling: first, "to preach to the Gentiles the unsearchable riches of Christ" (3:8); and second, "to bring to light for everyone what is the plan of the mystery hidden for ages in God, who created all things" (3:9). The apostle does not have carte blanche owing to office or charism but has a constrained calling; for Paul, who is "an apostle of Christ Jesus by the will of God," his ministry gains not only its impetus but also its shape or form by the will of God.

Paul considers the task of preaching Christ to be a grace, which can too easily be overlooked. The task of teaching and leading through the ministry of the word comes not primarily as a result of human strategic, political know-how but first and foremost as a grace of God. Preaching and office are not mere choices, as if the early church (or its leaders) simply judged it to be the best pathway, one more accidental determination of ecclesiastical history. No, the apostolic task lodged in the preaching office is a judgment of the church's Lord, the risen Christ (→4:7–11). In this regard, Reformed Christians especially claim that God's word provides a sketch of a polity or ecclesiology, rather than sketching an underdetermined vision that can be filled out later via ecclesiastical prudence ranging more widely (as in other communions). All manner of forms and circumstances require prudential wisdom and surely vary in diverse times and places, but the essence of the office is determined as a gift of the risen Christ. As John Calvin observes, "If the Church is built up by Christ alone, it is also for Him to prescribe the way in which it shall be built" (1965b: 181).

This grace also involves the privilege of commending "for everyone" that which has been a mystery given to Paul. The ministry of the word cuts against any sort of gnostic elitism that might hesitate to spread the word or to commend the word to every sort of person. The word brings demands. The word kills and makes alive. The word can only be handled or heard by those who come humbly. But the word is to be sowed across all manner of terrain (see Mark 4:3–9). Paul not only highlights that this is for all, but roots that global concern in the character and identity of God. The God who speaks gospel now through Paul and others is the one who spoke creation into existence in the beginning. Thus, the one who "bring[s] . . . light" now is also named as the one "who created all things." Paul elsewhere connects creation and new creation; for example, "for God, who said, 'Let light shine out of darkness,' has shone in our hearts to give the light of the knowledge of the glory of God in the face of Jesus Christ" (2 Cor. 4:6). Here too the imagery is of creational power, of light for knowledge, and in both texts it is the sign of Christ's face that serves as the matrix for this movement. Indeed, preaching "the unsearchable riches of Christ" here (Eph. 3:8) and the "glory of God in the face of Jesus Christ" there seem to coalesce inasmuch as Christ makes himself known now through his proclamation.

Paul has a sense not only of his purpose but even of God's grander design—namely, "so that through the church the manifold wisdom of God might now be made known to the rulers and authorities in the heavenly places" (3:10). The terrain of this battle is spiritual, not fleshly (→6:12), though this contrast does not so much mean to push our view away from the material world as to press our vision through and beyond it. What then might "the rulers and authorities" refer to in this verse? As with 6:11–12, the phrase highlights our struggle with the demonic forces of "the devil"; with 2:1–3, it does not thereby thin all struggle to the spiritually cosmic but can also be thickened by mediation through social or physiological or individual or natural entailments and instruments. Paul here highlights the demonic to note that the apostolicity of the church's mission will not merely have consequence here on earth but will even be apparent ("made known," *gnōristhē*) "in the heavenly places."

Preaching has occurred and is occurring (in written form), and Paul provides a retrospective account of its composition. But that which gave life and vitality to this preaching was not something reducible to his rhetorical force or moral pathos; rather, it was God active and involved in this work of authorized proclamation. "God is his own evangelist, and it is a pleasure for the Church to be used in his service" (M. Barth 1959: 161).

3:11–13 This was according to the eternal purpose that he has realized in Christ Jesus our Lord, in whom we have boldness and access with confidence through our faith in him. So I ask you not to lose heart over what I am suffering for you, which is your glory.

Paul wraps up this fourth instance of divine power and speaks to the "boldness and access with confidence" that can now be experienced. Gospel ministry manifests gracious power as much as resurrection, saving grace, and social reconciliation, at least according to the reformer Erasmus Sarcerius:

> The ministry of the gospel must be the work of the power and strength of God, and not surprisingly, because it must be effective by the preaching of the gospel against the devil, sin, death, hell, damnation, the world and so on. A powerful work demands a powerful creator; powerful effects depend on a powerful cause. The ministry of the gospel is given according to the effectiveness of the power of God, which governs and controls it, so it is not surprising that it runs smoothly,

that no one can stamp it out and that it is successful. Note here what the ministry of the gospel is—it is the gift of God's grace that is given according to the efficacy of his power. (*Annotations on Ephesians* 3.7, cited in Bray 2011: 308)

If we hesitate to make such bold claims, then perhaps it is no surprise that we are less prone to herald preaching of the word of God as itself the word of God (Second Helvetic Confession, ch. 1). Preaching can be viewed as mere rhetorical instrument, whether against the compelling oratory of late antiquity or now of the digitalized West. In such approaches, it is not at all shocking that preaching seems impotent, even foolish. Neither in that setting nor in our own day would apostolic proclamation bowl over other rhetorical expectations; indeed, it seems weak, antiquated, or inept. Paul would name that foolishness (1 Cor. 1:26–2:5).

Yet the foolishness may well be wisdom from on high. The apostolicity of Paul's ministry, and of his heralding the gospel near and far, brings hope and promise because it is impelled by God's own eternal will and resolve. Christian preaching and apostolic ministry heralds the life and work of a God on high— heaven brings its own rhetoric, which is marked by indication and by witness. Christian preaching, therefore, plays out in a rather self-effacing manner. Note that this does not equate to a self-annihilating posture, but it does espouse good news in drawing attention up to the heights where Christ is, drawing the sight of the audience up by its ears to the heavens. This word does draw together a congregation, though it does so by alerting disparate women and men, Gentiles and Jews, to that which transcends them all and yet fills them all.

John Webster regularly observed that much of modern theology (and we might add church practice) can be recited as the lapsing of trust that Jesus lives and speaks now. He described ways of getting back to the space and time wherein Christ was an agent, either through ethical or hermeneutical activation.

This vivid sense that the risen Jesus is speaker astonishes us or perplexes us. Where we are tempted to be embarrassed by its fervor, the apocalypse is not at all embarrassed to talk in very direct terms of the vocal presence of Jesus. Our perplexity, of course, is rooted in the fact that we find ourselves in a culture which functionally and theoretically has ceased to expect divine speech. The conviction on which the apocalypse is based—that God in Christ is a speaker, and that if we are to interpret human history we have to listen to the voice of God—is to all intents and purposes not an operative one for us. We work on the assumption that God is silent. If true words are to be spoken, we ourselves have to say them. (Webster 2011: 157–58)

Ephesians 3 jars these modern assumptions. The manifold wisdom of God will be heralded through the church, Christ's own body, and this pronouncement owes to the distinction (though not separation) of head from body, to which he alone can ensure and pledge not merely viability but also victory. Again, this will soon be elaborated on in 4:7–11, but here we see that the apostolic ministry and its consequent effects among the Gentiles are not merely subject to the vagaries and turbulences of history but ultimately sure in the steady hand of the Lord.

Paul identifies our blessings as including both "access" (*prosagōgēn*) and "confidence" (*pepoithēsei*)—divine promise centers on the experience of divine presence. Puritan theologians such as John Owen speak of the gospel gifts of both union and communion to alert us to this sort of scriptural language.[3] Union with Christ describes a reality wherein one is a member of the body, a part of the family, a citizen of the kingdom. But in this time—viewed at least through the lens of the divine economy, wherein we are in the state of grace but not yet of final glory—those united to Christ sometimes, indeed regularly, behave or walk apart from this reality as if they were severed from his promise and unaware of his presence. They do not always commune with him, that is, by enjoying the comfort of his pledge: "Behold, I will be with you always, to the end of the age" (Matt. 28:20). In those seasons of relational distance and therein of personal contradiction (behaving as that which one is no longer), the summons to access or to communion is no small thing. Indeed, this confident access unpacks an earlier term, "boldness" (*tēn parrēsian*), which speaks to the manner in which Christians are to approach the throne of God (see also Heb. 4:16).

These blessings are rooted not merely in Paul's strivings, nor even in the episodes of Jesus's life alone, but ultimately in God's "eternal purpose." That purpose was one that "he has realized in Christ Jesus our Lord," to be sure, but it has roots that run all the way down into eternity. While the notion of God's eternal will was most prevalent in 1:3–12, it recurs here. So the sequence must be traced: first, eternal purpose in the recesses of the inner divine life; then the decisive action of the risen Son who proves himself to be Lord; finally, God's purpose proclaimed from the mountains by the people of God, caught up in the vigor of the Spirit. While Protestants and Roman Catholics developed this theology of the Holy Spirit in far more detailed forms during the Reformation and the post-Reformation era, such can be found in seed form in early Christian theology. Irenaeus identified the

3. Owen, *Of Communion with the Father, Son, and Holy Ghost,* in *The Works of John Owen,* vol. 2, *Communion with God* (Edinburgh: Banner of Truth Trust, 1965).

giving of the Spirit to the church as ingredient to the gospel: "This faith which, having been received from the Church, we do preserve, and which always, by the Spirit of God, renewing its youth as if it were some precious deposit in an excellent vessel, causes the vessel itself containing it to renew its youth also.... For where the Church is, there is the Spirit of God; and where the Spirit of God is, there is the Church and every kind of grace."[4]

Christians have traditionally spoken of the appropriation of these moments in the economy, each to one of the three persons of the Godhead. So Eph. 1 identifies the Father as the blessed one who wills this plan and elicits the purpose of life that shall be made and then made God's own. Ephesians goes on to speak of that eternal will terminating in the historical acts of redemption and atonement, whereby Jesus Christ is the human name that manifests God's heavenly purpose. And this movement outward also echoes back or returns humanity to God because the Holy Spirit enacts "the working of his power" (3:7) and ensures the communication of the divine gift on the intended people of the promise. Visible are one gospel and blessing—one divine will—three enmeshed moments wherein the varied divine persons play more or less prominent roles, much like a chorus singing harmonically with one part occasionally sounding a more foregrounded note. If Eph. 1–3 has centered on the connection of Father and Son, with mention of the Spirit intermittently seasoning the letter thus far, then we will see that Eph. 4–6 concentrates more regularly on that connection of Son and Spirit, with less frequent mention of the Father from whom all good gifts come (Jas. 1:17).

We should also observe the coordination of prepositions here in Eph. 3:12, wherein we enjoy these blessings "in him" and "through our faith." Through the centuries it has become somewhat common to speak of the difference between the material cause and the instrumental cause of our salvation. These speak to distinct realities, as there is rather little impetus to read *pisteōs* as Christ's own faith (contra Wallis 1995: 128–34). While that concept plays a crucial role in the apostolic faith, it would be jarring to allude here to the human trust that Christ placed in his Father, not merely because there is a focus in this context on the Christian's experience (with boldness and confidence returning dependently to God) but also because of the text's portrayal of the work of the exalted—not the humiliated—Christ. Verses 12 and 13 mean to contrast Christian suffering now with Christ's own realization of his purpose as a way of invigorating steadfastness.

---

4. Irenaeus, *Against Heresies* 3.24.1, in *The Ante-Nicene Fathers: Translations of the Writings of the Fathers down to A.D. 325*, ed. Alexander Roberts and James Donaldson, 10 vols (Peabody, MA: Hendrickson, 1994), 1:458.

These blessings also evoke a particular posture to which Paul exhorts his audience: "So I ask you not to lose heart" (3:13). He asks "so" or "in this manner." Steadfastness does not come as a bare or discrete demand; rather, it fits just so with the way in which we enjoy the very presence of God in the heavenlies. Paul envisions a way in which their resolve may be buffeted, even battered, by the struggles of the Lord's servant. Indeed, a glance sideways toward Paul's sufferings (which he catalogs in 2 Cor. 11:23–30) might stun the saints, and so Paul summons them to another sort of vision: attentiveness to what is theirs in Christ in the heavenly places (→2:5–6; see also Col. 3:1–2).

Paul's particular concern is that they not fret or lose heart regarding "what I am suffering for you." Indeed, his pains are "your glory." Suffering and glory might seem strange bedfellows but for the evangelical redefinition of *gloria* propounded so insistently by Jesus himself (Mark 8:31; 9:31; 10:33–34). Martin Luther speaks of the sinful bent toward a "theology of glory" that believes glory can be perceived transparently and directly according to expectations (and, frankly, to our predilections and preferences). We are hard pressed not to interpret the modern culture of self-affirmation as being a particularly vigorous instance of this kind of theology of glory. Yet Luther, in the Heidelberg Disputation, suggests that such a theologian of glory is not worthy to be called a theologian. To be a theologian—at least one worthy of the task—one must follow the "theology of the cross," which is to realize that one's perception of glory and of God, of any ideal or transcendental, must be mortified and vivified. Such discipline was challenging in Jesus's journey through Palestine, and that struggle echoes through the centuries and reverberates around the globe everywhere the self-enclosed bent of the heart addled with sin finds witness. But Paul offers a contrary statement, a testimony to glory amidst suffering, and he has learned this from the one who confronted him on that Damascus Road. While Jesus's redefinition of glory was initially met with baffling stares (Mark 8:32–33; 9:32), eventually the experience of his death and resurrection brought clarity and would lead Paul to affirm that "this light momentary affliction is preparing for us an eternal weight of glory beyond all comparison" (2 Cor. 4:17). Not only does the incarnate King suffer before entering into his glory, but this proves to be a paradigm for his subjects who also experience momentary afflictions and then find that those afflictions are a pathway to heavenly, eternal bliss.

3:14–19 For this reason I bow my knees before the Father, from whom every family in heaven and on earth is named, that according to the riches of his glory he may grant you to be strengthened with power through his Spirit in your inner being, so that Christ may dwell in your hearts through faith—that you, being rooted and grounded in love, may have strength to comprehend with all the saints what is the breadth and length and height and depth, and to know the love of Christ that surpasses knowledge, that you may be filled with all the fullness of God.

Paul returns to prayer, having begun in 1:15–19 and initiated a rerun in 3:1. It is unusual for an epistle to turn to prayer midway, and we see that this prayer draws the first half of the letter to a close. Paul speaks not merely of praying here, but of "bow[ing] my knees before the Father" (3:14). In 1:16 he used verbal language of "giving thanks" and "remembering you in my prayers"; here he turns to embodied language of a particular posture. Might it be that the repeated, elaborated focus on our dependence on God's power has heightened or accented the way in which prayer involves deep supplication before the King? The posture of kneeling instantiates self-awareness for those who must come prostrate and exposed. Prayer lays us bare before the watching, active presence of the King who hears, who is near, and who holds a position of power above us.

Paul's adoption of this suppliant posture is rational. "For this reason" (*toutou charin*) Paul turns again to prayer. What renders it rational? What is the antecedent to "this" (*toutou*)? One may take the broadest possible angle, wherein the totality of 1:20–3:13 serves as its referent, or one might read it as a much more specific allusion to a statement or series of statements within the paragraph immediately prior. Syntax will not solve the problem, and we do well to pay attention to other features of the immediate context. Given that the next verse turns to elaborate the Father's identity as one "from whom every family in heaven and on earth is named" (3:15), the referent likely relates to God's global concerns, specifically as involving the Gentiles. While "this reason" for Paul's prayer may well take in the totality of Eph. 1:20–3:13 indirectly, then, it likely refers most directly to the more recent description of the mystery (3:6) of which Paul has been sent as an ambassador to the Gentiles. That God is named as Father of the many families of the totality of the created world (the merism of heaven and earth surely signals the notion of its totality) presses our imagination to turn directly to the inclusion of the Gentiles. While this has been a direct concern from 2:11–3:13, with a soteriological-theological analysis in 2:11–22 and an apostolic-missiological analysis in 3:1–13, these later sections hang on the prior mighty deeds of the Father in raising Jesus (1:20–23) and saving sinners (2:1–10). There is a deep magic that runs through the cosmos, in its totality rendering this kneeling supplication rational and fitting.

In both 1:17 and 3:16 the Father to whom prayer is made is identified as glorious. Paul, not least in the so-called disputed epistles, names God as glorious (e.g., 1 Tim. 1:11). His glory is praised in Eph. 1:12, 14; indeed, even the glory of his grace is acclaimed (1:6). In the Roman world, ascribing *gloria* to one whose power has been regaled and recounted at length would not be surprising, and so it is here. The Father raises the dead Christ to life. Glory, hallelujah! The Father makes alive those dead in their sins. Glory, hallelujah! The Father stitches together those who had otherwise been rendered asunder. Glory, hallelujah! The Father startles Paul such that he not only converts to Christ but calls the Gentiles to life in him. Glory, hallelujah! With each powerful step, the Father manifests glory.

In both 1:18 and 3:16, the prayer involves request for the "riches" or "inheritance" set aside for the saints. In 1:18 Paul employed an extended version, "the riches of his glorious inheritance" (*ho ploutos tēs doxēs tēs klēronomias autou*), and in 3:16 he uses the more compact statement "the riches of his glory" (*to ploutos tēs doxēs autou*). The latter surely refers back to the former construction, such that the riches here are a divine estate granted eventually to the children of God. Thus, there is an expectation that the prayer will be answered, because it has already legally been pledged for these sons and daughters. It is their rightful inheritance. Two things are notable in this regard. First, the *gloria* of the blessed Father will not be his alone, at least not if this suppliant request is granted. In a world of competition, where glory often displays itself in one winning out over another, such extension or—better put in moral terms—generosity is no small thing. Second, the language of inheritance goes a significant step further by signaling the way in which this generosity is not merely rational but expected and legally appropriate. Paul prays for those riches to be disbursed in the form of God's granting what Paul will request specifically in 3:17–19. And why is it theirs? A second infinitive expresses or explains the strength that is to be theirs: "that Christ may dwell in your hearts through faith" (3:17). By faith they are united to Christ; still further, by faith Christ inhabits or lives within them. The verb employed relates to a permanent dwelling, not a merely temporary tabernacling (*katoikēsai* rather than a variant of *skēneō*).

Both 1:17 and 3:16 identify the Spirit as the agent of enlightenment or comprehension. The Spirit here is only identified as "his Spirit," but this is no small affair. "His Spirit" does strengthen them inasmuch as he is, at least in some significant sense, in them—that is, "in your inner being." Reference to the Spirit appears throughout this epistle, whether in reference to the "seal[ing] with the promised Holy Spirit" (1:13) in the initial blessing or later in allusion to the word of God as "the sword of the Spirit" and the call to "[pray] at all times in the Spirit" (6:17, 18). The Spirit, then, has been granted (or sealed), is given as a gift external to us (like a sword or word that we receive in hand or ear), and is the principle of our action (as the one in whom we might pray, for example). Other references fit in these varied categories, this range of ways in which the Spirit may be considered. Here the Spirit is given as a gift that is external in its source, though internal in its effect. In other words, the Spirit comes as an agent, a person, a divine character acting on us, who can in no way be identified with or reduced to our own moral being or vitality or subjectivity. And yet this Spirit who is given to us comes to dwell within us and to work from within us, taking action "in [our] inner being" (3:16). The Spirit does not act on us from the outside but acts inside us, such that his power works with the grain of our being and does not cut against the fabric of our volition. This verse speaks of the Spirit acting on us in what we might call a subconscious or subvolitional manner.

In both prayers the overarching request is that Christians increasingly know the love that God has committed to their cause—indeed, know it in such an interior and personal way that it can only be described as "that you may be filled with all the fullness of God" (3:19). Paul has returned to the notion of blessing, the blessing that is God's properly and by his grace becomes that which will be shared with his children, albeit not to his diminishment in any way. Before we get to that language of filling, though, we need to consider the focus on knowledge. Knowledge plays a key role in being filled with God, and so Paul insists we take them in turn.

Knowledge suffers rather badly now, for a variety of reasons. Access to data digitally makes knowledge seem somewhat beside the point. Once that rather superficial or thinly utilitarian rebuke of knowledge fritters away, a deeper worry tends to set in: Does lack of knowledge really constitute either *a* or *the* problem for churches today? Are we not more in danger of being hearers only rather than doers (Jas. 1:22; see also Luke 11:28; Rom. 2:13)? With every clergy scandal and seemingly incessant historical exposé of Christian immorality (whether on the large or the small scale), rightful outrage is tempted to treat that moral issue as an ultimate or primary issue. The pain can be shared within and beyond the religious community, and it receives a significant social outcry, heightening our sense of its severity. Forget deepening doctrine or contemplation; triage demands a prioritization of moral and social concerns of immediate (read: real) consequence.

Such concerns about a focus on knowledge are only compounded by what we know of how humans learn. Recent studies in human formation and pedagogy have highlighted the role of protocols and habits. Knowledge seems so very cranial compared to liturgical or missiological rhythms into which we can be apprenticed. Neurophysiological data can be marshaled to identify ways in which we are social and ritualistic animals, shaped more by what we practice doing than by what we hear and ponder. A number of accounts seeking to gather and commend this frontline scientific data to a wider (especially religious) audience have garnered much attention, rightly so.[5] The contemplative study of theology—that is, of God and his works, in the most basic definition—does not always fit snugly with such analyses.

The penchant toward practical reasoning surely fits snugly with various sentiments of our age. Practical change has observable qualities and perhaps more widely appreciated value. While a sense of spiritual, personal direction or purpose may serve as a genuine spark at the individual level, it is hard to quantify and still harder to grant value to such an inner reality. Unlike a moral crisis that may well receive a feedback loop of outrage from those within and without the church, a theological error will fail to receive such widespread concern. Debates about divine immutability or triunity rarely rate mention on non-Christian media or analysis from the wider academy, so those areas of concern are not incentivized in the same manner. Not surprisingly, perhaps, they are often not incentivized by those within the church either, for many people in the church are shaped (malformed) by that wider culture of concern.

The retooling of the secularization thesis is pertinent here. Whereas the classic form of the secularization thesis falsely posited that technological advance brought a decline in religion, a retooled version suggests that religion, by design but also by unintended consequence, has been secularized itself, constricted to fit the world of technological and immanent concern. Genealogical discussions are not our concern here, but we do need to observe that the secularizing tendency of modern religion (indeed of much modern Christianity) will obviously incentivize and sentimentalize projects that have more immediate and empirical payoff: moral projects, therapeutic protocols, relational reconciliation. Knowledge will tilt toward such practical and, frankly, immanent concerns.

Perhaps an example helps bring matters into relief. Miroslav Volf and Matthew Croasmun argue that "Christian theology has lost its way because it has

5. See Jonathan Haidt, *The Righteous Mind: Why Good People Are Divided by Politics and Religion* (New York: Pantheon, 2012); David Brooks, *The Social Animal: The Hidden Sources of Love, Character, and Achievement* (New York: Random House, 2011); James K. A. Smith, *Desiring the Kingdom: Worship, Worldview, and Cultural Formation*, Cultural Liturgies 1 (Grand Rapids: Baker Academic, 2009).

neglected its purpose" (2019: 11). They refuse any triumphalist depiction of academic theology today and seek to show that it fails to commend a flourishing life. They itemize the crisis in terms of a shrinking professorate and audience and a diminishing reputation for theologians. These external challenges are often matched by equally severe internal threats, whether in the form of adopting a foreign commitment to *Wissenschaft* (theology as "science") or advocacy (of a progressive or conservative bent). As a response, Volf and Croasmun both widen and narrow the vision for theology. First, they widen it by reminding us that redemption, whether construed as forgiveness or liberation, does not suffice to name the subject of theology (which does emphasize such matters but ranges more widely also). Second, they remarkably narrow the task of theology when they argue that "Christian theology shouldn't be mainly about God because the mission of God isn't mainly about God—neither about God apart from the world (*theologia* in the patristic sense) nor about God in God's relation to the world (*oikonomia* in the patristic sense)" (Volf and Croasmun 2019: 64). Human flourishing comes to sit front and center in place of theology as the study of God.

Over against such a proposal and even more so in the face of such cultural shifts, Paul prompts us to double down on our concern—and, frankly, to join him on our knees in prayer to the Lord—for knowledge of God. Surely this prayer is not unattached from his desire that his epistle enjoy a thoughtful reception.

Now this contrarian position need not entail any diminished concern for what exercises others. Many pietistic or activistic calls will rightly arise to show one's love by what one does, and Paul will match them (→5:1–2). Practical concerns may be seen not least in one's observation of that which falls short; here too deepening knowledge of God proves crucial. In fact, by calling for deeper knowledge of God, Paul will actually enable a more profound lamentation of the tragedy that is moral failure or civil injustice (→2:1–3). As Cornel West has regularly said, there's a significant difference between claiming to have "issues" and identifying someone or something as suffering a "catastrophe": the difference is a matter not merely of degree but of qualitative divergence. Deeper theological contemplation actually sparks a more pained experience of sorrow, then, by whetting our appetite for genuine goodness, beauty, and truth, against the vision of which we discern the turbulence of our inconsistent lives. It is not for nothing, perhaps, that the greatest theologians of the Christian tradition (e.g., Augustine, Thomas, Luther, Calvin) have turned to the book of Psalms as a compendium of Christian theology, not least in its over seventy lament psalms.

This prayer for expanding knowledge does not equate to a cranial or right-brained approach, as if it were somehow divorced from ritual practice in liturgy or from moral formation across one's daily life. Such a divide dominates the Enlightenment era with its valorization of dispassionate inquiry and universal (unprejudiced) reason, but the New Testament nowhere suggests that wisdom and knowledge, maturity and discernment, attention and love can be possessed apart from formation in virtue by walking a particular "way." We do well to remember that Christianity was classed as a philosophy in the ancient world for a variety of reasons, suggesting that it involved an intellectual aspect but also a moral way of life. Early Christian theologians viewed theology as a task and calling both contemplative and active, ascetical and formative, spiritual and ethical.[6] Also, theological knowledge is both personal and social. The communal character of this knowledge is accented by Paul, who locates comprehension "with all the saints" (3:18), a congregational matrix about which Paul will have much more to say in the next chapter (→4:12–16).

More recently, a range of approaches have sought not merely to highlight the crucial place of practices or disciplines in Christian formation but have done so with a robust pneumatology. Reinhard Hütter (2000: 95–145) brilliantly argues that theology functions as a church practice enlivened by the Spirit, though he takes a fairly strong *communio* approach to the Trinity that struggles to register the qualitative distinction between God and creature. Over against that and weaker versions of the communion ecclesiology and the tilt toward thinking about ecclesiology via the concept of church practices, John Webster (2006: 153–94) seeks to reassert the axiomatic status of the Creator-creature distinction. Ephesians perhaps pressures us to register the concerns of both sides. Practices play a key role in God's gracious formation of a people, though God remains a saving agent who is not bound to such practiced modes (→4:15–16).

We also do well not to become naturalists regarding human transformation as we engage data from the physical sciences. The data of neuroscience serves as perhaps a looming threat to pastoral and spiritual practice inasmuch as it has been claimed by some to relay our moral formation in entirely natural and material rhythms. A range of objections can and have been raised to such a metaphysical and philosophical program from an epistemological angle.[7] Ephesians 1 and 3,

6. For a helpful sketch of the intellect in early Christian theology, see A. N. Williams, *The Divine Sense: The Intellect in Patristic Theology* (Cambridge: Cambridge University Press, 2007).

7. See Marilynne Robinson, *Absence of Mind: The Dispelling of Inwardness from the Modern Myth of the Self* (New Haven: Yale University Press, 2011).

however, prompt us always to ask whether we have accounted for divine power: divine power to make, to sustain, and, yes, also to remake and transform the mind such that it can be called spiritual (see also 1 Cor. 2:14–16). Divine power often works with the grain of the everyday, rightful repetition leading regularly to what we might call acquired virtue (including acquired intellectual virtues, which might relate, e.g., to learning to ask appropriate questions—who, what, when, why—of a text or situation). Yet Ephesians lifts our gaze up still further to occasions where heaven breaks in more jarringly, transgressing our expectations or normal patterns of gradualism by infusing virtue (including intellectual virtue). We not only have recourse to the language of infused virtues to help alert us to this category of spiritual transformation, but we have the so-called gifts of the Spirit (drawing on Isa. 11:2) to prompt us still further to various human powers that can be granted miraculously, it would seem, by the presence of the Spirit. Most pertinent for immediate purposes, those gifts of the Spirit prioritize matters of knowledge.[8]

In Paul's prayers the increasing knowledge of God's love requires power and the Spirit. Having already asked that "he may grant you to be strengthened with power" (3:16) and that "Christ may dwell in your hearts through faith" (3:17), Paul now prays "that you, being rooted and grounded in love, may have strength to comprehend with all the saints what is the breadth and length and height and depth" (3:17–18). In that first request, while this powerful strengthening is to be internal ("in your inner being"), its source is wholly external and specifically named: "through his Spirit." In this next request, Paul addresses the internal operation of that externally sourced strength. He desires not only that they would be capable or fit for knowing but that they would indeed know or comprehend in a certain manner. A parallel may be seen in Paul's claim that "it is God who works in you, both to will and to work for his good pleasure" (Phil. 2:13); "to will" and "to work" parallel the two requests here: fitness/desire and exercise/action, both of which are objects of his prayer.

What is the object of this comprehension? Paul begins by sketching something of its scale, with reference to the varied dimensions of "breadth and length and height and depth," though he then restarts by saying directly "the love of Christ" (3:19). So the dimensional is defined by the christological; put otherwise, the love of Christ that is to be known is precisely that which races outward in each of

8. "And the Spirit of the LORD shall rest upon him, the Spirit of wisdom and understanding, the Spirit of counsel and might, the Spirit of knowledge and the fear of the LORD" (Isa. 11:2).

these four directions, so much so that we are told it "surpasses knowledge" (3:19). Love sounds pedestrian; even the term *agapē* or *agapaō* appears in a whole range of settings and, contrary to much etymological mythology, cannot be blithely defined as a uniquely Christian or selfless form of love (the word appears, e.g., in 2 Sam. 13:4 LXX). But this love is differentiated from others. It is the Messiah's love, it ranges extravagantly in all directions, and it exceeds the bounds of our knowing.[9] It is ineffable; its depths cannot be plumbed.

The purpose of these prayers finally turns to that phrase that we encountered above, "that you may be filled with all the fullness of God" (3:19). The syntax leading here is complex and could be construed in a number of ways, though we have found the translation of the ESV to be quite plausible. The theological syntax is equally complex, for this filling cannot be extricated or removed from the notion of christological indwelling. There is an identification, it seems, of Christ's dwelling with the fullness of God filling us. In other words, there is the closest possible identification of Christ with God's fullness. That this Messiah's love cannot be known, at least not fully, helps us keep our bearings in speaking of what it means to be filled by God's fullness. This participation in God's own life does not involve becoming something other than a human creature, inasmuch as omniscience does not enter the equation. It involves transfiguration of our being (as human creatures) by grace rather than any transubstantiation toward a different sort of being (say, that of the Creator). It is no less evangelical and miraculous for showing the way in which grace restores and perfects nature, though it also gives real integrity to that gracious character of our transfigured or "filled" state in that we never outgrow the need for divine gift or grace. What we are filled with is "all the fullness of God" and yet the filling continues evermore, for the knowledge that it involves "surpasses knowledge." One is reminded of Gregory of Nyssa's teaching that perfection itself consists of eternal progress in the good—that is, in God himself—precisely because God's being so outstrips any advance we have yet made (Gregory of Nyssa 1978: 31, where the claim about eternal progress in section 10 follows from his account of God's infinitude in section 7).

This filling happens—or is beckoned to be in prayer—in a robust trinitarian fashion. God is addressed with humble supplication (3:14) by those named as his own via adoption and destined for his inheritance (3:15); thereby he grants to them favor, strength, and power like his own (3:16). In this way we become

---

9. The genitive is taken subjectively (*tes agapen tou christou*), for the passage is emphasizing the display of God's agency that we are to know, rather than any moral call that we are to know (though that comes very soon).

like nothing less than God's own character, even as we live dependently on him. That filling of might occurs "through his Spirit in your inner being" (3:16), for this Gift has been granted not merely to rest on but to dwell within those who are "being built together into a dwelling place for God by the Spirit" (→2:22). Finally, the account terminates with a christological focus, for the Son himself makes his habitation within us and "dwell[s] in [our] hearts through faith" (3:17). That indwelling and influx of spiritual power prompts a markedly richer knowledge of "the love of Christ that surpasses knowledge" (3:19). Father, Spirit, Son—each is pointedly and specifically involved here in the communicating of God's gifts to his adopted family.

3:20–21 Now to him who is able to do far more abundantly than all that we ask or think, according to the power at work within us, to him be glory in the church and in Christ Jesus throughout all generations, forever and ever. Amen.

Ephesians 3:20–21 offers a benediction and in so doing marks a transition in the epistle, in many ways closing the sustained argument of 1:3–3:19. Frequently, modern preaching on the epistle suggests that chapters 1–3 address the indicative whereas chapters 4–6 turn to the imperative, as if the first half describes God's saving action and the second half focuses on Christian morality. Major themes do cluster in such a way that this approach seems viable, and yet matters are more complex. The latter half of the epistle does linger patiently over morality, and yet it also highlights divine action in various spots (4:4–6, 7–11).

The benediction directs itself toward God, specifically toward the one "who is able." The acclamation commends God's potency or power, fitting given the repeated illustration of God's mighty power at work in various episodes of redemptive history. God is mighty, powerful, able. The outlets of that strength range: conquering physical death and overcoming the curse of sin (1:20–23), outbidding the claims of spiritual death and saving sinners by grace (2:1–10), making peace and forming one body through the cross (2:11–22), and converting a violent troll and redeploying him as a gospel emissary (3:1–13). The mighty acts first and foremost reveal something of God's character and being. While they do have obvious effects—described here at length and with rich texture—for human life and history, their primary role voices accolades of the divine being.

God's power exceeds expectations. He "is able to do far more abundantly than all that we ask or think." The power that has been communicated in four specific ways is said to exceed our thinking or even inquiring. What does 3:20 lead us to say of the power illustrated in resurrection, salvation, reconciliation, and calling? Those were illustrations from which we are to take not a sufficient or comprehensive definition or description of divine power but a necessary and illustrative depiction of its character. The implication of receiving those illustrations ought to be awestruck wonder, leading us to ask, "What might he do next?" Of course, those mighty acts chart a course; indeed, they rest on a divine predestination, so divine power will not be moving forward in arbitrary or tangential directions. Yet we are warned against assumptions that we know or can project what the next step would be in God's powerful provision for his kingdom's purposes. Being warned in that regard, we are invited to wonder and to wait expectantly for what that power will enact.

The emphasis on the divine power turns inward, then, to help trace the pathway for our wonder to move, for this excessive power is said then to be the "power at work within us." The power of heaven has touched earthly affairs in four ways as charted in these three chapters; in many respects, chapters 4–6 will tease out this phrase more fully as we see the epistle describing in concrete detail what it looks like for divine power to work within the Christian and the congregation. The plural term "us" (*hēmin*) has both personal and congregational or social consequence inasmuch as the group cannot be severed from the persons who constitute it. Power will shape life in the body and as the new self in various ways; that strength will also be something by which Christians are called to live (→6:10).

This powerful God shall receive glory, both in the church and in Christ Jesus, now and evermore. Glory has been a frequent feature of God's character and action (most recently →3:16). Interestingly, glory will not appear in the remainder of the epistle. While this God is glorious in eternity in and of himself, glory may be given to him throughout the passing of generations. The God who has his own fullness and is not thereby affected by the passing of time and its historical accidents is nonetheless given glory and magnified (as 1:3 says, he is "blessed") by those living within the constraints of time. We see here that God's fullness and transcendence do not distance him from creation or from genuine communication with his creatures; they mark the way in which he can engage them intimately and sovereignly.

God's glorious presence in history takes two forms. First, God is glorified in Christ Jesus. Jesus prayed to his Father, "I glorified you on earth, having accomplished the work that you gave me to do" (John 17:4). The Son's willingness to take upon himself the calling of his Father, his reliance on the Father's word when tempted, his offering prayer to the Father especially in times of weakness and trial—each of these elements of the evangelical story give glory and blessedness to the only wise God. As in Paul's other epistles, rather little is said of the earthly life of Jesus even here in Eph. 1–3, which relies on the gospel accounts and surely on broad descriptions circulating in oral testimony. The text instead fixes on the exalted work of the Son to save, reconcile, and send others according to the purpose of the Father.

EPHESIANS 4

4:1-3 I therefore, a prisoner for the Lord, urge you to walk in a manner worthy of the calling to which you have been called, with all humility and gentleness, with patience, bearing with one another in love, eager to maintain the unity of the Spirit in the bond of peace.

We do not here enter a new world in epistolary terms, but Paul does lay out in a fresh manner the texture of the new world created by the gospel. Chapter 4 will begin to lay out the lineaments of that people of whom it is said that God's "power [is] at work within [them]" (→3:20). While the benediction concluding chapter 3 alerted us that God "is able to do far more abundantly than all that we ask or imagine" (3:20), such divine excess does not take the form of ambiguous abundance. Far from it. The apostle now turns to sketch the shape of gospel power, which brings to pass a particular set of creaturely realities by transfiguring our earthly frame with heaven's own might.

In laying forth those particularities, the apostle reminds us that he does so as "a prisoner for the Lord." In taking up this name, he reverts to that which he already stated a chapter before when he said, "I, Paul, a prisoner for Christ Jesus on behalf of you Gentiles" (3:1). Why restate his location in jail? Why reframe his identity not merely as an apostle but as one appointed to suffer on Christ's behalf and for their good? Paul does so as a means of alerting them again—albeit in a way that will immediately turn from the second to the first person, from the abstract to the imminently personal—to the calling of God. Paul's calling led away from opposition toward service to the gospel of Jesus Christ, but it also led to the still further gift of suffering for Christ (see esp. Phil. 1:29–30, a text that also speaks inclusively of how the congregants are given the grace of joining Paul in the calling of Christ, even to suffer for and with him).

The mood here is exhortative: "I . . . urge you to walk in a manner worthy of the calling to which you have been called." This urging (*parakalō*) evokes not merely command but earnest plea. A similar call comes elsewhere in the Pauline corpus: "We exhorted each one of you and encouraged you and charged you to walk in a manner worthy of God, who calls you into his own kingdom and glory" (1 Thess. 2:12). Like the apostle, the Christians have been called or summoned. They have been given not merely a status but a summons, a task, a mission, and a vocation.

Martin Luther emphasized the fact that calling (the Latin term *vocatio* led to the language of vocation dominating later literature) was not merely a gift for the religious—that is, for those devoted to full-time Christian service as monks and nuns, priests and bishops. Luther argued that calling was a divine provision for all Christians, lay as well as religious. In his setting, this note was a jarring one, inasmuch as many laypersons had either assumed or been told that vocation was a privilege for the priestly caste. While there are all sorts of misleading ways in which the language of the priesthood of all believers can be heard (→4:11–12 for address of the most-common failing in this regard), Luther's theology of vocation did restore the apostolic task to the whole church.

Divine concern for daily life ranges as broadly as can be, with every human bearing the image of God and the task of imaging faithfully (Gen. 1:26–27), in contrast to those ancient Near Eastern settings where "image of God" language would be restricted to the elite, say, to the monarchic class. In this way, dignity has been granted to all; in being dignified, however, each one has been given responsibility. New creation is no less global than original creation in its provision and its concern. I do not mean that redemptive grace is given to each and every human being, in what we would deem a universalistic soteriology. Rather, new creation is global in concerning all sorts of persons, "from every nation, from all tribes and peoples and languages" (Rev. 7:9), for "there is neither Jew nor Greek, there is neither slave nor free, there is no male and female, for you are all one in Christ Jesus" (Gal. 3:28). Similarly, new creation is global in addressing the totality of the redeemed—that is, every bit of them and every inch of the cosmos. "Behold, I am making all things new" (Rev. 21:5). Thus, Abraham Kuyper and the Neo-Calvinists have spoken famously of the fact that there is not one square inch of this globe that Christ does not claim personally as Lord. We should add, to pair a personal note with that cosmic note, that there is not one nook or cranny of the redeemed self that the triune God does not make new.

This exhortation to "walk in a manner worthy of the calling to which you have been called" looks backward and forward. The backward glance provides structure:

there is "the calling to which you *have been called.*" God has already summoned. The gospel has already beckoned. The new life has already been born within you. In a world where purpose can be fleeting, these Christians have now, always, already been identified as those who "have been called." In the face of temptations within and without to forge their own pathways and identities (whether depicted as the curse by Nietzsche or the play by Foucault), they are first and foremost those who "have been called." The forward look prompts hope in the face of moral and personal despair: you have *"the calling to which* you have been called." Whatever settled character marks their identity as those who have been called, it is as those who have a calling. Christian assurance, then, is not complacency and surely not satisfaction with the status quo. The calling given to these women and men can be depicted as nothing less than apocalyptic and transfigurative; they are meant for—nay, they are destined for—glory and nothing less.

The summons beckons for them to "walk" and to do so in a manner "worthy" of that calling. Both terms demand care and attention. The language of the walk has appeared earlier in the epistle. Speaking of the people's death and sin, the apostle has already said that these were the spaces "in which you once walked" (2:2). The combination of the term "walk" (*periepatēsate*) with two *kata* clauses ("according to" or "following" first "the course of this world" and second "the prince of the power of the air") accents the fact that this term speaks not of a lackadaisical jaunt or stroll but of a directive outing. That depiction of death in sin contrasts with this portrait of life by grace, for they now walk in a new God-given calling. Indeed, they are beckoned to walk "worthily" (*axiōs*)—that is, to live as they are in Christ, to behave as they have been transformed. The notion of correspondence or fittingness serves well to display the kind of moral coherence of our creational character and salvific character by God's merciful action. The evangelical rule here is this: as you have been made, indeed remade in Christ by the Spirit, so shall you walk.

This calling is gracious, but not because it is ambiguous or undefined. Christian freedom cannot be understood as a sphere within which we experience autonomy (see G. Ziegler 2018; Yeago 1993; Webster 2003: 101–4; Hütter 2004: 111–44). Slavery to sin is matched by slavery to justice (Rom. 6:16, 18) and thus slavery to God (Rom. 6:22), just as the Israelites were delivered from slavery under Pharaoh's oppressive hand, that they might be delivered to service in Yʜwʜ's gracious kingdom (e.g., Exod. 3:12; 4:23; 8:1). It has been a while since it was stated in Ephesians, but this heavenly calling takes the form of a familial inheritance (→1:5, 11, 14). The language of adoption and sonship throughout the Bible speaks not only of rights and privileges but of moral and social expectations. Hence Jesus says, "Blessed are the peacemakers, for they shall be called sons of God" (Matt. 5:9); in making peace, these men and women show themselves to be something of a chip off the old block, those bearing the image of their Father in heaven and comporting themselves in a manner worthy of their callings as heaven's own.

Such vocational structure to which we are accountable clashes with two cacophonous but ever-present tones in our cultural milieu. As Reinhard Hütter says:

> After Kant, Fichte, and Nietzsche on the one hand and Marx, Darwin, and Freud on the other, we find ourselves as late moderns caught on a manic-depressive roller-coaster ride between the ghost of the Promethean daydream of freedom, by now turned desperate and therefore dreaming of autocreativity—that is, of designing our bodies, of choosing our gender, our values, and our destinies freely according to our idiosyncratic likings and longings—and the Hades-like nightmare of endless victimization by "the system"—by anonymous economic, political, and cultural power structures, by our own genetic makeup, and by the will to power of everyone else around us. (2004: 123)

The apostle neither lauds autonomy nor lambasts social or genetic determinism. Instead, he celebrates divine calling and calls for moral action, indeed manifesting hope that the former invigorates the latter. The evangelical summons demands that we put to death our insistence on a freedom that would have all the definition of an etch-a-sketch, always capable of reconfiguration at whim, and that we receive anew the conviction that true freedom may be found only in fitting correspondence or axiomatic coherence with the ones whom the only living and true God has made us to be.

Epistemological implications follow. Wisdom, maturity, discernment—these categories will play a major role in reflecting on the deepening Christian conscience and doing so in a way that does not reduce moral theology to mere divine command theory, which would only flatten the way in which holy scripture instructs us ethically and shapes us vocationally. Ephesians (chs. 4–5, esp. 5:10) will honor the place of Christian (especially lay) discernment, morally speaking, and cannot be shoehorned into a simple, fundamentalistic sort of command theory where every moral quandary has a textually direct answer. Other texts also speak to this need for mature judgment (e.g., Rom. 12:1–2; Heb. 5:14). Yet mature judgment also avoids utter ambiguity and its frequent twin, purported charismatic discernment, which can be used to justify all manner of action. While the will of God is frequently not laid out word for word in answer to all our personal queries, the word of God nonetheless guards our pathway of discernment by providing guardrails of sorts, sketching out the shape of a life that would be worthy of our shared calling. Discernment cannot be severed from law and principle, or else it is mere preference and not divine wisdom from on high.

Note that the apostle does highlight a shared calling. Though he has hearkened to a personal iteration of that calling in alluding to his imprisonment, even that providential experience is one in which he discerns a common summons (again see Phil. 1:28–29). The point to which he calls his readers, however, is not a personal project or an individual iteration; he summons them to the calling of Christian love, of moral integrity, of other-minded self-sacrifice. In 5:1–2 he will step back and relate this project to the calling of imitating God's action in Christ Jesus, an exemplary summons to which all Christian women and men are called by grace. While it is not inappropriate to speak of individual iterations of vocation for God's sake, we do well to note the more focal and repetitive character of shared callings in holy scripture.[1]

If 4:1 lays out something of a melody line, then 4:2–3 adds harmony with varied movements that are "worthy" of that central calling. The worthy life will be sketched throughout chapters 4–6 in a variety of ways, describing the experience of the body (4:11–16), the contrast of the old and new selves (4:17–32), the contrast of walking in darkness or light and in foolishness or wisdom (5:1–6:11), and finally of the spiritual warfare that is to be waged by the Lord's might (6:10–19). That we should read this section as a unit is signaled by the fact that we do not have another benediction (as in 3:20–21) until the very end of the epistle (6:23–24). Also, we see the language of walking recurring in this section (4:17; 5:2, 8, 15).

Paul begins with virtues (to which he will return in 4:31–32; see also parallels in Phil. 2:2–4). This worthy walk proceeds "with all humility and gentleness" (4:2). While later commands may seem, at least on the face of it, typical in the culture (as is often said about the household codes), these virtues were not widely celebrated. Humility marks a selflessness that would stand out for its demure character in a culture marked more by the celebration of machismo and the pursuit of *gloria*. Gentleness contrasts with unrestrained power and raw force, the kind of reactivity that manifests self-exertion. In both terms, the apostle signals a posture that is not self-exertive or domineering.

1. Gary Badcock, *The Way of Life: A Theology of Christian Vocation* (Grand Rapids: Eerdmans, 1998).

The apostle adds another pairing: walk worthily also "with patience, bearing with one another in love." Whereas the strong would fly off the handle and react to the first provocation, those who adopt a gentle walk respond patiently. But patience cannot be had free of charge; therefore, Paul goes on to speak of "bearing with one another." Bearing what? Bearing how? Bearing the cost of patience—that is, absorbing the pain that marks out the belligerent or simply self-enamored thoughtlessness of those around us. To do so, to bear that, to walk this way—this can only occur in a certain manner: "in love" (*en agapē*). Love reemerges when the apostle pauses his moral exhortation, coming up for air to offer something of a summative or programmatic statement in 5:1–2, wherein imitation of God in Christ means to "walk in love, as Christ loved us and gave himself up for us, a fragrant offering and sacrifice to God." These virtues must be enacted via love, precisely because they always involve an existential, relational, and moral cost. Love sacrifices for the sake of the other, taking up the vocation of imitating God himself (→5:1–2).

A final virtue is mentioned in 4:3: walk worthily as those who are "eager to maintain the unity of the Spirit in the bond of peace." There is unity, which will be discussed much more fully in the next few verses (→4:4–6), but it demands maintenance, just as these Christians have been called and need to walk worthily. This unity has been described at great length earlier, a discussion to which the phrase "the bond of peace" clearly alludes (→2:11–22; note that "peace" is mentioned there in 2:14, 17). This eagerness or zeal for maintaining relations with others involves a profoundly other-centered concern. One is not self-protective, first of all, but fixed on guarding the relationship or bond with others.

There is an ethical order in the grammar here. This virtue and the previous one are expressed in participial form, suggesting that they modify the terms in the previous verse (which are introduced with recurring prepositions [*meta*]). So not only "bearing with one another in love" but also being "eager to maintain the unity of the Spirit in the bond of peace" marks out the manner by which one would be humble, gentle, and patient. The virtues are coinherent, first, and ordered to the priority of peace and love, second. But that moral order is not the only shape discerned here. If love is described later as a christological gift (→5:1–2), then peace is highlighted here as a distinctly pneumatological provision (this "unity" is that "of the Spirit" [*tēn enotēta tou pneumatos*], the genitive likely depicting its source and/or sphere). So the order is trinitarian, but the order is also moral: love and peace are meta-virtues that inflect the others and apart from which the others cannot truly exist in Christian form.

4:4–6 There is one body and one Spirit—just as you were called to the one hope that belongs to your call—one Lord, one faith, one baptism, one God and Father of all, who is over all and through all and in all.

The mood shifts from exhortation to explanation. The apostle does not herein summon to action or beckon zeal; he professes and proclaims what is reality in the land of the gospel. For all the appropriate emphasis on Eph. 4–6 focusing on moral theology, it must not be forgotten that the text continues to offer truly moral *theology*. Bare command or pious proverbs do not come; rather, exhortations and wisdom sayings are located in description of moral reality. John Owen writes in his remarkable account of pneumatology that the scriptures summon believers to a distinctive sort of religious integrity called "evangelical holiness."[2] Sticking with the idiom of Eph. 4, we are led to say something similar: the apostle here depicts an evangelical worthiness that only makes sense within a given state of affairs brought into being and sustained by the living presence of the triune God.

The language of unity or oneness dominates. It is a perfect unity, a sevenfold oneness that marks the present reality of Christians. Oneness marks the body, the Spirit, the hope, the Lord, the faith, the baptism, and the God and Father. How can such oneness truly exist? The sixth verse ends in a flourish, for this "God and Father" is described first as being "of all" and second as "over all and through all and in all." Surely the threefold latter phrase (echoing vaguely the threefold iteration of Rom. 11:36, as only one preposition is an exact match) means to expound on the brief "of all" (*pantōn*). In doubly depicting the global or full impact of the Father, the text seems to suggest that the presence of unifying realities in these other areas is wholly owing to his being and action. That is, for example, as God is the Father over all (not merely Jews but Greeks as well), "there is one body" through the work of the cross (→2:16). Similar connections could be teased out with regard to each of the first six gifts: body, Spirit, hope, Lord (that is, the Christ or Son of God), faith, and baptism. In each case, they are a fruit of the inheritance we share by his grace.

In recounting the riches of their inheritance, Paul specifically reminds them again of their calling (reiterating language of 4:1). In doing so, he personalizes the reality statements: "you were called" and this hope "belongs to your call." The language impresses immediately on the hearer or reader that this is not proclamation of something back then or over there. The apostle's pause, rightly marked off

2. Owen, "Pneumatologia," in *The Works of John Owen*, vol. 3, *The Holy Spirit* (Edinburgh: Banner of Truth Trust, 1965).

as a brief excursus or tangent, signals something that is indicative of the entire passage. "Just as" (*kathōs kai*) with hope, so with the body, Spirit, Lord, faith, baptism, and God and Father: in each case, these are unifying realities of import to "you." The tangent actually draws out a personalizing principle that bears on each and every one of these claims.

Admittedly, these purported realities that we enjoy now seem somewhat far-fetched and, in some cases, run against much of the empirical evidence of daily experience. Even Christian theologians may feel impelled to question whether these are present realities as opposed to future ideals or prayerful hopes. To take but one example, the notion that there is one body may seem Pollyannaish in the face of modern schismatic Christianity, wherein churches and communions have splintered into literally thousands upon thousands of institutional bodies.

In his manifesto *The End of Protestantism*, Peter Leithart notes, as have many in recent decades, that ecclesiology must be shaped by the high priestly prayer of Christ and its way of attesting the evangelical character of churchly unity (John 17:21).[3] This prayer request elicits a vocation and a pursuit: "Jesus prayed that the church would exhibit this kind of unity. . . . Each church should dwell in every other church, as the Son dwells in the Father." So far, so good, and frankly nothing surprising. Then comes the showstopper: "This is what Jesus wants for his church. It is not what his church is" (Leithart 2016: 1). Leithart turns in the next few pages to consider possible programs of playing down that claim: perhaps doctrine, fundamental tenets, sacramental rituals, or polity express an underlying unity. In each case, though, he comes back to this judgment: "In reality, every apparent point of unity is also a point of conflict and division" (2).

Leithart's first claim, that the church is not united, is telling in terms of the underlying logic of his argument, inasmuch as it is sociological and not theological. The prayer of Jesus in John 17:21 is a summons, though this unity is not presently the case. "Every mark of unity is also a sign and site of division. Jesus wants his church to be one. But we are not" (Leithart 2016: 3; see also 1, 166). Of course, there is a sense in which Leithart is getting at something profound here—namely, the festering wound that is Christian divisiveness and ecclesiastical alienation. Most of us, sadly, know the debilitating effects of estrangement, and such ailments occur institutionally as well as personally. But Leithart's sociological/empirical

3. The following paragraphs draw from Michael Allen, review of *The End of Protestantism* by Peter Leithart, *Reformed Faith & Practice* 2, no. 1 (May 2017): 100–109.

assessment here is markedly limited by its theological thinness. At a theological level, his assessment is not profoundly helpful, for it ignores the most central claim respecting its subject—namely, Paul's words to the Ephesians: "There is one body and one Spirit—just as you were called to the one hope that belongs to your call—one Lord, one faith, one baptism, one God and Father of all, who is over all and through all and in all" (4:4–6).

Leithart does not ignore this text altogether, of course, but addresses it within his call for "Reformational Catholicism," or what he terms "evangelical unity" (2016: 17–20). He rightly notes that "the unity of the church is not an invisible unity that renders visible things irrelevant" (19; see also 21, 33, 41) and helpfully warns against "unrealistic expectations" by "emphasizing the eschatological dimension of unity" (19). But he does ignore the text's most crucial claim. He moves from saying that the "factuality of the church's unity" does not render its visible life irrelevant (18) to his central claim that the church is not united (1, 3). But the law of the excluded middle proves helpful here, for those are not the only two options nor even the most likely options. Why would we not explore an eschatological description of the church's life that attests its unity as its most fundamental claim and therefore takes Christ's testimony to the character of his own body given in Eph. 4:4 ("there is one body") as more definitive and fundamental than our own perceptions of reality relationally and institutionally? Starting there actually makes other experiences more tragic, not less, precisely because it enables us to say that these divisive experiences do not simply cut across our divine design, the summons of divine law, or even across the arc of eschatological history, but that they straightforwardly oppose reality. But the "evangelical" shape of unity must begin with theological—not merely or primarily sociological—reflection and with the self-attestation of the risen Lord through his emissaries: in this case the apostolic testimony of Eph. 4:4, where unity is no mere summons or prayer but a present reality.

Leithart's program of "future church" begins with an empirical observation, he says, that the one church does not presently exist (2016: 1, 3). Drawing on figural hermeneutics of promise (101–15) and on the philosophy of Eugen Rosenstock-Huessy (14–15, 103, 168–69), he argues that this oneness will be eschatological and has a future "factuality" (18), and states that this reality does not exist at present. But, we may say in response, God reveals oneness first as a gift in the present. This gift comes in the form of grace now and not yet glory or perfection (hence Eph. 4:4–6 must be paired with 4:1–3, as suggested by the soteriology sketched in 4:7–16). Unity must be maintained. Unity can be stretched and even scandalized. And we do feel the stretching and breaking of unity's embrace in personal and institutional forms. But we do well to allow Christ to set the terms of our intellectual approach by means of his revealing instrument, the apostolic scripture. To Leithart's empirically based approach (where our relational perception seems to provide the initial orientation of what is not reality), we need a theological ecumenism.

While our more activistic impulses may fret at its potential misuse, such an approach is going to need to make fuller use of categories like the distinction between the visible and the invisible church. That potential areas of unity are also sites of division does not negate the complex reality that they very well may be both unifying and dividing in various ways; indeed, the fact that they are places of unity is precisely why disagreement prompts such division. In other words, the visible-invisible distinction not only flows from exegesis of texts like Eph. 4:4–6 and 4:1–3 but also makes better existential sense of the liveliness of ecumenical debates. If we worry that talk of invisible unity leads to a lethargic embrace of the limits of the present (as do many of its critics), we might listen again to the way that Augustine of Hippo, in *City of God*, articulates that distinction in a time of crisis. He employed it not to provide a cop-out but to properly frame the call to order our loves, organize our common life together, and move ahead with zeal and expectancy. In his own way, Calvin's discussion of the distinction in book 4 of his *Institutes of the Christian Religion* also prompts an active lifestyle of ecclesial repentance rather than (as many sociologists seem to suggest) a program of presumption and arrogance by the purportedly elect. Admittedly, professing that Christ has redeemed a church that is one even as Father and Son are one (see not only Eph. 4:4 but also John 14:20) demands faith in the face of empirical challenge, but that is a wager that Christians are willing to take up. The Nicene Creed reminds us of this wager every time we confess belief (note: not sight!) of "one . . . Church" in its third article. The church's oneness is not a delayed reality (like the way we look to the resurrection of the dead and life everlasting) but a present gift that we trust to be true.

Perhaps, though, it is not for nothing that the tangent that pauses the litany of oneness in Eph. 4:4 singles out the special gift of a shared hope. Even when the body cannot be discerned easily and the Spirit may be cantankerously debated at times, "there is . . . one hope." Here too we do well to remember that we are not beyond the time for joining the apostle in his prayer: "to comprehend with all the saints what is the breadth and length and height and depth, and to know the love of Christ that surpasses knowledge" (3:18–19).

4:7–12 But grace was given to each one of us according to the measure of Christ's gift. Therefore it says, "When he ascended on high he led a host of captives, and he gave gifts to men." (In saying, "He ascended," what does it mean but that he had also descended into the lower regions, the earth? He who descended is the one who also ascended far above all the heavens, that he might fill all things.) And he gave the apostles, the prophets, the evangelists, the shepherds and teachers, to equip the saints for the work of ministry, for building up the body of Christ, . . .

Here we find the christological center of the ecclesiology of Ephesians. In speaking of Christology, however, we do not solely fix our sights on the virgin birth, life, death, and resurrection of the incarnate Son but also take in what has been called his post-existence—namely, his ascension and heavenly session. In confessing his post-existence, the text links that present reality with his past glories, his ongoing activity with his completed accomplishment.

The transition into this section comes contrastively. "But" (*de*) grace will be spoken of now. Yet the realities described in 4:4–6 are gifts, so it may not be obvious where the contrast lies. The shift occurs not in some move from human to divine action or ethics to theology or even church back to Christ; rather, the shift occurs in the move from unity to diversity or, we might say, from the church viewed as "one" in that sevenfold litany to the church viewed as a congregation of particular persons. Ephesians 4:7 is frontloaded, with the syntax actually saying, "But to each one of us grace was given" (*Heni de hekastō hēmōn edothē hē charis*), such that the ESV does not adequately capture that shift by its modification of the word order.

What is to be made of this grace given to each and every particular person in the church? Grace was given "according to the measure of Christ's gift." The giving has occurred in the past, and it has a rule or principle by which it was enacted ("the measure" [*to metron*]). Lest we somehow interpret this measure or canon in any extrinsic capacity, wherein it befits the global needs of a religious culture (i.e., gods provide this, religion provides that), a genitive statement clarifies or locates the nature of that rule: Christ measures out this gift to each and every man and woman. Christ is the giver, and Christ is the one who measures the allotment of each gift.

Ephesians 4:8–11 will elaborate the character of this giving by Christ, thus showing that a particular sort of giving is meant by the apostle (to which others presumably have been or might be added). To pinpoint the shape of this giving, the apostle turns to narrative; to sketch the form of that narrative, he unsurprisingly takes up the language of Old Testament scripture. "Therefore it says, 'When he ascended on high he led a host of captives, and he gave gifts to men,'" the apostle says, drawing on Ps. 68. That psalm recounts a victory of the Davidic king, met by the crowds and celebrated for his triumph. He returns not only with his troops but also with "a host of captives" or prisoners of war who will serve as spoils of victory. He marches or, more specifically, "ascends on high" as one who is fit to leave the depths of battle behind and, having secured victory in the trenches of that breach, to take up the lofty heights of peace and power.

Paul does not merely quote the psalm, however, in trying to sketch the narrative of the Christ. He turns to the language of Ps. 68 markedly. That psalm goes on to say, "You ascended on high, leading a host of captives in your train and receiving gifts among men" (68:18). It tells of normal political events, where a triumphant general or king would be sent tokens of admiration by emissaries from other lands and peoples. They give such gifts as a way of currying favor, seeking quid pro quo to avoid the fate of the recently vanquished foes of this ascendant lord. Indeed, politicians practice this manner of gift exchange to this very day, even if it drifts at times toward merely tokenistic pomp and circumstance when ambassadors bring gifts to a newly inaugurated minister, president, or king.

The apostle does not find that psalm's language adequate, however, to express the gift-giving of the messianic victor. He twists that final phrase. Whereas the psalm speaks of the victor receiving gifts, here we read that "he gave gifts to men" (*edōken domata tois anthrōpois*). We must catch the import of this move, for this phrase is the very reason for the quotation to begin with; it is here that the psalm connects with the apostle's broader concern (mentioned in 4:7) with the grace-giving of the Christ. The verb has shifted from passivity to activity as the apostle speaks of the triumphant messianic King giving rather than receiving.

Ephesians 4:9–10 will clarify the timing of this giving. These verses function parenthetically; hence the ESV and other translations appropriately tend to bracket them in parentheses. They pick up on the language of ascent in 4:8, expounding it as that which follows his descent "into the lower regions, the earth" (*eis ta katōtera merē tēs gēs*). That final phrase, "the earth," speaks epexegetically to clarify the nature or location of these lower realms—our domicile here on earth is defined, in terms of the Messiah's story, as the "lower regions." While we might bristle, not merely because we are used to and happen to like our earthly home, but especially because the psalms themselves train us to catch its God-given splendor, we must remember to take this judgment relative to this particular story. For the Messiah, this blessed earth represents a space into which he has descended from on high and from which he will return in ascent to glory. The apostle is not making a wholesale statement of earthly demotion, but, like the Epistle to the Hebrews' rhetoric again and again (e.g., Heb. 1:4; 3:3), he is making the argument from the lesser to the greater. This lovely earth is lowly in comparison to the greater glories of the heavens above, the home of the Messiah's exalted reign.

The narrative ends in 4:10 when it speaks of his post-descent ascent "far above all the heavens"—that is, to and beyond the breaking point of our cosmological imaginations. Remember that "the heavens" are a part of creation itself (Gen. 1:1), and so the Messiah exceeds even their majestic bounds in returning to God's own glory. His exaltation, picked out in the language of ascent here, is not lauded merely for what it says of the incarnate Son and Messiah. This ascent has purpose: "that he might fill all things." The language of filling (*plērōsē*) picks up a theme that has bounded the first half of the epistle (1:23; 3:19, which both read *plērōma*).

Many gifts might have been intended in speaking of the Messiah. He came preaching peace, taking up the words of the prophet Isaiah when coming to his own (Luke 4:16–30). He came in power to heal, to cast out demons, to proclaim good news of the kingdom (Matt. 4:23–25). He forgave people's sins and raised the dead (Matt. 9:2, 25). He gave his own life—no one could take it from him (John 10:18). These representative iterations of giving are overwhelming and yet emblematic of the excessive nature of the Christ's gifts. Surely we recall the words that bring one gospel account to its close: "Now there are also many other things that Jesus did. Were every one of them to be written, I suppose that the world itself could not contain the books that would be written" (John 21:25). And yet the apostle here fixes his focus on one gift at one time: the risen, ascended, exalted Christ, who is now at the right hand of the Father, gives gifts that he has measured out for each Christian, whether in Ephesus or across Asia Minor or the Mediterranean basin or throughout this whole apostolic era.

Again, we might wonder which gift, even of this exalted era of the Messiah's life, is being referenced. The ascended Lord sent the Spirit as a helper (John 16:7). Jesus will not abandon his church in its conquest of hell's own gates (Matt. 16:18). He is the "great shepherd of the sheep" through whom "the God of peace" will "equip you with everything good that you may do his will" (Heb. 13:20, 21). In all sorts of ways, then, the ascended Christ's heavenly session offers grace upon grace to his people. But, again, the apostle fixes his focus on a particular gift here: 4:11 tells us, "and he gave the apostles, the prophets, the evangelists, the shepherds and teachers." While other gifts are worthy of attention (→6:11–18 for a litany of other provisions), here our minds are drawn to attend to the church's officers and its polity as a provision from on high.

Ephesians 4:11 describes officers who equip the saints. Apostles, prophets, evangelists—these officers do the work of pointing and drawing women and men to Christ, and therefore toward each other, such that a congregation is formed and founded. Shepherds (or, as we say today, pastors) and teachers do the work of building up and sustaining that congregation with the same Word by which it was initiated. When speaking of polity, our first word must always be a particular word of confession: Jesus Christ is Lord of the church. Such affirmation does not speak to antiquity and our founding. It does not offer a mere recounting of our roots. It affirms the dependent character of all earthly governance now and pinpoints the heavenly reign of our first officer. While there are shepherds and officers here in our midst, he alone is "the great shepherd of the sheep" (Heb. 13:20).

Karl Barth says, "To say that Jesus Christ rules the Church is equivalent to saying that Holy Scripture rules the Church" (*CD* I/2, 693). That gets the notion of authority right in part, affirming the dependent and subordinate character of those administering offices in ecclesiastical polity, underneath the "living and active word" (Heb. 4:12–13). But it only makes sense when paired with the affirmation that Jesus rules his sheep by his word, and he builds up his sheep with that word through the ministry of those he sends as officers of that very same word. They are unique offices, five of them, though they bear a commonality in that all five minister the word of God. Reformational Christians turned to the distinction between ministerial and magisterial authority to express the character of these offices: they work under and bear the authority of another, not of themselves. They are gifts of the one of whom alone we might say that the buck stops with him, the great Lord of the church who continues his reign from on high. Thus, the ministry of any such officer always sits underneath and finds itself accountable to that of the risen Lord.

The purpose of these offices—of Christ's own gift—is spelled out in 4:12: "to equip the saints for the work of ministry, for building up the body of Christ." Punctuation is interpretation here. Some argue that these are three ways of describing the same goal: officers equip saints, do ministry work, and build up Christ's body. There are two *eis* ("for") clauses in the verse, which suggest a slightly noted shift from the first phrase to the final two phrases. Thus, the sentence structure militates against reading equipping and doing ministry work as being parallel or related epexegetically; rather, these activities seem to be construed sequentially as a staggered sequence of purposive actions: God gives officers so that they equip saints, so that those saints do the work of ministry (contra Horton 2011: 129–53). Most likely the second *eis* also speaks of this deeper purpose, again relating to the equipping done by officers. Thus, officers "equip the saints" with the dual purpose that those saints do "the work of ministry" and are thus "building up the body of Christ." It is possible, though, that the final *eis* speaks of a broader purpose that takes in the whole sequence: in such a case, the officers "equip the saints" so that they do "the work of ministry," with the effect that in all this activity each of them are "building up the body of Christ." In either case, the text alerts us to the ministerial calling given to all Christians as well as the unique role of pastoral officers.

Ministers equip laypersons with the word of God for the ministry (*diakonias*). They do not crowd out lay participation in ministry, but they help form laypersons and resource these men and women that they might minister well. Again, the ministry of the word is fundamental—definitional, we must say—for the calling of officers. And it is formative for the development of a laity capable of mature judgment or Christian discernment (on maturity, →4:13–14; on discernment, →5:9–17 [esp. 5:10]). The apostle will not elaborate here on the praxis whereby officers do this equipping; interestingly, the household code will not take up the language of pastoral authority and its appropriate order (though we could very well imagine pastors or overseers on the one hand and laity on the other hand being added to the litany of husbands and wives, parents and children, slaves and masters). The Pastoral Epistles expound further in that regard, however, by describing the calling and the responsibilities of officers. Here the apostle instead describes the way in which this ministry equips a laity who themselves grow, by God's own power, into maturity and fullness. That fullness is the purpose, after all, of the exalted Messiah (1:22–23; 4:10).

4:13–14 . . . until we all attain to the unity of the faith and of the knowledge of the Son of God, to mature manhood, to the measure of the stature of the fullness of Christ, so that we may no longer be children, tossed to and fro by the waves and carried about by every wind of doctrine, by human cunning, by craftiness in deceitful schemes.

Ephesians 4:13–14 offers a bit more specificity regarding the telos of this christological gift and ecclesial life. Put otherwise, the word "until" beckons us to consider the eschatological aim of it all. The eschatological or telic character of this section helps lean against any reading of the later household code (5:22–6:9) as endorsing the status quo or settling for common mores. Grace does not ultimately bring one to peace with battlefield conditions, but Christ's gift fits us for the eternal armistice and glorious peace that remains to be manifest.

The eschatological aim to be attained is "the unity of the faith and of the knowledge of the Son of God" (4:13). Interpreting the line is not necessarily straightforward for a number of reasons. Does it speak of a unity that is experienced by those who possess faith and knowledge *or* does it speak to the unity of faith and knowledge themselves? Further, how do we render the final genitive: as human knowledge about Christ or of Christ (an objective genitive of one sort or another) *or* as Christ's own knowledge (a subjective genitive)? The former question can probably be answered with a resolute answer—namely, that the unity spoken of is directly constituted by faith and knowledge themselves and not some discrete or other result of their pairing; the only plausible argument otherwise would link the verse all the way back to 1:10 and its mention of the unification of all things, a rather unlikely literary move. There shall be a unity of what we trust and what we know in the hereafter, as faith and knowledge become one. The latter question, however, is a good bit more difficult and demands further attention.

On the one hand, it is quite plausible that the text here lays out the first christological definition of our end—namely, the unity of faith and knowledge that were manifest in the human life of Christ himself. Here the final genitive is rendered subjectively, and the unity is itself constituted by faith and knowledge. On the other hand, this line may well call us to unite or pair our faith with knowledge— more than mere *notitia*—of the Son of God, as prayed for in 3:16–19. In this approach, the final genitive would be rendered objectively, though the unity is again constituted by the pairing of faith and knowledge themselves. The strongest argument for the former is that the text will turn almost immediately to defining our end christologically; this reading simply would enter that movement one line earlier. Yet the recurring references to faith and especially to knowledge throughout the epistle are consistently highlighting Christian faith toward and knowledge about Christ (rather than his own faith and knowledge). For that reason, the most probable rendering sees this as a call to grow up in one's faith in such a way that one also increasingly possesses knowledge with which that faith is paired or united. In this way, we are reminded that the apostle's sketch of maturity in chapters 4–6 really does expand on his prayer for God's power to work within us to increase our knowledge of God's love in Christ (→3:18–19). Such knowledge is the targeted goal of that divine *dynameōs* (1:19).

Nonetheless, the end is also defined christologically. Christ is not merely the fulcrum on which the ages turn, but he is also the frame and blueprint whereby we see "the measure of the stature of the fullness of Christ." The apostle stacks terms one upon the other here in an act of literary excess, with "measure" (*metron*) and "stature" (*ēlikias*) serving almost redundantly. While the term "fullness" is in genitive relationship, syntactically subordinate, it represents the material center. The text's concern with measurement and with stature circles round this notion of the "fullness of Christ" (*plērōmatos tou Christou*). The exalted Christ has ascended to "fill all things" (4:10), and this has long been expressed as an ultimate purpose of God in the epistle (1:22–23; 3:19).

Two descriptions relate tightly together: "mature manhood" is the positive way of asserting it, while "no longer . . . children" is the negative rendition. It is in these next verses (→4:15–16) that the text highlights the calling to grow up in Christ most bluntly. God's excessive power works here, not to bring things into being from nothing (as in 2 Cor. 4:5–6; Rom. 4:17), but to grow and develop that which is existent and death-ridden in sin's distortion. The first mark of maturity is to be anchored, as it were, protected from the waves of false promise and misdirected teaching. Such "waves" are described in three ways here: "by every wind of doctrine," "by human cunning," and "by craftiness in deceitful schemes." These temptations remain perennial, even if they had unique faces in first-century Asia Minor. The first threat is stated most generally ("every wind of doctrine" with no other adjectival descriptors), while the second accents its human (rather than divine) source ("human cunning"), and the third highlights its devious character ("in deceitful schemes").

4:15–16 Rather, speaking the truth in love, we are to grow up in every way into him who is the head, into Christ, from whom the whole body, joined and held together by every joint with which it is equipped, when each part is working properly, makes the body grow so that it builds itself up in love.

Having considered Christ's gift and Christ's goal, the text returns to something of a thick description of the ecclesial praxis wherein the heavenly pastor's care finds earthly expression. If Christians are mature enough to avoid being tossed about by this threefold battering of waves, then we do well to explore what they are strong enough for. To what sort of life does God's power enliven them? To what activity does their stature fit them? Ephesians 4:15–16 speaks mainly of the goal of growth.

As above, the apostle defines this end of maturity and growth in christological terms, for the aim is personal: "into him who is the head, into Christ." Body imagery arises, signaling the link between Christ and his people. Augustine would speak regularly of the *totus Christus* or "whole Christ," especially in regard to the psalms, wherein Christ and his people were united so intimately that he could speak for them or pray for them (in other words, the "I" speaking the psalms can be shared among that difference).

Body imagery does not function, however, apart from differentiation. Head and members are conjoined—that is, distinct and united. The language of "head" speaks to deliberative and discriminating authority, for a head makes judgments and determinations about the movement of a body; whatever other elements wax or wane in a given polity, this much is constant in the metaphor. But 4:16 speaks of the real integrity of the whole body's action here. The body is "joined and held together" and is "equipped" to that end. Even more so, the body "builds itself up in love." The language need not tilt Pelagian or autonomous—indeed, we shall see in a moment why it cannot do so—yet it does speak in a profuse and potent way of the necessity of bodily action and the real implications of that movement. In speaking of a body building itself up, the text nods at the fact that it is created and designed to be sustaining. "The whole body . . . makes the body grow" such that it is the congregated agency of the body with all its members that, "when each part is working properly," elicits development.

This emphasis on bodily action and integrity notwithstanding, the text also locates this human agency within a participatory context. The body's action in making the body grow and building itself up is all "from [him]" and tilted toward "grow[ing] up in every way into him." Christ is the context and the character of the body's growth. We have already sketched ways in which he is its character; the measure and stature of fullness are located firmly and singularly in him. We are conformed to the image of God in him. He is the second Adam and the one in whom we singularly see humanity transfigured before us. He is also, though, the context within which this transfiguration occurs, this conformity is extended, and this body is grown. Union with the exalted Christ serves as the animating reality for all ecclesiastical agency.

This christological participation marks healthy bodily life. The apostle also notes a qualification, though, which raises another aspect of christological provision. The text speaks of the body growing "when each part is working properly." The design of an integrated ecclesiastical body functions smoothly and effectively such that it "builds itself up in love." And yet daily experience, together with the testimony of all the apostle's other epistles, testifies that parts frequently do not work properly. The body can veer off course and stammer in its attempts to stick with the straight and narrow. To the creational need for christological power there is added then a second need for christological correction and instruction. "When each part is working properly" is syntactically parallel to "in love" here, so we can see something of the character of underwhelming ecclesiastical experience. We can speak of the body, or parts thereof, not working properly when they do not function in that love for God and for one another (→6:23).

It is not for nothing, then, that the church will speak of sustaining and conforming grace. Sustaining grace is the kind of grace that enables and empowers the normal function of human relational and moral agency, even when the body is functioning in a healthy manner (like the reality of caloric intake), while conforming grace intervenes in the not-infrequent crises when a part or parts become misaligned and require reorientation (which might be analogous to physical therapy). In the work of Christ, there is a reenergizing of who we were originally created to be, but there is also a transfiguration of that human shape such that glory is more than a mere return to Eden (see Allen 2017: 199–226).

Yet again human agency, in this case that of the communion of saints as a corporate, interconnected body, finds affirmation within a broader framework wherein Christ provides. In him we live, move, and have our action, we might say, turning the apostle's sermon to a more agential direction (cf. Acts 17:28). God's sovereign provision in making and remaking us—that is, in sustaining and conforming our moral agency—does not crowd out real human and ecclesial praxis that bears its own integrity. Far from it. As we have seen before, freedom and integrity are found in the right sort of dependence—that is, in increasingly conscious participation in the triune God's provision. While there is a wrong sort of dependency among creatures in society, in this unique relationship utter dependence remains metaphysically appropriate precisely because of God's singular transcendence and perfection.[4]

Ecclesiology must attend to both moments of this passage. The head must be honored. The head is not dispersed into or confused with the body as a whole. The head maintains integrity and discrete action. Jesus Christ is Lord of the church not just yesterday but today and forevermore (see Heb. 13:8). And yet that christological confession pairs with the body imagery wherein the head functions to give vigor and direction to an interconnected agential movement that has real integrity and effect. Those effects can be described as owing ultimately

---

4. See Kathryn Tanner, *God and Creation in Christian Theology: Tyranny or Empowerment?* (Oxford: Blackwell, 1988); William C. Placher, *The Domestication of Transcendence: How Modern Thinking about God Went Wrong* (Louisville: Westminster John Knox, 1996).

to the head, to be sure, but are also rightly traced to the body that "builds itself up in love," at least "when each part is working properly."

In his *Life of Moses*, Gregory of Nyssa defines perfection as endless progress. He does so because perfection is defined by conformity to and participation in an endlessly full God. Given that God is without bounds, surely the calling to be holy as he is holy is itself unbounded and thus unending. Reading this portion of the epistle jolts attention to such questions. Maturity does not find description here in a way that is easily cataloged or charted, nor in a fashion that admits of a terminus or end point. Maturity involves growth; wholeness contains the notion of being built up within it.

4:17–19 Now this I say and testify in the Lord, that you must no longer walk as the Gentiles do, in the futility of their minds. They are darkened in their understanding, alienated from the life of God because of the ignorance that is in them, due to their hardness of heart. They have become callous and have given themselves up to sensuality, greedy to practice every kind of impurity.

Again, Paul describes the foil for gospel faithfulness, herein depicting the walk of the Gentiles. In so doing he returns to the language of walking: he beckons the Christians "to walk in a manner worthy of [their] calling" (4:1), yet he had already described how "you once walked" in "trespasses and sins" (2:2, 1). While he is addressing a predominantly Gentile audience ("at one time you Gentiles in the flesh" in 2:11), he plainly here uses the term "Gentiles" (*ta ethnē*) to depict unbelieving persons who do not share in Christ. Chapter 2 described their walk as spiritual death (2:1–3) and their polity as separated from Christ (2:11–12); now the apostle turns to describe their psychology.

In turning to address this theme, he describes what he is doing: "Now this I say and testify in the Lord." Ephesians 4:11 has already prepared us to receive an apostolic word or testimony as being a gift not merely of a called human but ultimately of the exalted Christ (→4:7–11). Here Paul returns to that sort of self-conception as teacher and apostle in that he describes his labor not only as "saying" but also as "testifying"—that is, offering witness of another. Still further, he testifies "in the Lord," which is to say that he speaks as one who has been commissioned by another or, as he put it elsewhere, as "an apostle of Christ Jesus by the will of God" (1:1). The moral instruction to follow does not arise from a mere mortal; it has been sent by God on high. Especially given that this epistle soon turns to household codes that are frequently received today with suspicion (as if they merely parrot material from the wider cultural milieu and, in the eyes of some, fall short of the evangelical distinction of other New Testament writings, such as Galatians), it is not for nothing that Paul here flourishes his credentials as one who "testifies in the Lord."

As we trace that commissioned testimony, we see the apostle diagnosing and then prescribing. Ephesians 4:17–19 provides a thick, intellectually focused description of Gentile depravity. Descriptions cluster: "the futility of their minds," "darkened in their understanding," "the ignorance that is in them," "their hardness of heart." The thought life of the Gentile can be summed up as pointless/futile, cloudy/unclear, ignorant/unknowing, and unteachable/stubborn. Intellectual vice mars their moral judgment in a range of ways. In light of the ways in which the apostle's prayers turn again and again to intellectual longings (1:17–19; 3:18–19), it is perhaps not surprising that his lament over depravity and warning about Gentile behavior accents intellectual vice.

The ESV loses something of the parallelism in 4:18 in its efforts to avoid redundancy (*dia* plus the accusative translated "because of" and "due to" instead of simply "on account of" and "on account of"). These Gentiles are "alienated from the life of God," a tragedy owing to two conditions that are each identified with the same syntactical construction (*dia tēn agnoian tēn ousan en aoutois* and *dia tēn pōrōsin tēs kardias autōn*). Ignorance and hardheartedness each lead to this alienation, and they are expressed in parallel. It would be one thing to be ignorant but teachable, the kind of pupil with whom a docent can work, but it is another matter to teach a student who proves to be both ignorant and unwilling to receive instruction. Sadly, it is precisely the one who most needs correction who is here deemed the one least likely to be teachable.

The passage goes on to speak of results. "They have become callous," suggesting a waning sensitivity in moral terms. They have become accustomed to the ethically questionable and the morally depraved; such things no longer register warning bells. Conscience has grown stale within them. Their spiritual callousness opens them up to less constrained agency, as the internal governor for their moral deliberation has grown weak. Not surprisingly, then, they also "have given themselves up to sensuality." This phrase not only speaks of pursuing sensual delights, which would go without saying, but it speaks of offering or sacrificing themselves to those allurements. In living in such an unconstrained manner, they quite literally give themselves away.

By the end of the passage, they are "greedy to practice every kind of impurity." The description takes global form, much like that refrain in the flood narrative: "The wickedness of man was great in the earth, and . . . every intention of the thoughts of his heart was only evil continually" (Gen. 6:5; see also Gen. 8:21 for a recurrence of the "evil-thought clause"). A rapacious lust for impurity turns ceaseless and indiscriminate: their posture is "greedy," such that temptation taken is of "every kind." Greediness or covetousness marks them out as insatiably seeking and searching for more, never satisfied or completed. Like the sage's tragic seeking depicted in Ecclesiastes, the search for joy "under the sun" will turn to every sort or kind—yes, even of impurities in pursuing completion and satisfaction.

The most challenging statement surely relates to what may likely be another result. Owing to ignorance and hardheartedness, "they are . . . alienated from the life of God." Most likely, then, this participle ("being alienated") speaks of something brought about by their intellectual vice. While alienation has been mentioned earlier (→2:12), the phrase "the life of God" (*tēs zōēs tou theou*) is an outlier. When Paul and the wider New Testament witness speaks of "life," the word typically refers to "eternal life." That reference may be one term removed from "the life of God," but this is the one spot where the connection is made directly. It may speak of life from God (interpreting the genitive as source) or the life that is God's own and in which humans may participate (a possessive reading of the genitive). Both notions are attested elsewhere in the New Testament, albeit not in this exact idiom. A number of interpreters have argued, largely for unnecessary theological reasons related to suspicion of participation as a viable soteriological and metaphysical category, that this reference cannot speak to participating in God's own life (Hoehner 2002: 586; but see Fowl 2012: 148). Perhaps the strongest reason that makes it slightly more probable that it does refer to God's own life—in which we are meant to participate and from which these Gentiles are alienated—is that this claim appears alongside the tragic description of them as those who greedily seek satisfaction in every which way. Precisely because they have not found all-sufficient provision in God alone, they are seemingly doomed to taste and see how vapid the wares of the world are by comparison.

4:20–24 But that is not the way you learned Christ!—assuming that you have heard about him and were taught in him, as the truth is in Jesus, to put off your old self, which belongs to your former manner of life and is corrupt through deceitful desires, and to be renewed in the spirit of your minds, and to put on the new self, created after the likeness of God in true righteousness and holiness.

As with earlier passages (→2:1–10; 2:11–22), Paul pairs a negative portrayal of former life with a new vista wherein we can see the granular shape of living by God's grace. In his commissioned testimony (4:17) he now turns to speak prescriptively of that which is intended for those in the Lord. He speaks prescriptively to a group who are described in certain fashion. Three phrases qualify the appropriate audience for these prescriptions. First, he contrasts these Gentile ways as "not the way you learned Christ." So he speaks initially with the implicit syntactical assumption that they have in fact "learned Christ," likely alluding to the notion of discipleship. Second, he makes that implicit judgment explicit and hypothetical: "assuming that you have [second] heard about him and [third] were taught in him." These second and third descriptors serve as a kind of sieve, by which hearers might assess their own standing: Have they heard of Christ? Were they taught not merely about him but "in him"? Ephesians 4:21 is a tangent that provokes the listeners or readers to ask if this applies to them, for it has commanding significance if it does. To suggest that inviolability, the apostle here conjoins language of discipleship (prevalent in the gospels) with language of union with Christ or incorporation (dominant in the Pauline corpus).

Discipleship may seem woodenly moral to some, but it is worth noting that there are covenantal reasons to appreciate its significance. "The truth is in Jesus" (4:21) offers a metaphysical claim that locates truthfulness in a particular person who is Wisdom incarnate and God in the flesh. If ultimate spiritual truth cannot be separated from Jesus Christ, then locating oneself as a pupil under his instruction makes all the sense in the world. Discipleship comes not as a consumer choice, nor as a mere spiritual strategy. Rather, the singular claim to this one's truth makes discipleship a necessary epistemological way. Not surprisingly, then, 4:20 uses the language of being a disciple (*emathete*) in describing how one learned Christ.

Several phrases speak to what is learned in and of Christ: "to put off your old self" (4:22) speaks to mortifying that which is sin-ridden, while "to put on the new self" (4:24) attests to the calling to walk worthily of one's calling (→4:1; see also Col. 3:1–11). The "old self" is not wrong for being Gentile ethnically speaking, but because it "belongs to your former manner of life" (which does relate to Gentile religiosity and culture in certain respects) inasmuch as it "is corrupt through deceitful desires" (4:22). Likewise, the "new self" is elevated not for its ethnic distinctiveness but for its theological character as that "created after the likeness of God in true righteousness and holiness" (4:24). In saying it was fashioned "after the likeness of God," the text alludes not only back to Gen.

1:26–27 but more immediately to Jesus (see Col. 1:15).[5] The new life remains new in the heavens, but heaven has not yet come pervasively and exclusively to earth; thus, one can still be summoned to put off the earthly and old and to put on the heavenly and new.

The specific object of mortification and vivification is, in both cases, the self (*ton anthrōpon*). This "man" (to use the most wooden translation), "person," or "self" can be "old" (*palaion*) or "new" (*kainon*). The very phrase "the new man" (*kainon anthrōpon*) appeared earlier in the epistle: "he might create in himself one new man in place of the two" (2:15). That prior appearance spoke of a collective entity, "one body" (2:16), whereas this later instance speaks of a personal reference for each and every Christian (again see the parallel in Col. 3:9–10). That prior reference included language of mortification ("broken down") and vivification ("making peace") in speaking of society under the former sign of sinfulness and now under the sign of Christ's grace. Here, then, we have the personal and moral parallel wherein the apostle speaks of the person or self formerly under the reign of sin and latterly in the kingdom of Christ's gift.

The text speaks of the vivified life in two ways. "To be renewed in the spirit of your minds" conveys a sense of nature being revived, whereas "and to put on the new self, created . . ." interjects a measure of new creation and drastic divine intervention. The analogy for the one would be a home renovation that brings out the character of an existing dwelling, while the other would involve a knockdown and rebuilding job, which is a very different architectural and constructional task. Both idioms are used here as they are throughout scripture, and we must catch the imprint of each. Renewal conveys that it is the person—in their irreducible and particular identity—who is saved by Christ, while new creation communicates something of the stark and interruptive event that is conversion and union with Christ (see Allen 2017: 212–26).

The apostle does not invent this pairing—it runs all the way back into the Old Testament scriptures. Some prophecies speak of a bad heart being removed and a new heart being implanted (Ezek. 36:26), while others speak of the circumcision of the heart (Deut. 30:6) or the writing of the law upon the heart (Jer. 31:33). The former imagery seems to gesture strongly in the direction of new creation and even toward replacement, while the latter texts nod at restoration and renewal as apt descriptions. Similarly, the apostle would have learned as a

---

5. Note that this link is conceptual and not semantic, as the definition of this new creation after God's own likeness is expressed simply in a prepositional statement (*kata theon*) and lacks a nominal term for "likeness" that would allude back verbally to Gen. 1:26–27.

young child to confess in prayer, "Create in me a clean heart, O God, and renew a right spirit within me" (Ps. 51:10). This cry demands new creation, yes, but also renewal of that which is "within me," showing that the two sorts of images are not oppositional or mutually exclusive even if they are notably distinct and convey varied notions.

The language of new creation here connects with the apocalyptic imagery and cosmology that have so dominated recent Pauline interpretation (P. Ziegler 2018). Philip Ziegler and a range of Pauline interpreters (especially J. Louis Martyn) have seen the way this imagery fixes sights on the interruptive character of grace; salvation in this apocalyptic or new creational frame involves nothing less than bringing life from outside our cosmos. In that respect, apocalyptic theology returns Augustinian sensibilities (appreciated not least by Reformed forebears) to reading Paul on grace and salvation. Yet new creation is not the only word; the verse and passage also speak of renewal and restoration, which compels us to maintain a doctrine of creation and an appreciation for human nature. In so doing, we must glean our understanding of human nature from revelational teaching and never allow it to serve as a conduit for adopting or baptizing pagan instruction (under the guise of the mantra that the word of God instructs regarding new creation while other sources concern themselves with only creation itself). The word shapes our understanding of creation and nature too, so that this affirmation does not justify or warrant endorsement of extraneous theories (as in Barth's worried engagement of the so-called orders of creation during the time of the Nazis).

The apocalyptic new creation absent the restorative angle may well lead to moving human freedom into the realm of free play. Self-creativity would be unconstrained by any defined sense of human nature, of divine covenant, or of natural law. In many ways this would be to fall into the same tragedy experienced by those self-proclaimed "Radical Lutherans" who seek to expand the law-gospel contrast of Luther and the Lutheran and Reformed confessions into a systemic *discrimen* or principle (against which see the penetrating analysis by Yeago 1993). While each of those aspects, new creation and restoration, must be probed carefully and approached exegetically, they remind us that God's heavenly power does not destroy but perfects human nature (a truth no less heralded by Reformed theologians than by Thomas Aquinas; see discussion of Bavinck on this score, contra Barth, in Allen 2017: 135–40). Conversely, focus on restoration or renewal apart from that new-creational cataclysmic imagery fails to register the turbulence that grace involves. Discipleship and salvation are disruptive to the very core, for there is not one nook or cranny of the self that can proceed apart from the resurrecting power of heavenly grace. As ever, the call is to trace each apostolic word in its particularity and to feel its peculiar weight, but also to make sure we are attending to the breadth of holy scripture, not settling for one or the other image as if it were sufficient. Readers of Ephesians must be alert to what the apostle Paul said to the Ephesian elders: "I testify to you this day that I am innocent of the blood of all, for I did not shrink from declaring to you the whole counsel of God." Pointing to themes dominant in the epistle, he also said, "Now I commend you to God and to the word of his grace, which is able to build you up and to give you the inheritance among all those who are sanctified" (Acts 20:26–27, 32).

4:25–32 Therefore, having put away falsehood, let each one of you speak the truth with his neighbor, for we are members one of another. Be angry and do not sin; do not let the sun go down on your anger, and give no opportunity to the devil. Let the thief no longer steal, but rather let him labor, doing honest work with his own hands, so that he may have something to share with anyone in need. Let no corrupting talk come out of your mouths, but only such as is good for building up, as fits the occasion, that it may give grace to those who hear. And do not grieve the Holy Spirit of God, by whom you were sealed for the day of redemption. Let all bitterness and wrath and anger and clamor and slander be put away from you, along with all malice. Be kind to one another, tenderhearted, forgiving one another, as God in Christ forgave you.

Beckoning to us, then, Paul summons his hearers. The mood turns consistently subjunctive ("let us") so as to spark action. Ephesians 4:25 roots the call, yet again, in what has been accomplished already—in this case, "having put away false-hood." They have turned from "futility" and "ignorance" and are thus no longer "darkened" or "alienated." That shadow existence—promising yet delivering all the substance of a momentary vapor, enticing and yet so very fleeting—has been left, dismissed, repented of. Indeed, they have "put it off."

Biblical repentance always involves turning from a false promise for the sake of turning to a genuine hope. Abandoning sin's futility must be matched by pursuing the truth's pathway. Why? Because holiness is not a call simply to divest oneself of the unclean but also and ultimately about investing oneself in that last true devotion to God's own self (see Lev. 10:10). So here they "[have] put away false-hood" and "learned Christ"—remember that "the truth is in Jesus" (4:21)—and so they have put off the yoke of deceit and put on the burden of integrity. Seven exhortations illustrate this new manner of life that they have learned in Christ.

First, "let each one of you speak the truth" (4:25). Walking in truth demands speaking truth. Words are given weight and treated as bearing gravity here. They are not flippant play but are both expressive of one's own self and formative of one's own and others' selves. The apostle explains a reason for this kind of word care—namely, it engages one "with his neighbor" (*meta tou plēsion autou*). Neighbor identification here probably focuses on the Christian community more specifically, for the apostle goes on to say that "we are members one of another." The language of membership hearkens back to the image of the body (→2:15–16; 4:15–16). C. S. Lewis speaks of the miracle in others:

> There are no ordinary people. You have never talked to a mere mortal. Nations, cultures, arts, civilizations—these are mortal, and their life is to ours as the life of a gnat. But it is immortals whom we joke with, work with, marry, snub and exploit—immortal horrors or everlasting splendors. This does not mean that we are to be perpetually solemn. We must play. But our merriment must be of that kind (and it is, in fact, the merriest kind) which exists between people who have, from the outset, taken each other seriously—no flippancy, no superiority, no presumption.[6]

His observation is that the metaphysical and eschatological reality of the neighbor beckons forth a certain gravity. The apostle goes a step further, moving from a general affirmation of immortality to identifying the neighbor here as also a fellow "member" to whom we owe the kind of care that one body part offers another (see 1 Cor. 12:21–26). Thus, there is a particular gravity to our linguistic address among family and fellow heirs.

Second, "be angry and do not sin" (4:26). Anger is appropriate, not for selfish reasons, but, again, out of concern for truthfulness and integrity. Injustice and deceit warrant anger, whether from without or within. But anger turns on a razor's edge, and so the apostle warns them that they "not sin" in their anger. Admittedly, one way not to sin is to demonstrate anger appropriately and in proportion to legitimate causes. In other words, indifference and a lack of anger would be one pathway to sin. On the other hand, venting anger disproportionately or indiscriminately would be to exude the fire of anger but in an untargeted and unconstrained manner. Wisdom and discernment are needed here; not surprisingly, perhaps, anger and wrath are major concerns in Proverbs (see Treier 2011:

---

6. C. S. Lewis, "The Weight of Glory," in *The Weight of Glory: And Other Addresses* (New York: HarperCollins, 2001), 47.

92–95). A paired exhortation will follow (thirdly) regarding the governance of anger when it does arise.

Third, "do not let the sun go down on your anger, and give no opportunity to the devil" (4:26–27). If anger festers, it presents an "opportunity" or occasion for temptation. It enables the devil to create a rift or disjunction between those who are "members one of another." Thus, not only the existence but also the endurance of anger needs to be managed for moral and relational reasons.

Fourth, "let the thief no longer steal, but rather let him labor" (4:28). Past sin does not consign one to exclusion or ostracism. The thief is drawn into or kept within the Christian community, though the sin needs to be put away. It is addressed here amidst a focus on language, not least because deceit and thievery have a tendency toward obfuscation and outright lying, which would be as deleterious for the Christian congregation as when a body's immune system makes false judgments and, owing to an autoimmune disease, begins to unleash its own force upon itself. So thievery poses a serious threat within the congregation (see esp. Fowl 2012: 157). Here we have a direct illustration of the broader principle that mortification and vivification must be paired: this thief shall no longer steal and shall now labor or work. "Doing honest work with his own hands" is commended, as is a deeper purpose: "so that he may have something to share with anyone in need." Restoration of the thief does not stop short at ending burglary but goes on toward gainful employment; but it presses still further in directing that work so that philanthropy and self-sacrifice for others might follow. One may—even should—identify one with a track record of thievery as "the thief" (*ho kleptōn*), though only for the sake of intentionally fostering a social environment wherein the body diverts that person from thievery (*mēketi kleptetō*) toward honest employment and ultimately to neighbor love and self-sacrifice. Naming one's own sinful temptations (and past—perhaps habitual—failures) is not meant to burnish a sense of smug self-satisfaction, though it may well be essential to targeting a corporate and personal strategy of sustained repentance as one concrete illustration of building up the body.

Fifth, "let no corrupting talk come out of your mouths, but only such as is good for building up" (4:29). Again there is a return to the tongue and to the way in which conversation is meant to "build up." This imagery of building up gestures back to 4:16, where it says this of Christ: "from whom the whole body, joined and held together by every joint with which it is equipped, when each part is working properly, makes the body grow so that it builds itself up in love." The body apparently builds itself up by choosing encouraging words. Admittedly, context and circumstance matter, so it is not as though there are similar good words and bad words that can be plugged in and played piecemeal; no, discernment shapes the judgment about words that "may give grace to those who hear" (4:29). Just as 4:16 speaks of the integrity of ecclesial life in that the body "builds itself up in love," so here ecclesial language "may give grace" in speaking with the neighbor and fellow member.

Sixth, "do not grieve the Holy Spirit of God" (4:30). Here there is another reminder of the rationale: this Spirit is the one "by whom you were sealed for the day of redemption" (→1:13–14). What constitutes grieving this Spirit with whom Christians are sealed as heirs of God upon their conversion? The language of grief (the imperative *lypeite*) serves as a reminder that the Spirit is no mere instrument or force; while functioning analogously, the terminology rightly alerts us to the irreducibly personal nature of the Spirit's work, which can more easily be forgotten given the lack of a public face, as it were, to the mission of the Holy Spirit. While the Spirit has never assumed incarnate form, the Spirit seals us for glory in a thoroughly personal manner.

Stephen Fowl (2012: 158) argues that grieving the Spirit involves living at cross-purposes with the end for which the Spirit fits us; to speak in terms of 4:1–2, it would constitute walking *un*worthily of that calling or telos. He argues further that the sealing work of the Spirit (1:13–14) is next elaborated in reference to the Spirit's work with the community: "In him you also are being built together into a dwelling place for God by the Spirit" (2:22). To grieve the Spirit, then, would be to walk and work in such a way that this filial fabric is torn by deceit or rancor or burglary. Fowl's focus on communal malformation certainly has much to commend it, though he skips over the other reference to the Spirit's work, which is found in the prayer concluding chapter 3. In what way does Paul's pleading that "according to the riches of his glory he may grant you to be strengthened with power through his Spirit in your inner being" (3:16) also inform what he means by grieving the Spirit? Can interpretation fix on the social aspects to the exclusion of this more epistemological aspect?

Seventh, "let all bitterness and wrath and anger and clamor and slander be put away from you, along with all malice" (4:31). Here the apostle concludes with a range of debilitating and distancing attitudes and actions (see also Col. 3:8, 12–13). Three attitudes are excluded: bitterness, wrath, and anger. Two concrete actions are similarly denounced: clamor and slander. Finally, a fourth attitude concludes the list: malice is also to be cast aside. Note that while anger is to be practiced without sin (4:26), malice is never appropriate and ought to be excluded in its every occurrence. To speak of these terms in 4:31 as vices (Thomas Aquinas 1966: 191; Fowl 2012: 159) is appropriate but must be approached with a sensibility for the variety of ways in which they manifest (some as concrete action, some always at the level of motivation or attitude).

The final verse of the chapter actually introduces a transitional section that continues throughout 5:1–2. "Be kind to one another, tenderhearted, forgiving one another, as God in Christ forgave you" (4:32) does offer another hortatory call to action, and it picks up on the concern to maintain communal bonds. Thematically, however, it hews much more closely to the theme of imitating God's care for his family by way of sacrifice, as is sketched in 5:1–2, where we read, "Therefore be imitators of God, as beloved children. And walk in love, as Christ loved us and gave himself up for us, a fragrant offering and sacrifice to God." As this commentary turns to chapter 5, concern for the way of life that marks the body of Christ continues to fascinate the apostle and captivate his attention.

What is involved in this summative call in 4:32? First, there is a call to show kindness to one another—that is, to one's fellow heirs (note that sonship language becomes explicit in 5:1: "as beloved children"). Kindness flows from a subjective posture described as being "tenderhearted." Yet the apostle does not reduce kindness to an inner disposition of tenderheartedness that might play out in different ways. He goes on to specify the measure of tenderhearted kindness as forgiveness of one another. The passage quickly expands on the way in which imitation is significant: here briefly as "as God in Christ forgave you," then more fully as "as Christ loved us and gave himself up for us, a fragrant offering and sacrifice to God" (5:2). It is impossible to segregate this kind of tenderhearted kindness from the language of sacrifice, even though the apostle's rhetorical move is by way of analogy and not crass imitation as such. That sacrificial aspect (→5:2) demonstrates why tenderheartedness is so significant to kindness; given the cost of showing kindness to each other, the only person who will bear that sort of cost willingly will be the one who does so with a genuinely "tenderhearted" disposition toward others. With any hardened or distant manner of heart, one will be unwilling to do the sort of painful work that is involved in inconveniencing oneself for the sake of one's fellow members in the body. More on the theological logic herein will be addressed as we turn to the following two verses (→5:1–2).

EPHESIANS 5

5:1–2 Therefore be imitators of God, as beloved children. And walk in love, as Christ loved us and gave himself up for us, a fragrant offering and sacrifice to God.

The link between 5:1–2 and the preceding verse is signaled not only by parallel content (forgiveness and selflessness in 4:32 and 5:2) or merely by analogical reasoning (*kathōs kai* in 4:32 and 5:2) but also by "therefore" (*oun*) in 5:1.

Ephesians 5:1 beckons the audience to the imitation of God. Imitation marks the tradition, from Gregory of Nazianzus to Thomas à Kempis. The way of the cross shapes piety not merely during the Holy Week ritual but also in Reformational descriptions of the Christian life as a pathway of self-denial (looking to what Calvin calls "the model" of Christ in *Institutes* 3.6.1). In earlier centuries, imitation shaped the way in which Christians imagined their apprenticeship and discipleship along the way of the carpenter. The idiom seemed to arise most commonly when calling Christ's members to the more painful parts of his way—namely, taking up the cross and following him, enduring mistreatment for his name's sake, bearing the griefs of others, and so forth.

Imitation has gained critics, however, for at least two reasons, each of which deserves analysis. First, some—especially Augustinians and particularly Protestants—have worried that the gift of Christ might be reduced (à la Pelagius) to an example for imitation. In such a vision, Christ would remain outside us and move us by way of moral persuasion or motivational inspiration. He would not be head of a body, however, and he would not indwell or unite himself with our very selves, bearing burdens and offering himself as a sacrifice. He would not free us from bondage and deliver us over to the kingdom of God as the king and victor who has conquered sin, death, and devil in his Father's name. Whether imitation comes in the guise of an Abelard or a later Socinus or even a Schleiermacher, many Protestants (especially though not exclusively) have sought to counter by remembering the dictum of Luther: Christ is gift before he is example.[1]

Luther's emphasis can be seen in this text as well: "be imitators of God, as beloved children" (5:1). Imitation follows the pathway not of servitude but of inheritance. The language here is not that of sonship specifically but of childlike familial standing (*hōs tekna agapēta*). The kind of *mimesis* or repetition that is invoked does not come from one who is parroting the way of the original; rather, it is the imitation of one who has been parented by the heavenly Father. Ephesians has already used the language of the beloved: "beloved children" here evokes earlier mention that "he has blessed us in the Beloved" (*autou hēs echaritōsen hēmas en tō ēgapēmenō* in 1:6). Slightly more distant, though nonetheless significant, are the words characterizing the way in which God "made us alive together with Christ" "because of the great love with which he loved us" (2:5, 4, with the nominal and verbal paired: *dia tēn pollēn agapēn autou hēn ēgapēsen hēmas*). Indeed, love roots and grounds the audience (3:17) and demands still to be known more and more such that they might be filled with God's own fullness, for which Paul himself prays (3:19). Here we learn not merely of God's loving, nor of them having been loved, but that they are beloved children; their very character will be defined, in this sense, by God's great love for them.

Luther's dictum has often opened some up to forget that Christ, being gift, must also be example. Perhaps Radical Lutherans most poignantly illustrate this tendency when they juxtapose law and grace as competing *discrimens* for theology and suggest that the law-gospel distinction serves as a comprehensive rubric for all theological inquiry (for analysis and rebuttal see Yeago 1993). In such a frame, the word of imitation serves not to adorn grace but to undercut or oppose it. But resurrection brings new life and action this side of death, and transfiguration really does shine glory in the created order. Further, the Christ who carries burdens calls us also to follow him. The later Lutheran theologian Dietrich Bonhoeffer was captivated by this vision of the Christ who gives himself not only as sacrifice and victor but also as teacher and model and Lord: "When Christ calls a man, he bids him come and die."[2] While imitation can and has turned parasitic insofar as it is Pelagian at times, any shirking of imitation altogether has turned away from the particularity of the incarnate Son (on the link between grace and the discipline of following an example, see Allen 2017: 264–75).

1. Luther, "Brief Instruction on What to Look For and Expect in the Gospels (1521)," in *Word and Sacrament I*, Luther's Works 35, trans. E. Theodore Bachmann (Philadelphia: Augsburg, 1960), 113–24.
2. Dietrich Bonhoeffer, *The Cost of Discipleship* (New York: Macmillan, 1995), 89.

A second objection has arisen, largely in late modern times, regarding imitation. Here the concern is not that of grace being preserved free from works but that of individuality being kept from slavish mimesis. The patron saint of this concern might be Foucault as opposed to Luther, and the watchword might be self-stylization over against gift. The concern of these late modern critics of imitation is the homogenization of cultural mores, clipping the wings of one's daughters and sons by calling them to fly the routes of their parents. Christian moral restraint, in such a critical viewpoint, inhibits self-expression and mollifies moral discernment. The objection may be better caught by way of personal narrative than sociocultural expression.

In his memoirs, religious historian Carlos Eire tells his story not merely of immigration from Cuba but of deliverance from suspicion of imitation. In *Learning to Die in Miami*, he speaks of his frustration with this traditional language. The one gift accompanying him in his journey to South Florida was a copy of *The Imitation of Christ* by à Kempis, a provision from his mother. He hated that book, a reminder that she sent him away and a warning that the Christian way forward would not—should not—involve comfort or peace. As he eventually began to feel settled in a new home in Illinois, finally gaining some sense of security and shelter, the book served as a special challenge: "I have this book I carry around that tells me that I should let go of everything and everyone, including myself. It's the book my parents gave me when I left home, *The Imitation of Christ*. An awful book, really. They don't come much worse than this one. It scares me to death, every time I try to read it. Let go of everything, says the book. But everything in my life right now is everything I've always wanted" (Eire 2010: 248). Having traveled to "the land of the free and the home of the brave," Eire sensed that the call to imitate Christ would lead back to tyrannical bondage and implicate him in moral cowardice (such were Kant's invectives against Christian moral realism in "What Is Enlightenment?").

Eire eventually turned to the book, telling of how he would open it at random and surprisingly find it insightful. Again and again, the way of the crucified seemed to speak tellingly of what would bring life. Finally he testifies:

> Everything changes, from top to bottom. A veil rips loudly, and light pours through, and nothing looks the same. For the first time in my life I feel as if I'm the master of my own destiny, not because I feel more highly of myself but just the opposite: Accepting my own limitations is key. So is accepting it as an unquestionable fact that some higher power is eager to help me overcome whatever the world throws at me, both from without and within.

It's close to Easter. My mind is reeling and so are my heart and my will. I'm in Bizarro World now, where everything is the opposite of what it should be. I'm no longer who I was two months before, and neither is the world itself.

Jagged is smooth. Bitter is sweet. Sorrow is joy. Dark is light. Black is white.

> The unseen illumines what is seen.
> Absurdity rescues logic.
> Love of self leads to anguish.
> Self-loathing leads to elation.
> Abstinence becomes the highest thrill of all.
> Praying becomes the only conversation that makes sense.
> Believing becomes as natural and unstoppable as breathing.
> Doubting becomes as unsurprising as exhaling.
> Forgiving becomes the only sensible option.
> Temptation drops its mask.
> Remorse claims its crown.
> Loss loses its sting.
> Pain gains its wings.
> Now becomes forever. Forever begins now, forever. (Eire 2010: 258)

Eire paints the eschatologically transformative impact of knowing himself to be illumined by that which is above and powerful. Life in light of the benediction of Eph. 3:20–21 involves a walk that makes no sense apart from that wonder-working power from on high, and that begins the apocalyptic reversal of values that seems so very scandalous. It is not for nothing that Eire speaks of this transformation as "close to Easter," for that moral illumination is tethered by the very gift of life from death. This testimony casts into relief the way in which imitation in all its christological particularity can seem oppressive, threatening, or death-dealing when viewed from a remove. But it also goes on to confess its life-giving, clarifying, freeing summons when heard this side of Easter, wherein one hears the call now no longer in a tone disconnected from the promise forever. This is what Eugene Peterson has termed the summons to "practice resurrection" in walking with the call of Ephesians.[3]

So Paul summons sons and daughters to be "imitators of God." Imaging the divine—that is, mimetic imitation of their heavenly Father—will take what may be strange form, so it is not surprising that 4:17–6:9 ranges widely over the moral

---

3. Eugene Peterson, *Practice Resurrection: A Conversation on Growing Up in Christ* (Grand Rapids: Eerdmans, 2010).

terrain in which Christian heirs are called to walk. It does not shock either that this instruction returns to contrasts, whether of Gentiles and Christians (4:17–21), the old self and the new self (4:22–24), or darkness and light (5:8–14), for the moral summons gains credibility with the self-awareness of adoption and the illumination of life within the family home, an experience only enjoyed on this terrestrial globe by those who are adopted in and come to know by grace this new way of walking. Imitating God—not a mere mortal—cuts against the grain of sinful proclivities, even of earthly morals. We have seen already that the virtues and habits of the Christian sometimes overlap with but frequently diverge pointedly from those of Greco-Roman society (→4:1–3).

Most immediately, 4:32 and 5:2 highlight ways in which the triune God is to be imitated: "Be kind to one another, tenderhearted, forgiving one another, as God in Christ forgave you. . . . And walk in love, as Christ loved us and gave himself up for us, a fragrant offering and sacrifice to God." The former sentence has already been examined (→4:32), so attention should be paid to the latter sentence now. Again the audience is to "walk" (→4:1; 5:8, 15), and here the call is specified as doing so "in love" or "by [means of] love" (*en agapē*). The same apostle who defines the right walk as a worthy one (4:1) also values love as a mark of that movement, so the audience dare not play off the seemingly objective against the subjective, or the purportedly enduring against the spontaneously authentic. Love here involves the benefiting of others out of genuine concern for their good, even as it demands weighty self-sacrifice. The larger portion of the verse provides an analogy: "as Christ loved us and gave himself up for us." Love will be defined christologically: the incarnate Son *acted out of* a personal desire to bless "us" and *acted to* a personal diminishment by offering himself up as a sacrifice.

The language of sacrifice (*thysian*) and of a fragrant offering (*osmēn euōdias*) locates the love of Jesus in the frame of Old Testament law. The imagery points to the liturgical practice of the priests. The term "sacrifice" translates a number of Hebrew terms, located most formatively in Exodus (e.g., Exod. 12:27 pertaining to Passover and 29:34, 41–42 regarding priestly sacrifices as regulated at Sinai). In Leviticus, however, "sacrifice" is first frequently paired exactly with the phrase "fragrant offering" (e.g., Lev. 1:9, 13, 17; 2:2). Jesus loves his people, Greek as well as Jew, by offering himself according to these scriptural stipulations, thereby fulfilling or bringing to its determined goal the law of God (Rom. 10:4). In fulfilling that lawful demand, Jesus confirms the validity of the law as a matrix for moral discernment inasmuch as his expression of love does not come ambiguously or autonomously; even he, the incarnate Son of God and the one who is greater than Moses but is also nonetheless depicted as a new Moses, submits himself to the revealed will of God (for that will expresses his own: see Ps. 11:7). Christians are not called to offer themselves as sacrifices for sin, for Christ has performed the perfect offering in that respect (Heb. 10:1–18), but they are called to make sacrificial offerings (Heb. 13:15; see also the clear liturgical parallel in Rom. 12:1 and the oblique parallel in Col. 1:24 regarding sacrifice for missiological purposes). Therefore, the exegetical imagination must be as broad and variegated as Leviticus, for sacrifice was never restricted solely to sin and guilt offerings (see Lev. 1–3).

God shall be imaged, and God beckons imitation. Long before reaching these verses, the epistle has already reaffirmed the singular glory that is God's own and the fullness that he uniquely possesses. Talk of imitation, then, must be disciplined by an axiomatic commitment to that Creator-creature distinction, wherein the blessed and only King of kings and Lord of lords is not to be blurred with or set alongside any of his creatures, even those blessed in his Son. Fowl attends to this principle while also noting the demand of Eph. 5:1: "Obviously, humans cannot imitate God in all respects. All human imitation of God must work on the basis of analogy rather than strict mimesis. At the same time, God's desire is that we participate in the divine nature (2 Pet. 1:4). It is important, therefore, that on the one hand Christians avoid all attempts to transgress the boundary between Creator and creature, and on the other hand that they not sell short their calling to participate in the life of the triune God" (2012: 161).

To guide us in a non-idolatrous imitation of God's own life, the apostle points specifically to the incarnate God's love, for in the action of Christ we see that process of mimetic contextualization already begun and in fact perfected; he is "the founder and perfecter of our faith" (Heb. 12:2), and he also defines and distributes love in an imitable manner. Just as God has "give[n] the light of the knowledge of the glory of God in the face of Jesus Christ" (2 Cor. 4:6), so the triune Lord has displayed the costly shape of human love in the sacrificial work of the Great High Priest.

5:3–5 But sexual immorality and all impurity or covetousness must not even be named among you, as is proper among saints. Let there be no filthiness nor foolish talk nor crude joking, which are out of place, but instead let there be thanksgiving. For you may be sure of this, that everyone who is sexually immoral or impure, or who is covetous (that is, an idolater), has no inheritance in the kingdom of Christ and God.

Paul here speaks to that which has no place for those imitating God in Christ. This is the rare occasion where the apostle speaks explicitly of "the kingdom of Christ and God" or any such variant. For all the frequency of kingdom language in the gospels, the idiom is relatively rare in Paul's writings. Romans 14:16–17 is the parallel text: "So do not let what you regard as good be spoken of as evil. For the kingdom of God is not a matter of eating and drinking but of righteousness and peace and joy in the Holy Spirit." In that passage, three things are conveyed. First, the moral judgment of the kingdom is under threat (such that verse 16 must be stated). Second, the kingdom's ethic will not include continued practice of Jewish dietary law (see Rom. 14:1–23 as a whole). Third, the included items in this list of moral concerns range over matters pertaining to the second table of the Decalogue, specifically the seventh, ninth, and tenth commandments.

These verses in Ephesians manifest the same concerns as that passage in Romans. First, the danger now that the good might be called evil will be addressed in what follows via the distinction of light and darkness (→5:6–16; note also that this use of light/darkness found its place in Rom. 13:11–14). Second, there is no mention here of anything that distinguishes Jew from Gentile per se, whether circumcision or dietary law or festival-keeping. In this regard, Paul again works within the judgments rendered by the Jerusalem Council (see Acts 15:28–29 on the council's letter following the testimony of Peter in 15:8–11 and James in 15:19–20), which have been described at length already in this epistle (→2:11–22). Third, the moral teaching can rightly be seen to range across the second table of the Decalogue. Remember that the sixth and eighth commandments have already been addressed in Ephesians (→4:26–27 and 4:28, respectively). So the section running from 4:25–5:6 covers the terrain of the second table, interrupted by the programmatic discussion of imitating God in Christ in 4:32–5:2.

Prohibition of "sexual immorality" (*porneia*) appears elsewhere in Paul (1 Cor. 6:18; Gal. 5:19) and refers widely to that which is unclean and inappropriate (described variedly in Lev. 18). Pairing the term with the next, "all impurity" (*akatharsia pasa*), alludes powerfully to Leviticus, where both terms play such a frequent role (the pairing appears also in 2 Cor. 12:21 and Gal. 5:19). Interestingly, the verse relates impurity with "covetousness" (*pleonexia*), a term drawn from Exod. 20:17. Ephesians 5:5 will identify covetousness and idolatry, picking up on the notion that coveting is loving an earthly good in a disordered or disproportionate manner (as if possessing that earthly good in a way that cannot be paired with possessing the heavenly good of God, who has not seen fit to give that lesser good now); one thinks no doubt of the primal sin in Eden, where

Adam and Eve coveted the forbidden fruit as though it could be had apart from God or as if it were equivalent to having God himself.[4] The exact statement here is not merely that these ought not be practiced but that they "must not even be named" (*mēde onomazesthō* in 5:3), a claim that likely refers not to prohibiting speaking of them (as if Christians cannot speak of evil) but to not identifying themselves as participants in them (as if pagans might accurately name them as doing such things).

If 5:3 speaks to the way in which the body may be employed lustfully, then 5:4 addresses the misuse of the tongue. It does not focus on deception, the overt form of the ninth commandment, though it addresses wasteful and distracting or even foul speech. Putting off and putting on mark the discipline of this member. Put off "filthiness" and "foolish talk" and "crude joking," for these are "out of place." Other passages speak of the treachery involved in navigating threats to good speech (see Jas. 3:1–12), though this Ephesians passage offers a notable focus on "thanksgiving," presumably for such grateful speech could be said to be *in place* (the inverse of being "out of place"). The call is not merely to avoid outright sin (whether filthiness or crudity) but to devote one's speech in thankfulness to God (similar to what is said of earthly things in 1 Tim. 4:4, for they are good in and of themselves and shall not be rejected if and when done thankfully). Silence is not the response to the sins of speech; the response is the sanctification of the tongue (putting off foul talk or superficial jabber, instead putting on grateful and encouraging words "for building up," on which →4:29). More will be said later regarding the way in which this thankful speech happens in contexts of congregational gatherings (→5:19–20) and in one's prayer (→6:18).

The triad of terms in 5:3 reappears in 5:5—"sexually immoral or impure, or who is covetous"—in the guise no longer of an imperatival exclusion ("let there not . . .") but of an indicative declaration ("there is not . . ."). Two reasons are given for this declarative statement. Verse 3 uses the language of propriety ("as is proper among saints"). There is conceptual overlap between the terminology of worthiness (→4:1, "walk in a manner worthy of the calling to which you have been called") and this reference to propriety. In both idioms, the fit between ontology and ethics finds expression: one should live worthily of what one has been made, and one should act properly relative to what one has been given. A second reason appears when 5:5 speaks of kingdom inheritance: "For you may be

4. For more on the central role of idolatry, see R. R. Reno, "Pride and Idolatry," *Interpretation* 60, no. 2 (2006): 167–80.

sure of this, that everyone who is sexually immoral or impure, or who is covetous (that is, an idolater), has no inheritance in the kingdom of Christ and God." This claim shows some parallels with 1 Cor. 6:9–10: the construction of a list of evil persons who shall not inherit the kingdom is present in both passages, though the exact list only overlaps in part (e.g., both texts address sexual improprieties, but 1 Corinthians lingers over matters of greed and consumption/drunkenness whereas Ephesians turns to matters of speech [having already addressed acquisition and consumption: →4:28]).

5:6–14 Let no one deceive you with empty words, for because of these things the wrath of God comes upon the sons of disobedience. Therefore do not become partners with them; for at one time you were darkness, but now you are light in the Lord. Walk as children of light (for the fruit of light is found in all that is good and right and true), and try to discern what is pleasing to the Lord. Take no part in the unfruitful works of darkness, but instead expose them. For it is shameful even to speak of the things that they do in secret. But when anything is exposed by the light, it becomes visible, for anything that becomes visible is light. Therefore it says, "Awake, O sleeper, and arise from the dead, and Christ will shine on you."

If 4:25–5:5 addresses behavior, then 5:6–14 turns to the way in which that behavior plays out as Christians must and shall live among others. Piety cannot be defined by opposition, lest it simply assume the categories of its alternatives (e.g., Christianity is not simply the antithesis to pagan polytheism, as if it assumes the category of "god" understood by pagans and merely disagrees regarding the number, identity, and nature of these "gods"). Piety must be defined by its own peculiar terms. And yet piety cannot be practiced, not for long at least, apart from a conscious awareness of a Christian community's relationship to the wider world, precisely because that world is not neutral and disinterested. While Christians do right to avoid construing the world in antagonistically violent terms (for instance, avoiding imprudence in conflating language of religious warfare with nationalist or patriotic causes), Ephesians will not allow us to overlook the reality of an ongoing conflict that exceeds our neighbors but does include them (→2:1–3; 6:12).

Who are these others? They are "the sons of disobedience" (5:6) and "darkness" (5:8). They participate in "the unfruitful works of darkness" (5:11) and "do in secret" that which even reporting is "shameful" (5:12). Ultimately they must be named "O sleeper" (5:14), those who are dead and gone and need nothing less radical than to "arise from the dead" and to be resurrected from death's own clutches. The images and terms vary quite a bit, taking in a variety of descriptions that are united only in their pejorative character: "dark" means one thing, "unfruitful" something very different, but they do share a rhetorical emphasis on futility and failure.

What are the dangers? The apostle warns of the danger of deception (5:6). Apparently these "sons of disobedience" have a way "with empty words" (*kenois logois*; see also Col. 2:8). What makes their words empty? The background to the term does not emphasize vanity per se (that is, fleetingness) but empty-handedness (Gen. 37:24; Exod. 3:21; 5:9; 23:15). The notion seems to be that their speech is effectively empty-handed and thus has no hope. On such persons comes "the wrath of God."

How shall these Christians then live? "You are light in the Lord"; therefore "walk as children of light" (5:8). The apostle repeats his earlier calls to them to "walk in a manner worthy of the calling to which you have been called" (4:1) and to "walk in love, as Christ loved us" (5:2). They are light; therefore, their walk ought to be light. Being precedes doing in this evangelical logic, but doing must follow and manifest that being. Being does not precede doing because of some self-sufficiency; these passages do not suggest that essence precedes existence, in other words. Rather, being precedes doing precisely because this human and Christian being is a gift from God on high. Therefore, Oswald Bayer can speak of the primacy of what he calls "categorical gift" before any summons to action; the all-sufficiently full God fills them (1:23; 3:19; 4:10) so that they can then act accordingly, walk worthily, and love imitatively.[5]

In walking this way, Christians also flee. They are not to be "partners with them" (5:7). Indeed, the text actually says that they shall not "become partners" (*mē oun ginesthe symmetochoi*). The prohibition seems to forbid something intentional and conscious here, because it is not rooted in their common past. They used to be darkness with these others (5:8: "at one time you were darkness"), yet the text does not merely warn against remaining or lingering in some ties or links with them. In other words, it does not simply say that they ought to further their turn away from paganism; it speaks against a new partnership and rules it out of court. Christians are not to presume upon their difference and view themselves as above the fray; they are to remember that they remain within this drama of sin and salvation. Prudence demands that they be self-aware enough to avoid

5. Oswald Bayer, *Freedom in Response: Lutheran Ethics; Sources and Controversies*, trans. Jeffrey Cayzer (Oxford: Oxford University Press, 2007), 13–20.

walking wayward paths, whereby they might fall into temptation, or journeying in such places that they bring contempt on Christ's own name. In this regard, partnership here functions similarly to what Paul says about the danger of dishonoring the body of the Lord (1 Cor. 6:15–20). As with those words to the Corinthians, here the apostle wants to expand the way in which they imagine their bodily and social behavior to have significance of a heavenly and spiritual register. These are not merely mortal or ordinary matters; they have conflictual import for good or for ill.

The heightening of concern continues, for the text does not merely call for avoidance and distance. "Expose them" (5:11), we read. How can one expose the behavior of others without falling prey to the shamefulness of even speaking of them (5:12)? This pairing of commandments does seemingly suggest a contradictory posture, yet each call can be interpreted such that it presents a harmonious picture. When Paul writes of the shamefulness of speaking of their behavior, he conveys the way in which even the pagans would grow ashamed were they to own up to their behavior in public. He attests that others are ashamed by mention of that behavior. Thus, Christians are called to expose the deeds of darkness not by running investigations and seeking to find out their evil but by living differently, by being light in the Lord. The very image of light has this effect naturally—namely, that it shows the darkness to be what it is.

What motivates such behavior? The apostle offers carrot and stick alike here. The text does offer the promise that "now you are light in the Lord" (5:8). Yet the overarching bent of the passage fixes on the warning in 5:13–14 that Christ shall return in judgment. Reading 5:14 is complicated by the fact that Paul introduces a quotation here (for a parallel →4:8), yet the purported quotation does not match any Old Testament passage exactly (Isa. 26:19; 60:1 are the nearest approximations, though they are partial at best). Some assume that there must be later Jewish or early Christian hymnic material behind this text (Thielman 2010: 348–49), though arguments are conjectural in whichever direction. Shy of some closer parallel being discovered, we are probably stuck with simply reading the text as it is, without any real benefit from a source text (Fowl 2012: 172).

The more significant question regards whether 5:13–14 continues to speak of the exposure and judgment of nonbelievers or whether it shifts to attest a judgment and vindication and even blessing of Christians. Some argue that the presence of Christ's light in 5:14 suggests a shift in the passage (Thielman 2010: 351). That said, the rhetorical impact seems strengthened by the quotation offering a wholly negative example. It is not evident that becoming visible is a beneficial thing or that arising here is anything more than the general resurrection of all for judgment (Talbert 2007: 128, though he oddly limits the context to exposure of sin in a worship setting [likely tying this tightly to 5:17–21 and reading it in light of potential parallels]). Determination is difficult here. This reading is complicated, no doubt, by the fact that the language of light is used first to depict "children of light" who act in regenerate manners (5:7–9), while it then speaks of sheer transparency or visibility that comes on all—the righteous as well as the wicked—and it fixes on those wicked whose evil cannot remain hidden at the day of final judgment (5:13–14).

The text does motivate with warning, then, but its end is discernment: "try to discern what is pleasing to the Lord" (5:10). It is easy to assume that God takes pleasure in his redeemed children and to reduce all divine pleasure to that global delight taken in the saved; yet passages such as Eph. 5:10 and Heb. 11:6 seem to suggest that God also takes delight and pleasure in particular actions that are befitting and worthy of the redeemed. God's love is a many-splendored thing, falling on the redeemed *tout court* as well as fitting redeemed lives to match their new divine family's *modus operandi*.

This language of discernment fits with what was said earlier about Christian— even lay—ministry or service (→4:12). The ministry of the word of God equips for this service or *diakonia*, but it does not provide a simple and straightforward commandment befitting all determinations to that end. Ministers of the word equip all the saints so that they can, in all circumstances, discern or judge appropriately what is "good and right and true" (5:9). While Ephesians does elevate the clergy's role inasmuch as it speaks of ecclesiastical office as a direct gift of the exalted Christ (→4:7–11), it shows that the limits of ministerial service must be paired with a rich expectation of lay wisdom and discernment. The body of Christ functions symbiotically in this regard: ministers do not usurp lay judgment, though laypersons' discernment has been shaped authoritatively by ministerial proclamation of the full word of God.

Even churches of the Protestant Reformation continue to struggle with this dynamic. The momentum toward guru culture and a minister-dominated approach to Christian faith and practice is powerful, not least now because of the reach of much theological and pastoral media in the digital sphere. A Paul or an Apollos may have garnered a following in the first century (1 Cor. 3:4–9), but we can only imagine their brand influence in an age marked by streaming and social media. For all that Protestants may warn of clericalism in hierarchical or episcopal churches (of the West or the East), a guru mentality and a domineering authoritarianism can easily set in within even nondenominational churches where pastors speak to every issue and answer every query. The microphone is a seductive thing. Yet this passage reminds us of the inviolable duty for Christian women and men—laypersons—to exercise discernment and to grow up in Christ such that they can maturely make moral judgments about the good, the just, and the truthful (see also Rom. 12:2; Heb. 5:14). Ministers may not go beyond the word of God to bind the conscience of laypersons, for such would be the homiletical or pedagogical sin of commission, though ministers must also preach the "whole counsel of God" to acquit themselves of malpractice by way of omission (see the Westminster Confession of Faith, ch. 20, for one classic expression of this ministerial-lay symbiosis). Laypersons cannot outsource the task of discernment; mature judgment remains an essential element of the struggle against evil and darkness as all grow up in Christ.

5:15–21 Look carefully then how you walk, not as unwise but as wise, making the best use of the time, because the days are evil. Therefore do not be foolish, but understand what the will of the Lord is. And do not get drunk with wine, for that is debauchery, but be filled with the Spirit, addressing one another in psalms and hymns and spiritual songs, singing and making melody to the Lord with your heart, giving thanks always and for everything to God the Father in the name of our Lord Jesus Christ, submitting to one another out of reverence for Christ.

Ephesians 5:6–14 addresses social relationship to the pagan world at large, and now 5:15–6:9 turns to address the way in which Christians conduct their own polity: as a congregation in 5:15–21 and by extension among their scattered relationships at home and work in 5:21–6:9. These first few verses in 5:15–21 will speak broadly about the life-giving Spirit and the way of wisdom before 5:21–6:9 unpacks some particular relational contours of that path.

What is the danger? Foolishness (*asophoi*) marks the false start. The juxtaposition here is stark and simple: *sophoi* or *asophoi*, wise or unwise. The black-and-white register hearkens back to earlier Jewish texts that portray the moral pathway as life and death (Deut. 30:19) or righteous and wicked (Ps. 1; →2:1–3 for earlier discussion of these juxtapositions). Paul himself will trade in such polarities: old self and new self (→4:22–24) or flesh and spirit (Gal. 5:13–26) or things above and earthly things (Col. 3:1–2). Pauline pairs tend to address reality in cosmological or eschatological distinction (e.g., the person with respect to Christ as opposed to the person with respect to Adam, *or* the human corrupted by sin compared to the human regenerated by the life-giving Spirit, *or* reality as viewed in this sinful world versus the world to which heaven has come). Here the polarity of unwise and wise signals an equally sharp divide related to how one makes judgments. Some discern in a foolhardy capacity, lacking keen judgment; the apostle longs for Christians to walk wisely.

Wisdom is meant to mark their "walk"; this term appears yet again to describe their journey or way (→4:1; 4:17; 5:2; 5:8). To that end, however, the immediate summons is to "look carefully" (*blepete oun akribōs* in 5:15) or intentionally perceive how they are going about their daily affairs. Not for nothing do we see daily matters as significant, for the wise and alert person will be one who perceives time appropriately. The manner of walking alertly depicted here is "making the best use of the time" (*exagorazomenoi ton kairon* in 5:16). An interpretive decision lurks when we see the "best use of the time" further elaborated by or grounded in the statement "because the days are evil" (*hoti hai hēmerai ponērai eisin*). Does the evil character of these days demand a particular posture (e.g., protective), or does the evil character of these days alert one to a coming day or days that are otherwise and therefore promote another posture (e.g., confident)?

What guides the way through these evil days, at least in this passage, is "understand[ing] what is the will of the Lord" (5:17). The Lord's will sometimes comes on us like lightning, wherein the prophet has a word placed on his very lips (Jer. 1:9) or the layperson receives a dream (Joel 2:28–32; Acts 2:17–21). Does this verse seek to suggest that we are to pursue a transgressive word from above to answer our daily need? Perhaps the reference in the following verse to being filled by the Spirit coalesces here with this word to summon us to a more charismatic experience? However appealing such a reading may well be, it is unlikely. The paragraph begins with the contrast between wise and unwise, terminology that is less shaped by possession of a discrete mandate than by personal character and habitual judgment of a keen sort. The wise person is not necessarily the knowledgeable person, surely not necessarily someone with a "word from the Lord" delivered by a fleece or the like. The wise person is the one well planted, not easily blown about, mature and sensible (→4:14). When the apostle speaks of "the will of the Lord," then, he likely does not refer to particular mandates pertaining to specific daily decisions but to the principles, parameters, exemplars, and songs that shape one's moral imagination. The verses that follow speak to particular practices through which that imagination is meant to be cultivated (→5:19–21), while earlier verses speak of the divine intent to equip the saints in this regard (→4:7–16). Again, the text reminds us of the significance of a well-catechized and mature laity who know "the will of the Lord," not because a minister has told them what particular choices to make but because a minister has instead equipped them with the word of the Lord and has led them in a community marked by these formative rhythms.

Days are evil, so a coping mechanism will be sought. "Do not get drunk with wine" but rather "be filled with the Spirit" (5:18). Apparently these are the options: the pathway of dulling the senses or of deepening one's perception and resolve. The enticement of wine comes not first in joviality, though that may follow, but in its mellowing or dialing back sensory powers, providing a buzz that removes the bite of the evil day. Not surprisingly, that dulled perception positions one to be less competent in knowing when to quit, so it is not illogical that mention of wine can be so quickly related to drunkenness. While it is quite possible to drink wine or any alcohol without turning to excess, the beverage does make such moral restraint physiologically more difficult. The apostle knows also that a new sense of the days being evil will only heighten the temptation to turn to drink—again and again—so as to cope with the tragedy.

A different way presents itself, however, in the apostle's command: "be filled with the Spirit." The divine desire to fill all things or to fill his own people has appeared repeatedly (→1:23; 3:19; 4:10), though this particular form of "filling" language also has deeper roots. The language comes from the Gospels and Acts, wherein we learn of Jesus being filled with the Spirit or being full of the Spirit repeatedly (Luke 4:1) and then of apostles and Christians being filled with the Spirit (Acts 2:4; 4:8; 9:17; 13:52). Paul does not employ the exact phrase elsewhere, though he speaks aplenty of the Spirit's work on and in Christians. The Spirit does not numb one to the day's pain, evil as it may be, and so this presents a very different manner of coping with this epoch. Spiritual existence actually provokes deeper perception of pain, like the way in which improvements to one's central nervous system would make heightened pain more possible. The Spirit does not cause pain, but the Spirit does illumine and intensify our awareness of pain and suffering. This is why Christians have been behind artistic movements such as the blues, having learned from the Spirit's gift and the example of the Psalms to better express our tragicomic experience and to lament the evil days.

What are the relevant practices? Note the participial phrases subordinate to the imperative "be filled with the Spirit." Three participles describe the manner or means of this grace. Back in 4:12–16, the body of Christ is said to "[build] itself up in love" (→4:16), which speaks of the social and specifically ecclesial character of "grow[ing] up in every way into him who is the head, into Christ"

(4:15). But that bodily self-building—remember that the body builds itself, the language being intrinsically active in 4:16—takes a particular form: "when each part is working properly." Improper bodily life does not lead to building up and growing up; proper function creates space and relations within which such maturity does advance. So the church does not possess carte blanche to determine its own protocols and practices, as if spirituality were a grab bag for one's procedures and preferences. Such was the way of Nadab and Abihu (Lev. 10:1–2). Such also was the reason that the Israelites, fleeing the religion of polytheistic Egypt and en route to equally religious and polytheist Canaan, have to be given not merely the first but also the second commandment, pertaining to how you worship the true and living God (Exod. 20:4–6; Deut. 5:8–10).

Reformed theologians speak of "means of grace" whereby God communicates spiritual benefits to particular persons via ecclesial actions. The 154th question in the Westminster Larger Catechism provides a classic exposition: "What are the outward means whereby Christ communicates to us the benefits of his mediation? A. The outward and ordinary means whereby Christ communicates to his church the benefits of his mediation, are all his ordinances; especially the Word, sacraments, and prayer; all which are made effectual to the elect for their salvation." The answer points to a centered set wherein certain practices are "especially" highlighted, though that very term also suggests that others fit the bill too. All such means of grace are means of Christ's action and are "made effectual" not by the humans but ultimately by the triune God himself. In this regard, the language of the means of grace helps accent two facets of Ephesians' teaching: first, there are the practices that concretely sketch the proper functioning of the body wherein it is building itself up (4:16; 5:19–21); and second, these practices convey a power that exceeds their immanent strength, for "Christ . . . makes the body grow," and these are means of "be[ing] filled with [his] Spirit" (4:15, 16; 5:18).

Modern persons may struggle at just this point. We live in a world where "acts of God" are those spaces that lack clarity about immanent causality, so that the natural disaster can be described by an insurance company as an "act of God." That colloquialism fits snugly in a wider philosophy wherein moderns are willing to affirm the agency only of the "god of the gaps." In such a schema, situations where we can tease out causal agency in a materialist or historicist or social framework are situations absent God's involvement, but it is only when we lack any such immanent description of causal force that we can and may speak of God's agency or presence (i.e., in such epistemological gaps). And yet Ephesians will not allow us to segregate God and history in this way. Here classical Christian metaphysics alerts us to the fact that God's transcendence differentiates him from creaturely agency, though it does not distance him from it. Indeed, precisely as God is holy and distinct, God may and does act in and through creaturely causal relations. So here Christ makes the body grow and the Spirit fills us toward maturity precisely as we lean into the life of certain animating practices; those practices become conduits of life-giving power, not for their own innate strength but because of God's electing love, whereby his power is disposed to light up the ecclesial power grid, as it were (Tanner 2010: 274–301; Allen 2017: 227–56). This layered approach to ecclesiastical action makes sense of the fact that particular practices are commended and that the warning was issued about parts of the body "working properly."

Just as the human body brings with it nature and thus design, apart from which it may function physiologically though it will not image God appropriately, so the ecclesiastical body has been given a nature within which it builds itself up. All this is from God (2 Cor. 5:18), for new creation is his watchword and action, even as the message and means of reconciliation have been granted to his ambassadors and emissaries (2 Cor. 5:19–20), who even receive the privilege of "working together with him" (2 Cor. 6:1). That fellowship is never equivalence, does not involve reciprocity as peers, and must be pursued therefore with fear and trembling. But it is true fellowship—not merely of an inheritance but also of a mission and vocation. What Paul has said of his personal vocation in this regard (→3:1–13) here finds corporate expression, for these practices cannot be pursued in individualist fashion, as if one could address one another by oneself or submit to one another by one's lonesome. Rightly directed functioning of social relations manifests faith in God and thereby images God well by showing forth the conscious and active dependence that befits creaturely existence.

The first Spirit-filling practice is "addressing one another in psalms and hymns and spiritual songs, singing and making melody to the Lord with your heart" (5:19). Songs are depicted in three forms: psalms drawn directly from the Psalter in the Old Testament, hymns, and spiritual songs. These later two forms seem to speak of circulating and perhaps spontaneous or lesser-known formulas of musical confession of God's worth. While the verse calls for "making melody . . . with your heart," the material shape of what is sung does seem to matter too. Word and spirit both matter in the practice of sung worship (John 4:23). All songs are to be taken up for two purposes, which may at first blush seem opposed. First, this corporate singing involves "addressing one another" in these words. Second, in so doing, those gathered are to be "singing and making melody to the Lord with your heart." Christian song to and of God also directs itself toward sisters and brothers, thereby taking up the summons elsewhere to "[encourage] one another, and all the more as you see the Day drawing near" (Heb. 10:25). In a parallel passage in Colossians we read this: "Let the word of Christ dwell in you richly, teaching and admonishing one another in all wisdom, singing psalms and hymns and spiritual songs with thankfulness in your hearts to God" (3:16). Again, singing thankfully to God takes form also as bodily address of "one" member to "another"; interestingly, that passage describes this whole nexus as a call to "let the word of Christ dwell in you richly" such that congregational exhortation (i.e., by laypersons) and song form the means whereby the Lord's word takes residence within the body and to very great—that is, rich—effect. Reading Eph. 1:23, 4:10–12, and 5:18–19 together leads to the same nexus wherein God desires to fill us with his riches, Christ fills all things by sending his word to equip all the saints, and all those saints are filled by the Spirit through the means of grace.

Second, a related but distinct means of grace is "giving thanks always and for everything to God the Father in the name of our Lord Jesus Christ" (5:20). Here a practice of prayer—a certain form of prayer: thanksgiving—is specified and, by extension, so is a certain posture of living, which might be called prayerfulness. Every time is fitting for thanks to the Lord, "in [whom] we live and move and have our being" (Acts 17:28), and for doing so in Christ's own name, given that "in him all things hold together" (Col. 1:17). Those metaphysical claims of divine providential direction bespeak a liturgical mandate: because all fits together only in this one, so they are all to be directed or taken up to him in praise and fear. Colossians employs the pairing "all things were created through him and for him" (1:16)—metaphysics shaping moral ends.

Christians may have special warrant to wonder whether "all things" can be taken to God in thanks. As noted above, Christians will be tempted toward self-coping with drink precisely because life is painful and divine illumination brings into greater relief the pangs of this evil age, both without and also within (→5:18). Can we, of all people, really speak of all things warranting thanks to God on high, when we can speak not only of natural disasters and physiological expiration but also especially of spiritual warfare and indwelling sin and the cacophonous silence of human creatures' praise of their God on high? Again, this second practice ought not be considered apart from the first discipline; singing psalms, in particular, shapes one for prayerfulness and thankfulness in all things, for the psalms train us to take all situations before God. The psalms deepen our lament, showing the real tragedy at play in situations, but their lament is the kind of convivial blues that comes from one who possesses hope (see, e.g., Ps. 13:5–6 present even in that remarkable lament). Like Joseph, then, Christians trained by singing and being sung to with psalms (and with other songs that are similarly redolent of the whole spectrum of Christian experience, highs and lows) will be able to discern beneath the vagaries of human experience a divine hand to whom "all things," even those perpetrated by others, ought to be returned in thanks (Gen. 50:20).

Perhaps the most debated line here is the third and final practice: "submitting to one another out of reverence for Christ" (5:21). It is a transitional line. It points backward for it is syntactically subordinate to the summons to "be filled with the Spirit," modifying it and charting one course whereby such filling occurs (alongside the practices of song and thanksgiving). It points forward to repeated mention of submission in various relational webs (5:22, 24, 33; 6:1, 2, 5, 7, 9). Because this practice is expounded at such length, we will examine it further in subsequent sections.

Before moving into the first such scenario (wives and husbands →5:22–33), the location of this verse must be highlighted again: submitting to one another in relationally appropriate manners is a means of grace whereby one is "filled with the Spirit." These relationships may be defined in modern life, as in many antique settings, as secular, having rather little to do with how one engages the gods. Here, however, we see that it is not only corporate worship (in the form of corporate singing to one another) that serves as a conduit of divine grace but also dispersed thankfulness exercised personally (in the manner of prayerfulness throughout the day and week) that fills out such an instrumental role for the Spirit's life-giving agency. Finally, then, the Spirit works to fill us up and Christ works to grow his body as we relate to each other appropriately. Thus, submission, respect, and obedience must be addressed, as self-sacrifice, discipline, and leadership must also be considered; these give shape and texture to the sort of relationships within which we live together.

These relationships do not serve as automatic conduits of life-giving Spirit or of Christ's making the body grow. Recent years have seen a notable and welcome spike in analyses of systems (familial and economic, religious and political) wherein relationships have gone wayward, and frequently the results are not merely problematic but catastrophic, a distinction of kind that the philosopher Cornel West regularly notes. Here too we see the significance of paying attention to all the ways that Ephesians addresses our social life. "When each part is working properly," the body "builds itself up in love" (4:16)—proper function plays a definitive role in serving as an instrument of God's powerful grace. While God can and does shoot straight with a crooked stick, such mercy should not be presumed upon and empirical observation shows that kicking against the goads of nature (in terms of relational order) leads to chaos and real detriment. Christians, of all people, should be at the forefront of observing, first, and lamenting, second, the ways in which human relationships fall short at just this point. Yet Ephesians tells us precisely why such occasions are so tragic and painful; wayward disorder in relationships (through the abuse of power or the subversion of authority, each in varied and distinct ways) disrupts divine design, displaces spiritual empowerment, and manifests a lack of trust in Christ's plan for growing us up. No wonder such instances lead to pain and harm.

The final thing to note here is that this call to submit one to another (in varied contexts) shall be pursued "out of reverence to Christ." Again, there is no secular. Just as relationships with family or workplace colleagues cannot be held at a distance from the call to discipleship, so the posture or manner in which Christians approach them cannot be defined on their own terms. One engages a parent or child, a husband or wife, a slave or master with Christ himself as a relevant figure in that relationship. Inasmuch as we all submit in certain relationships (not least in that we are all children of parents, whatever positions of authority we may later hold at given points or in certain other relationships), we are called one and all to submit specifically for the sake of revering Christ himself. Doing so does not discount ways in which we may have responsibility to be mindful of the excellencies or deficiencies of an authority figure, but submission is not ultimately premised on such observations.

5:22-24 Wives, submit to your own husbands, as to the Lord. For the husband is the head of the wife even as Christ is the head of the church, his body, and is himself its Savior. Now as the church submits to Christ, so also wives should submit in everything to their husbands.

Here we enter what is often called the "household codes" (see also Col. 3:18–4:1; 1 Pet. 2:13–3:7). While they overlap significantly at points with social mores in portions of the Greco-Roman or Jewish worlds, they also offer distinctively Christian inflections and judgments. Indeed, it would be rather surprising if the moral theology offered thus far from 4:17–5:20, with its constant contrasts of old and new, light and darkness, and wise and foolish, would suddenly be turned into a straightforward commendation of the mores of a pagan culture. Some have argued that such was necessary for apologetic reasons, to show that Christianity was no threat to the wider society (e.g., Lincoln 1990: 356–60). Fowl has shown briefly why that is less than compelling given that the text in no way gestures at an apologetic purpose but keeps its sights on ethical behavior for its own reasons (2012: 180–81).

In reading 5:22–24 (and 5:22–6:9 as a whole), we are expounding that summons from the previous verse: "submitting to one another out of reverence for Christ." The call to "submit" appears again and again, whether explicitly or by means of synonyms (5:22, 24; see also 6:1, 2, 5, 7 for synonyms). The entreaty that this relational submission occur not with respect to competence or rank or wealth or morality but "out of reverence for Christ" also finds echoes in that those called to submit are repeatedly to do so "as to the Lord" (see also 6:1, 5, 7). More debated today, as noted above (→5:21), is the notion of submitting "to one another": whether this upholds purportedly hierarchical social structures, or levels the social playing field by calling for something approximating what has been called mutual submission.

What would mutual submission involve here? Mutuality would involve each person in a pair or network submitting their own personal interests to others, loving others as they love themselves and "count[ing] others more significant than yourselves" (Phil. 2:3). Submission here takes perceptional form, not organizational or institutional shape. Indeed, mutual submission cuts against the grain of hierarchical organization and presents a way of radical equality where union with Christ Jesus subverts social mores and expectations. "For as many of you as were baptized into Christ have put on Christ. There is neither Jew nor Greek, there is neither slave nor free, there is no male and female, for you are all one in Christ Jesus" (Gal. 3:27–28). Some would suggest that Eph. 5:21 provides the seed for a later subversion of the more patient, incremental moral reform expounded in 5:22–6:9.

Does mutual submission actually fit the texts? How likely is it that Paul would expound a particular principle of mutual submission in 5:21 and then speak of directional submission in a series of relationships in the next section? Directional submission helps clarify that, in each of these three relational settings, the apostle uses the term "submit" or its synonyms ("respect," "obey," "honor") in a call to only one party consistently. More is said to directly challenge the other party in each case, and Paul also consistently addresses the one who shall submit first. The very basis for submission differs from other philosophies or moralities, so there is plenty here nonetheless to subvert the sociopolitical status quo and to challenge the patricentric character of the first-century Greco-Roman world of Asia Minor. Yet there is no transitional suggestion that Paul moves to address that which he will subvert, and no signal that 5:22–6:9 comprises anything other than some illustrations of the principle taught in 5:21.

Three things should be caught in the imperative of 5:22. First, wives are addressed first—no small thing in a patricentric milieu. The apostle does not bother to address the husbands first, as convention might have it. Leaving the men to the side for the moment, he turns rather to wives and acknowledges both dignity and duty. They warrant moral address as they are called to image God well. They are not mere members of their husband's household, to be addressed after him or even by and through him. They are Christians in their own right, and the way in which they conduct themselves has remarkable bearing on the name of Christ. With every challenging instruction given to these wives (or women who may someday be wives), the apostle shows that their lives, even the intricacies of their daily household management, matter to God.

Second, wives are told to "submit to [their] own husbands." The term "submit" (*hypotassomenoi*) relates most closely to the term employed later in the summative statement at the end of the section, "respect" (*phobētai* in 5:33). Submission does not come as a blanket posture that marks all female relationships to all men. A wife submits to her specific husband and no other (at least in this respect, though political and economic relationships may overlap). The passage does not root this command in some generic or global hierarchy of the sexes. The text does call for a respect of one's own husband as husband, however, which takes the form of submission to authority in that singular, specific relational context.

Third, this submission to one's own husband shall be "as to the Lord." What may be perceived as a horizontal command relating to interpersonal behavior among mere mortals here joins with a vertical aspect. One's posture before the Lord will be manifest in one's manner to one's own husband, if one is a married woman. A wife shall treat her husband, out of faith, as the Lord would have him treated, even if the husband is not particularly appealing or especially competent. Fowl (2010: 187) suggests that "as to the Lord" functions like the head metaphor in 5:23–24 to beckon submission "willingly and out of love," but that is to conflate matters. A deeper metaphysical point is made here: in submitting to this human being, one shall be revering one's heavenly Lord (see also Rom. 13:2). Such a link does not give the leader or authority figure carte blanche to reign terror under the name of God. Various societies and cultures make allowance for different forms of protest and recourse regarding any such tyranny or abuse—indeed, this very chapter is about to raise the standard to which authority figures are held—but creaturely authorities are a means of divine provision nonetheless (Austin 2010).

Ephesians 5:23–24 provides reasons and an imaginative frame within which this imperative makes sense. The basis, which the apostle presumes would not be controversial, relates to the ordered union of Christ and church. "The husband is the head of the wife even as Christ is the head of the church." Christ has a body (see also 1 Cor. 12:12–31), which speaks to integral unity, and that body has diverse parts, which attests to diverse integrity (1 Cor. 12:14). Jesus Christ is the body, and Jesus Christ is the head (*kephalē*) of the body. Texts do speak first of the whole body being identified with him ("now you are the body of Christ" in 1 Cor. 12:27) and also at times locate him within that body as the "head" (here in Eph. 5:23). While union with Christ brings about remarkable oneness, that mystical union never runs roughshod over the distinction between Creator and creature. The incarnate Son alone serves as head in the church, and this authoritative place serves as the analogy for the husband. Marriage brings about a one-flesh unity (Gen. 2:24; 1 Cor. 7:16), though that flesh exists in differentiated harmony.

The sort of rhetorical argument here works imaginatively. It shapes the way in which one views or contextualizes one's own moral judgments. And it does so by means of comparison or analogy. "Now as . . . so also" frames the claim of 5:24. Submission to Christ befits the kind of relational order that his own enjoy (his position warranting submission from his body), and the apostle capitalizes on that vision: "Now as the church submits to Christ, so also wives should submit in everything to their husbands." And yet this submission of wives to husbands occurs "as to the Lord." The husband nowhere fits the mold of Christ. If we catch the "as to" passage and miss the "now as . . . so also" pattern, then submission will not really be directed to this particular human being, the husband of a particular wife. On the other hand, missing the "as to" line and grasping the "now as . . . so also" comparison sets one up to expect too much of the husband, as if submission stands or falls on his capacity and competence to be like the Lord.

Fowl argues that because the patriarchal order delineated here would be widely assumed in the first century, this analogy is somewhat beside the point. He says, "Christ's unquestioned preeminence relative to the church certainly can underwrite a wife's submission to her husband. In a first-century context, however, it is not clear that such a comparison really says much. The paterfamilias would have already been considered the head of the household" (2012: 187). So he suggests, therefore, that this image says more to the husband than to the wife (188). But this is not the image used to address husbands; when we get to 5:25–33, the image turns from the head/body image to the one-flesh image. And the apostle here addresses wives. Fowl is right that a first-century crowd would have assumed the patricentric approach here, so we do well to ask what more is going on. Most likely, Paul is here providing a theological ground for what might be otherwise taken as merely a set of social mores. He will work within the regnant social mores, chastening them from inside and at times even laying the groundwork for their eventual overturning (→6:5–9; see also Philemon). So here he seems to be showing his cards—namely, that this cultural structure, at least in its principle, is not altogether happenstance (see also 1 Tim. 2:13–14 for theological arguments—distinctly Christian—to undergird what would have been an assumed cultural practice anyway).

Submission really involves tangible respect given to particular persons; the parallel term translated "respect" (5:33) might be rendered "fear," though its connotation is "a disposition to obey" (Fowl 2012: 183). Submission does not equate to self-denial, though submission is one such means of expressing self-denial. Indeed, it soon becomes apparent that self-denial fashions those in positions of leadership as well (in whatever sphere: marriage, childrearing, employment; →5:25–28). Submission does mark the life of one who embraces a walk of conscious dependence, first, before the Lord and, second, among fellow humans by God's providential design. This "submission" is meant to flavor "everything," though its concrete form is not elaborated here. Surely that brevity and that underdetermined definition is meant to help encourage wives to discern (→5:10) what submission would involve in their given situation.

5:25–33 Husbands, love your wives, as Christ loved the church and gave himself up for her, that he might sanctify her, having cleansed her by the washing of water with the word, so that he might present the church to himself in splendor, without spot or wrinkle or any such thing, that she might be holy and without blemish. In the same way husbands should love their wives as their own bodies. He who loves his wife loves himself. For no one ever hated his own flesh, but nourishes and cherishes it, just as Christ does the church, because we are members of his body. "Therefore a man shall leave his father and mother and hold fast to his wife, and the two shall become one flesh." This mystery is profound, and I am saying that it refers to Christ and the church. However, let each one of you love his wife as himself, and let the wife see that she respects her husband.

These remaining verses in chapter 5 shift to address the husbands. Again, three things ought to be observed. First, husbands are addressed second, after wives have already been addressed. Second, husbands are called to "love [their] wives." Third, this love of a husband for his own wife shall be "as Christ loved the church and gave himself up for her." Thus, the apostle offers moral instruction that may overlap in its cultural consequence with elements of wider household management in the first century, but it breaks rather starkly at points that show its distinctly Christian pedigree.

The following verses depict the manner, the analogy, and the mystery of this love. Love is the watchword, though it is not the specific vocabulary employed (*agapaō*) that manifests that singularity (contra Fowl 2012: 188). The manner of this love is described as "lov[ing] your wives as your own bodies." Metaphysics shapes ethics, and so here the declaration that man and woman are one has consequence for behavior.

The analogy of this love begins with an unpacking of Christ's love for his church. He "gave himself up for her" in order "that he might sanctify her" (5:25–26). Purity results, Christ "having cleansed her by the washing of water with the word" (5:26). His ultimate aim is "that he might present the church to himself in splendor" (5:27). That splendor is depicted by her purity: "without spot or wrinkle or any such thing, that she might be holy and without blemish" (5:27). The work of Christ is to her growth and benefit, that she might be holy and splendid. His was the cost, offering himself and his very life as a sacrifice: therein he "gave himself up for her."

There is always danger, of course, in reducing the sacrificial work of the Christ to something sentimental. Christians rightly worry about translating "taking up your cross" into any which frustration, as if it were a trite or blasé reality rather than a truly horrific and altogether unique agony. And yet the New Testament plainly and regularly calls not merely for the imitation of Christ but also for the most singular facets of Christ's way to be imitated or followed: "take up [your] cross and follow me" (Matt. 16:24) or "walk in love, as Christ loved us and gave himself up for us, a fragrant offering and sacrifice to God" (→Eph. 5:2; see also Phil. 2:5). Here is one specific example of that general call from earlier in chapter 5 to all Christians that they must emulate the self-sacrificial love of Jesus—namely, that those with authoritative power in a marital relationship, the husbands, should wield that authority not to use others for their benefit but to bless others by their self-sacrifice. In our cynical age, it is hard to imagine leadership and power being marshaled in a costly manner, but such is the vision repeatedly offered in these household codes, wherein authority structures are upheld, to be sure, but are radically relativized inasmuch as those in authority are to view their function as a means of self-denial and self-sacrifice for the sake of others. In this case, a husband's preferences ought to be the first to go, as needful, for the sake of blessing his wife and seeing her grow and flourish to holiness (parallels will be seen shortly regarding the use of power in other social relations; →6:1–9).

This analogy goes a step further, though, in that the apostle then says, "In the same way husbands should love their wives as their own bodies" (5:28). Just as the church is Christ's own body (the *totus Christus* concept), so the wife and husband "become one flesh" (5:31). One loves one's own body—the text assumes readers will agree—and thus in giving oneself up for a spouse, one is actually loving oneself in the other. The notion of selflessness is then reframed. Self-denial is paired with one's own self being tied to and related with that of another. Again, both words must be heard. A person does hear the call, if a husband, to give himself for his wife. But he also receives this reminder that he is one flesh with her, so in giving himself up for her, he is also acting in a way motivated by his own identity and being. In many ways, the text flips the language of *eudamonia* or self-interest by simply reconstruing the social relationship of marriage in this covenantal union that involves real identification.

The text names this a "mystery" (*mystērion*)—that is, something christological that has been revealed in apostolic proclamation after being hidden or kept behind a veil in the past. Here we can see that the marital union of Christ and church was signaled by the Song of Songs especially and by the whole Old Testament employment of marital imagery for God's relationship with Israel (e.g., Hosea employing the marriage gone sour to convey the notion of covenant-breaking before God), though the prophetic or proleptic element of these texts was not clear. We have seen this term "mystery" employed earlier (→3:3–5) to convey something of the newfound revelation about the gospel. In this instance, the apostle identifies a latent purpose in human marriage that goes beyond procreation and societal cohesion and romantic love and sexual restraint and all the other purposes that might be rightly noted. Here he draws out from Gen. 2:24 a christological principle—namely, that the leaving and cleaving of a man to his wife signals the way in which the eternal Son has sought out and united himself to his bride, the church. The apostle says this verse "refers to" or (otherwise translated) "is" Christ and his church, not merely that it parallels or serves as an analogy; he is drawing this union mysteriously from that very verse with its reference to the leaving and cleaving of husband to wife. In so doing, he has taken upon himself the very humanity of that church through the miracle of the virgin birth, wherein he now has skin in the game, so to speak, and has truly assumed our nature. And his body—the many members of the church—is truly united to him in all his glory through this mystical union.

Ephesians 5:33 summarizes both subsections in saying, "Let each one of you love his wife as himself, and let the wife see that she respects her husband." Here the husband is addressed, as is the wife; they are both to relate to the other in particular ways. She submits to him in respect, and he employs his authority in a loving manner (not using her or assuming his preferences over hers, but treating her "as himself"). While the authority structure parallels that of other household codes in this antique setting (e.g., Plutarch, Dio Chrysostom), the existence of the structure has been given positive theological grounds rooted in creation (though these do remain underdetermined in the sense that they are not expounded) and in the christological union of new creation; and the exercise of the structure has been chastened by distinctly Christian morals shaped by Christ's own providential rule and exercise of self-sacrifice for the sake of loving his own.

EPHESIANS 6

6:1–4 Children, obey your parents in the Lord, for this is right. "Honor your father and mother" (this is the first commandment with a promise), "that it may go well with you and that you may live long in the land." Fathers, do not provoke your children to anger, but bring them up in the discipline and instruction of the Lord.

Instructions for the household continue (parallel to Col. 3:20–21) by turning now to the relationship of children and parents. Here too is an opening to "submit to one another out of reverence for Christ" (→5:21), as children may respond appropriately to parental authority, and conversely as parents may exercise authority in a godly and loving manner. Some find a conflict here; Ian McFarland has argued regarding the relationship of 5:22 to the rest of the household code, "The problem is that this summons to mutual subordination in Christ appears to be inconsistent with the writer's ensuing argument for the unilateral subordination of wives to husbands" (2000: 349). But that is to view this one relationship apart from the web of social orders mentioned here (which are not exhaustive either but could include others: citizen and ruler, on the one hand, or layperson and ordained Christian, on the other hand). As with the discussion of marriage above (→5:22–33), differentiated relational roles shape the way in which Christians are called to submit mutually in varied relations; mutuality does not bespeak egalitarianism *within* a relationship, as if to level distinctions between husbands and wives and parents and children, but speaks of egalitarianism *across* relationships, as Christians will submit in some relationships and exercise authority in others, matching their varied stations in life. So all Christians have a relational call to honor parents, while some of those children will also be called to exercise authority over children in adulthood (which would not be the case for the celibate or the otherwise childless); a wife submits to a husband, though she may also have children over whom she is meant to express authority; a slave is summoned here to obey a master, though a slave may hold a position of authority vis à vis his or her own child. Again, mutuality does not mix responsibilities in a given relationship, though it does relate to our overlapping and varied duties in a range of settings (over time or even in a given time).

Children are commanded to "obey [their] parents" and "honor [their] father and mother." Language of obedience appears here in 6:1 and shortly thereafter in 6:5 regarding slaves' obedience to their masters. Notably, it did not occur in discussion of wives and their submission to their own husbands; the term *hypokouete* likely evokes too much of a social differential to appear in that context. While a wife is to submit in respect, a child is called to honor via obedience; the two forms express variants of submission (as manifestations of that pattern identified in 5:21) that are notably different: between two peers in the former case and between those of different generations in the latter. This diverse description of submission (which will veer even further when discussing slaves and masters) helps put the lie to the notion that mutual submission involves the undoing of social differentials. Submission, as a means of being filled by the Spirit, takes the form of a number of distinct relational orders consciously inhabited in a particular manner.

What is that manner? This behavior with respect to parents must be "in the Lord" (→6:5 for similar reference to slaves' obedience of masters). What does it mean to obey a parent in the Lord? One does not merely obey in the family— that is, with strategic judgment about the propriety and wisdom of obeying this man or this woman. Rather, one deems the most pertinent context for moral deliberation to be the presence of the Lord: the prudence of honoring this parent is not indexed by the intellectual, social, or moral capacity of that parent alone but ultimately by the providential presence of the almighty Lord. In this regard, obeying a parent manifests faith, not primarily in that parent in him- or herself, but in the triune God—even more specifically, in Jesus Christ (for "Lord" here likely refers to the Second Person of the Trinity, as in Paul's typical usage).

These verses are the context for the rare use of the language of *dikaiosynē* in Ephesians; 6:1 concludes by saying "this is just" or "this is right," either translation of which renders the term *dikaion* faithfully. This sort of generational respect and honor accords with reality and is not merely a strategic decision that might be otherwise—say, if the accidental cards of one's context played out differently. Right behavior fits the very fabric of our interpersonal existence (see Ps. 11:7). Though the rest of the epistle does not overtly turn to the Mosaic law or the

Decalogue specifically (→2:15 for a seemingly negative mention), perhaps it is not for nothing that here the language of justice appears just when the text will speak next of fulfilling that law and one of those ten commandments.

A parenthetical statement comes—"this is the first commandment with a promise" (6:2)—and the apostle takes his time in actually relaying that promise from Exod. 20:12: "that it may go well with you and that you may live long in the land" (Eph. 6:3; cf. Deut. 5:16). Paul includes this promise long after the entry to the land, after the prayer for future rest in Ps. 95, even after the exile. He restates it to a group composed of Gentiles who live in Asia Minor (whether Ephesus specifically or a range of churches in the area), to those who have inheritance in the heavens and not in the Middle East. While this may seem a fairly trite episode of prooftexting, with the apostle simply affixing a reference to God's promise of blessing to this command, something far more specific seems to be in play here. Paul does not mention generic blessing along the lines of a "God helps those who help themselves" mentality. The promise here is of blessing in the promised land, and yet it is recited again in the New Testament.

Is it too much to suggest that a particular hermeneutic is demanded for this citation to make sense? If the Old Testament promise was merely for an earthly home, would the apostle Paul mention it here? Other questions arise as well: Why would Ps. 95 continue to speak of a rest yet to come when it was sung by one who was in that promised land already? What more did the psalmist await? While other texts have to be considered to think through that question (see Heb. 3:7–4:13), the broader hermeneutical point must be addressed here. The text of 6:2–3 suggests that "you" are a subject receiving that original fifth commandment and that "you" are given that initial promise as well, even if you are plainly not a recently freed slave from Egypt on the way to Canaan.

Some recent interpreters have argued that Christian readers need to avoid lapsing into Marcionite readings and thus need to appreciate the earthy hopes, rooted in Old Testament promises (such as Gen. 12:1–3), that find fulfillment in apostolic proclamation (Middleton 2014). It is true that the New Testament picks up and even extends those earthy elements in the salvific promises of God; for example, the promised land of the Middle East expands to become the whole "earth" in Matt. 5:5. And yet Ephesians seems to be depicting more than mere real estate: we have inherited the heavenly places (→2:6). John Calvin provides a salient counterexample in that he offers a nonreductive reading of these Old Testament promises that also manages to catch the apostolic priorities of texts like Ephesians.

Calvin repeatedly shows that Old Testament saints longed for more than merely earthly blessings, such as the promised land of Canaan, because they knew the God of Israel promised through figural signs more than meets the eye. But in so doing, Calvin never suggests that the earthy figures were inconsequential or mere signs lacking real substance (*Institutes* 2.10.1–2.11.8, in Calvin 2006: 1:428–57).

That the Christians addressed here by the apostle can anticipate good life in that land suggests that the sign of Canaan does point toward the "heavenly places." That rest and that provision, symbolized powerfully by culinary panache, abounding storehouses, and military fortification, find their mysterious terminus in the land where the Lord dwells. Not surprisingly, the battles for the promised land are also symbols for a deeper sort of warfare, and the apostle will soon turn to remind us that our opposition is not ultimately flesh and blood, not an Egyptian or a Canaanite, neither a Jew nor a Roman. For Christians young and old, the good life in the Lord's land comes by trustingly inhabiting the order that God alone has woven into the fabric of our being and written into the mandate of our law.

After the exhortation to children, fathers are addressed specifically and secondly. First, they are named distinctly (over against mothers), likely because of the way in which fathers tend to behave. In a setting such as Ephesus or other cities in Asia Minor, fathers would have concern for the family name and might respond in rage to childlike waywardness. While mothers are morally bound to parent in an appropriate way too, the apostle emphasizes the divine governance over all parenting by noting that even the father is a man under orders from above. Second, the authority figure is addressed after the subordinate so as to reveal again this radical relativizing of relations. While the parent-child relationship remains, both parties are creatures underneath the reign of the Lord. If the child is to be obedient in the Lord, the father is to raise the child in the Lord; in both cases the individuals are to look away from the immediate interpersonal relation, as if facing the other could provide a sufficient register for the relational context, and instead to look upward to the engagement of the risen Lord in their midst.

Fathers are called away from provocation and summoned to divine instruction. Neither goes without saying. First, the aim of their role is the upbuilding of their children, not merely the itemized satisfaction of their duties. In other words, fathers are not there to "just do something," and their aim is not to rest satisfied at day's end that they attempted to parent. They are called to foster a space within which children will grow and mature and flourish and be transformed; apparently anger is an alternate reality or end, provided that a parent provokes their child. A father ought not call out every wrong, and a father dare not chide his child for failures he himself provoked. Instruction is meant to be revealing and convicting, taking a pedagogical and not cynical posture. Just as the father is to govern the occasions and ends to which he disciplines and corrects, so the rubrics of that instruction are given shape here.

Second, fathers function as instruments in the Lord's hands to bring up children "in the discipline and instruction of the Lord." We might be inclined to trace this back as a statement of pedigree: God has revealed previously what humans ought to be and do, and so now parents teach by reiterating those old divine instructions. While there is nothing false in what that says, it does not sufficiently attest what it means to speak here of the Lord's discipline or of the Lord's instruction. The risen Christ teaches even now, through the school of suffering enacted in his providential lordship and through his ongoing prophetic ministry to effectuate the way of his holy word. The human parent does not inculcate his or her own dreams or mores, then, but participates in God's own training of this young man or young woman by drawing attention to God's principles, morals, and ends. To be a father, then, is a call to relinquishment of one's own preferences or dreams, that one might be fully invested in summoning one's child to something greater—not merely to family customs but to divine callings. In this regard, like the husband's self-sacrificial giving of himself so as to sanctify the wife, here too the father (and by extension the mother) constrains his own likes and foibles, that he might manifest to his own children the ways of the Lord (and not merely of him- or herself). While parents hold an interpersonal authority with respect to children, then, parenting is nonetheless a form of submission with and to others, for it too becomes an occasion for self-denial and self-renunciation before the Lord. In that strategic and social weakness, that self-emptying of one's own preferences and mores, the filling of the Spirit may mark and deepen his sanctifying work on a father or mother.

6:5–9 Bondservants, obey your earthly masters with fear and trembling, with a sincere heart, as you would Christ, not by the way of eye-service, as people-pleasers, but as bondservants of Christ, doing the will of God from the heart, rendering service with a good will as to the Lord and not to man, knowing that whatever good anyone does, this he will receive back from the Lord, whether he is a bondservant or is free. Masters, do the same to them, and stop your threatening, knowing that he who is both their Master and yours is in heaven, and that there is no partiality with him.

The final set of household instructions pertains to slave-master relations in the household business. Here we venture to the wider composition of the household, moving beyond familial relations to economic relations. Slavery was a widespread practice in first-century Asia Minor, so it is not shocking that this set of relationships would be addressed as one arena for moral formation. Aristotle addressed the same three pairings: husband-wife, parent-child, and master-slave (*Politics* 1.2.1–23, 1.5.1–23). Modern readers, particularly those in the United States, do well to realize that slavery then and there was not the same as later chattel slavery in the so-called New World. Slaves might find themselves in that position for many reasons, though slavery was not largely race-based. Slaves could be severely and horrifically mistreated—notably, slaves were to be sexually available at the master's whim—and yet they also had opportunity to build wealth, to buy freedom, to form families, and thus to find their way out of slavery.[1]

The updated ESV and NKJV render the term *douloi* as "bondservants," while others opt for "slaves" (HCSB, NASB, NIV, NRSV, RSV, and also the earlier version of the ESV). The argument for "bondservant" is that it rightly locates the term in the world of slavery but also registers divergence between ancient bond slavery and more modern variations in the Western world. While not all *douloi* were enslaved because of a debt, they were capable of being bonded out of slavery (by their own or others' payment). Of course, none of these arguments in favor of "bondservant" differentiate it from the term "slave." Further, it is a less common rendering of the term and loses the commonality with the more common usage of *doulos/douloi* across the New Testament and the Pauline corpus. The term "slave," then, more accurately fits the bill here.

Slaves are called to "obey," and this is later described as "rendering service." The language of obedience parallels that given to children (→6:1) and thereby differs from that offered to wives (→5:22, 24, 33). The notion of deference moves to the fore here, deferring one's priorities for the sake of serving one's master. However, the language of priorities raises the question of how the qualification to come shapes even this submission. The slave is to serve the master as though serving Christ, for Christ is Lord of all (both slave and master). This ultimate lordship relativizes any immoral or evil demands of the master, suggesting room for moral deliberation about how a slave might rightly relate to a master's demands for improper service. While the text does not elaborate on mechanisms for navigating such situations politically, much less any casuistry regarding protocols for

---

1. See Kyle Harper, *Slavery in the Late Roman World, AD 275–425* (Cambridge: Cambridge University Press, 2011), 33–66.

identifying such dilemmas specifically, it does prompt the need for such a category in ethical formation.

Similarly, great care is given, not to depict what concrete acts compose this obedience or service but to describe the manner of that submission. Ephesians 6:5–7 characterizes the posture of slaves' service with a range of expressions. "Fear and trembling" does not call for cowering before the master but for appropriate respect of the master's position as temporary authority (see parallel usage in Phil. 2:12–13, where salvation is to be "work[ed] out . . . with fear and trembling"). "With a sincere heart" relates the summons to integrity and not mere stratagem; one is to be devoted to one's work, even if it takes the form of servitude. The idea of sincerity is then extrapolated by way of a contrast: the apostle excludes what he terms "the way of eye-service [*ophthalmodoulian*], as people-pleasers [*anthrōpareskoi*]" and exalts the way of being "bondservants of Christ." The eye can be served by exalting or privileging that which is visible and can be observed by those around; hence, such service entails being a "people-pleaser." In this sense the rendering "eyeing the master" by Christopher Seitz (2014: 175) gets the term *ophthalmodoulian* backward, as the slave lives for the eye rather than eyes anything. But God alone sees the heart, and thus Christ is served by those doing God's will "from the heart" (*ek psychēs*). Finally, service is to be rendered "with a good will"—that is, a will that seeks the good of the one to whom it is rendered. This does not suggest that one's master is to be viewed with Pollyannaish lenses, but that the master—whether fair or unjust, friend or enemy—is to be loved. Only a way that calls for the love of enemies could summon a slave to such a posture.

As noted above, this service and the appropriate manner of this service are repeatedly said to be "to the Lord" or "as to the Lord." Each verse expresses the notion in its own way: "as you would Christ" (6:5), "as bondservants of Christ" (6:6), and "as to the Lord and not to man" (6:7). Repetition serves as a less than subtle schoolteacher, and readers do well to pay attention. There is a spiritual recontextualization of the slave's agency because there is a retrofitting of the slave-master relationship. The master is simply not the master, in the ultimate sense. The Lord is the master, and all others serve at his beck and call. Doing so does not obliterate the duty of slave to earthly master, but it does reframe and sublimate that social and economic order.

Ephesians 6:8 provides a justification for this posture before the Lord and its consequent mode of submission to the master: "whatever good anyone does, this he will receive back from the Lord, whether he is a bondservant or is free." The rule might speak eschatologically of that which shall be received in the next life alone, or it might speak proverbially (though not crassly) of rewards in this life, or it might speak in overlapping manner of rewards both near and far. In any event, the apostle intends to motivate by means of an undefined future promise of divine beneficence; while the specific shape of the gift is not sketched, it is "from the Lord" and thus in some way befitting of that Lord, which means it has marked definition.

Again, the authority figure is addressed secondly. Oddly, the command here is one of seeming similarity: "Masters, do the same to them" (6:9). How can the apostle speak of similar action when one character holds all the cards in their powerful hand? Where does the similarity lie? How can the apostle truly expect a master to behave like a slave? In this short statement may be found perhaps the most radical comment on slavery in the passage. Frank Thielman argues that this section actually tilts in the direction of mutual service—not merely of slave to master (6:5–8) but also of master to slave (6:9). While the overall structure of the household code employs various examples to show the diverse ways in which submission occurs, one to the other, in overlapping, temporary relationships, here the apostle says there is a "submitting to one another out of reverence for Christ" (5:21) within a single relationship.

Thielman (2010: 409) offers three arguments that warrant attention. First, Paul has already labeled the authority figure here an "earthly master" (6:5) and said in 6:8 that both slave and free have a heavenly master above, which levels their standing in the most ultimate terms. Second, "there was a strong conviction in early Christianity, originating in the teaching of Jesus, that those in positions of authority should adopt the role of slaves with respect to those under their authority (Mark 10:41–45; Matt. 20:24–28; John 13:1–17; cf. Luke 12:37)." Third, this phrase may plausibly be interpreted as originating from the common human struggle under sin expressed earlier in the letter. The three arguments would not differentiate this master-slave relationship from the two earlier relations (wife-husband, child-parent), which do not have any teasing out of mutual service within them. So a lingering, real question is how the leveling of authority before the heavenly master affects the exercise of a master's authority over a slave in the first century as well as the way in which Jesus's address regarding service might shape how we hear this passage.

Thielman's evidence does not provide a knockdown or sure line of argument that leads to mutual service within the master-slave relationship (as opposed to the asymmetry defined within the wife-husband and child-parent relations). Nonetheless, the phrasing is idiosyncratic within the wider household code and does seem, in some fashion, to say more than merely that masters ought to be kind to their slaves, as rendered rather blithely by most commentators. In this regard, Thielman's second line of argument merits further consideration, for texts such as Mark 10:45 do suggest a paradigmatic inversion of power dynamics. Jesus does not negate social hierarchies as such, but he does upend much of their logic. The Son of Man employs his position and presence to serve others, not to be enhanced by exploiting or engaging them to serve him (though, presumably, such service would be appropriate and due him). It is not a leap to link that paradigm to the example of Jesus washing the feet of his own disciples and commanding them to go and do likewise (John 13:15) and to see this as a Christian reframing of power by way of the cross. Here Martin Luther's distinction between a theology of the cross and a theology of glory may be helpful, reminding us that what is true and lovely finds its definition in Christ's own being and behavior, not in our intuitions or our cultural mores; indeed, our intuited sense of the true and good and beautiful needs to be killed and made alive again. Just as sinful logic may find it nonsensical madness to speak of a master serving a slave, so a theology that has undergone mortification and vivification in the crucified and risen Christ will find that protocol to fit with the grain of the universe.

The text does not summon masters to manumission (as the letter to Philemon does), though it does undercut a number of common practices, not least being the presumption of sexual availability.[2] The text certainly does not suggest that slaves ought to pursue insurrection, and it likely cannot imagine a sociopolitical context without slavery. The sort of parliamentary possibilities of centuries later, wherein Christians and others might pursue the political end of the slave trade, is not yet being engaged or envisioned (though it does fit with the basic convictions of a Christian anthropology). The apostle does reframe service in this sphere as an opportunity for spiritual formation, wherein the filling of the Spirit plays out in the selfless service of a slave who uses their agency with sincerity and wholeness. Augustine put it this way in speaking of these verses: "Paul does not try to turn slaves into free men and women, but bad slaves into good slaves" (2004: 63). That's almost right. Paul does not here seek to transform status (slave to free), but the change he calls for is more a matter of spiritual and Christian character than of economic quality per se. In other words, Paul cares less that they be good rather than bad slaves and more that they be Christian

2. Kyle Harper, *From Shame to Sin: The Christian Transformation of Sexual Morality in Late Antiquity*, Revealing Antiquity 20 (Cambridge, MA: Harvard University Press, 2013), 46–52.

slaves (which will surely have some spillover effects as various Christian virtues have economic or vocational benefit).

Coming to the end of 5:22–6:9, it is worth noting commonalities and divergences in these three social settings. In each setting, Christians are called to be filled with the Spirit by submitting to each other in relationally appropriate and distinct ways. These three representative (though non-exhaustive[3]) pairings enable the apostle to tease out the shape of a cruciform formation for both parties within each binary. The parties deny themselves in diverse ways in each case, but they are called to mutual accountability (though not strictly equivalent service) in each case. Just as the text radically challenges the exercise of power and authority in overt and understated ways (perhaps nowhere as punchy as in 6:9), so it also summons those lacking social capital to pursue the filling of the Spirit by receiving their situation as part of the tapestry of providence. Their doing so does not thereby affirm the moral value of the actions of those in power; providence often works through the vagaries of infidels' rule or the hypocrisy of righteous posturing. A colloquial proverb says that God can shoot straight with a crooked stick.

The three binary relationships do not parallel each other exactly, however. The husband and wife are described in peer relations in a way that is not mimicked by the parent-child and master-slave binaries; respect and submission are demanded in the former, but obedience is called for only in the latter two cases. It would appear that the lack of "obey" as a term employed in 5:22–33 is intentional given its repeated usage in 6:1, 9. So the kind of submission offered one to the other varies. The moral value of the binaries varies as well, and here the distinction breaks down differently. The apostle gives positive theological argumentation for the significance of the husband-wife relationship in the mystery of Christ and the church and for the binding character of parent-child relations in the Sinaitic promise of blessing; no such positive argument is offered to give credence to the institution of slavery. Slavery is a given social reality with a place in God's providence, but it has no claims to any divine mandate or positive theological legitimation. Not surprisingly, then, 6:9 suggests the one possible subversion of the power differential, one that will be teased out in other writings (Philemon) and in later times.

Must the church read this passage today? Some have argued that the household codes here are not meant to have modern application. Charles Talbert (2007:

---

3. The apostle does not choose to explore the political parallel here, though he has addressed it in Rom. 13:17, and the Petrine household code addresses it in 1 Pet. 2:13–17.

150–51) argues that the term *oikos* may be wrongly rendered today as a home or family when it actually refers to a household business; on this basis he then argues that these verses do not address, for instance, modern marriages or parent-child relations. While Talbert is right to observe that households entailed more than merely familial relations and do take an economic bent in both the classical and the specifically Jewish worlds, both affecting the life of early Christians, it is nonetheless strange to suggest that a nuanced reading of the word *oikos*, a term that does not appear in our passage, somehow nullifies this passage's modern impact.

Ian McFarland (2000: 347–48) argues that a canonical reading of the passage must deem Paul's argument here a failure (at least in 5:22–33) for not grasping the egalitarianism latent in the Christ event and expressed in other Pauline passages such as Gal. 3:26–28, though it is "profitable" as a beginning point from which those other texts prompt a movement. Of course, Ephesians is not early and appears canonically after Galatians, so the sequential reasoning doesn't get us far. McFarland deems only a christological argument satisfactory for any hierarchy in the New Testament, thus excluding creational arguments given in passages such as 1 Tim. 2:9–14. Perhaps an apocalyptic theologian would want to so excise other doctrinal foundations in nature and covenant, but there are good reasons not to take such a radical apocalyptic bent (see Macaskill 2018: 107–34). Indeed, even if one granted McFarland's Christocentric starting point, Eph. 5 offers an overt christological argument for its approach to marital relations. Even if one hesitates over the admittedly complex creational arguments offered in 1 Tim. 2, the argument here is much more straightforwardly christological in the case of husband-wife relations and covenantal in the case of parent-child relations. These relationships continue to bear significance not merely in times and places for sociological reasons but for specifically theological reasons.

Further, positive theological foundations are provided in varied forms for the husband-wife and parent-child relationships, while no such argument appears within the later master-slave discussion. McFarland challenges this claim, suggesting instead that "it should come as no surprise that the writer of Ephesians gives no further theological argument for the subordination of children to parents (6:1–4) or of slaves to masters (6:5–9). He does not have to, because his argument for the subordination of wife to husband provides a theological model of dutiful submission, complemented by paternal rule, that is readily transferable to other contexts" (2000: 353n32). But further argument does appear in one case. Paul quotes verbatim from Exod. 20 to note that there's a promise related to parent-child relations (→6:2–3); in fact, his moral argument stands out from

every other teaching in chapters 4–6 at just this point—namely, that he turns
to the Decalogue and does so that he might draw on that covenantal promise
given to God's people. God's word and that promise still stand. So there is a
christological argument given for the husband-wife relation and a covenantal
promise undergirding the parent-child relation. Notably, Paul offers nothing
by way of argument to ground the master-slave binary. This one sits on nothing
more than socioeconomic happenstance, to speak in moral and theological terms.
While Eph. 6 does not speak of the evil of slavery as such (though it does call for
a revolution of its protocols), it does throw into relief the fact that it cannot be
sourced to divine design (unlike marriage and family).[4]

What of this section as a whole? How might one summarize its value or contribution to apostolic teaching? Talbert (2007: 153) argues that household codes
were meant in general to help organize a family business to function efficiently.
That is true to an extent, though it would be wrong to exclude moral formation
and honor from the equation. He is right also to note that Paul's and Peter's
inclusion of household codes in various New Testament texts is meant to show
that the kind of Christian equality or unity expressed in a text like Gal. 3:26–28
does not mean that all social settings and relationships are flattened. That is true,
but that is only half the story. The apostle locates these relationships within a
discussion of moral formation by the filling of the Spirit (→5:15–21), such that
there is also a positive and revolutionized concern here.

The spiritual point, however, is not merely that life in Christ enables a new
inhabiting of social orders but also that social orders are used by the Spirit as a
means of further transformation. Sanctification or redemptive change continues,
and it is not merely prayer and song through which the Spirit fills and inhabits.
Those gathered activities are means of grace for the congregation, but there is
also an elaboration that the scattered church can still receive mercy from on high.
So again the text seeks to give its recipients new eyes to know the love of God in
Christ, shown powerfully in what Christ's own Spirit does in addressing Christian life in socially ordered relationships of various sorts. New ends are given to
these relationships that well exceed the typical household code's aim at economic
efficiency and social honor: not merely to help Christians avoid messing up their
social responsibilities, whether to avoid persecution by Rome or to enable more

4. It is not surprising, then, that in the long run Christians saw a text like Eph. 6 as gesturing toward,
first, the manumission of one's own slaves (as in Philemon) and, second, the call of Gregory of Nyssa
and others in later centuries for the global end to slavery on distinctly Christian grounds (see Talbert
2007: 153–56 for a helpful discussion of the difference between short-term and long-term expectations).

successful evangelism, but also to serve as a sphere within which all "do the same" (6:9) by inhabiting their own positions in various overlapping social relations as occasions for self-denial and for spiritual transformation.

6:10–18a Finally, be strong in the Lord and in the strength of his might. Put on the whole armor of God, that you may be able to stand against the schemes of the devil. For we do not wrestle against flesh and blood, but against the rulers, against the authorities, against the cosmic powers over this present darkness, against the spiritual forces of evil in the heavenly places. Therefore take up the whole armor of God, that you may be able to withstand in the evil day, and having done all, to stand firm. Stand therefore, having fastened on the belt of truth, and having put on the breastplate of righteousness, and, as shoes for your feet, having put on the readiness given by the gospel of peace. In all circumstances take up the shield of faith, with which you can extinguish all the flaming darts of the evil one; and take the helmet of salvation, and the sword of the Spirit, which is the word of God, praying at all times in the Spirit, with all prayer and supplication.

A finale returns here to the central thread of the epistle: power. The Christians are summoned to "be strong," and this strength shall be found specifically "in the Lord and in the strength of his might" (6:10). God's power needs to be known (1:19), but that knowledge needs to involve being empowered by God's own strength (3:16). This same Paul elsewhere says, "I can do all things through him who strengthens me" (Phil. 4:13), though that "all things" demands some focus and definition. While nothing lies beyond the pale of God's power, his force fits cohesively with his will: divine simplicity demands that we always interpret divine power with the grain of divine character. God cannot make a rock too big for God to move, to be sure, but what is of more interest is that God does not empower one by his Spirit to become evil or warped. In Phil. 4 Paul is addressing a specific range of things for which such empowerment comes—namely, the "secret" of being content whether he is "brought low" or "abound[s]" (4:11–12). In Eph. 4:1–6:9 he has described the shape of the mature or whole Christian life that is empowered by God in a much more panoramic view, taking in many areas of human life, both individual and corporate, bodily and cosmic. Now in 6:10–18 the apostle turns to describe the means by which God grants strength.

Again, this teaching about divine power within which Christians participate undercuts the ethic of Greco-Roman society. Paul inverts these moral expectations: "But he said to me, 'My grace is sufficient for you, for my power is made perfect in weakness.' Therefore I will boast all the more gladly of my weaknesses, so that the power of Christ may rest upon me. For the sake of Christ, then, I am content with weaknesses, insults, hardships, persecutions, and calamities. For when I am weak, then I am strong" (2 Cor. 12:9–10). The wider context of that boast repeats the language of foolishness (2 Cor. 11:1, 16, 17, 19, 21; 12:1). Strength is not innate, though it does inhabit. Christian power comes always from the outside, though this does not mean that it remains alien or other. That rooting in a divine power from above shapes the contours by which human strength is exercised, always in a self-effacing and humble manner. Not for nothing was the prayer and benediction in Eph. 3:14–21 followed by a summons to befitting or "worthy" behavior that involves "humility," "gentleness," "patience," and "bearing with one another in love" (→4:1–2).

Paul will elsewhere use the language of strong and weak in seemingly divergent ways (see Rom. 14:1–15:1). In that context he will speak of strength as a good thing that differentiates one from those who are weak. The timidity of 2 Cor. 12 has gone, and Paul does not hesitate here to own up to being strong (Rom. 15:1: "we who are strong"). Yet the strength there is a markedly different register: it is the strength of faith, not of internal gumption. "The strength in their faith is the degree to which they have been able to dissociate their faith in Christ from every norm or value that is not derived from the good news itself. . . . Faith stakes the self on God, and is stronger to the extent that it allows attachment to God to dissolve human attachments, whether in the form of reliance on human capacity or in the form of commitment to human systems of evaluation" (Barclay 2013: 203, 205). Faith's strength comes not in leaning on extraneous resources but in receiving and resting wholly on faith's object. As far as strengths go, this strength of faith stands out for being determined completely by the force of the face on which it is fixed, not the gaze of the one exercising it.

The text turns in 6:11 and 6:13 to the call to "put on" (*endysasthe*) and "take up" (*analabete*) "the whole armor of God." Interestingly, 6:10 also begins with an imperative: "be strong" (*endynamousthe*). Though this strength comes from above, it is not inappropriate or beyond the realm of rhetorical propriety for the apostle to summon them to be strong. Yet this strength is the Lord's strength and is possessed only "in the Lord" (*en kyriō*). That Paul goes on to specify this location or sphere of strengthening—"in the strength of his might" (*en tō kratei tēs ischyos autou*)—suggests that his emphasis lies there, in the divine provision of the strength. The phrasing here emphasizes not simply that God is the source of the strength, though this is surely the case, but also that this strength is God's own might. Here is the latest example: we have seen already that the wise God gives wisdom and the loving God gives love, and now the powerful God gives power. God gives what is his own, for God gives nothing less than himself. We must remember that evangelical logic stated bluntly earlier: "in him you also" (1:13; 2:22). Here we might say that 6:10–13 says something equivalent to "in his armor, you also possess his strength and might."

Ephesians 6:12 offers a hiatus of sorts, as the apostle pauses before reiterating his command and plunging ahead to describe the makeup of God's armor. In the face of secularizing temptations, the Christians are to remember that their battle is in heaven. Again, 2 Corinthians parallels much of this discussion: "For though we walk in the flesh, we are not waging war according to the flesh. For the weapons of our warfare are not of the flesh but have divine power to destroy strongholds" (2 Cor. 10:3–4).

Readings of the language of "powers" and "principalities" have developed quite the biography, particularly in recent decades. Some identify powers and principalities with demons. Some liken them to earthly power structures of varying sorts. Some view them as sin personified, a mythic kind of portrayal of the battle against evil in every time or even person. Some view these pictures as overlapping, at least in some cases. A moderate example would be this comment from Markus Barth: "The 'principalities and powers' are at the same time intangible spiritual entities and concrete historical, social, or psychic structures or institutions of all created things and all created life" (1974b: 800–801). A global view of evil surely involves something much like what Barth here describes: real demonic activity, social and even institutional malformation. Ephesians has already spoken of sin's consequence and transmission in a thick manner that sounds rather similar (→2:1–3).

Yet 6:12 says nothing that draws our attention to earthly structures or social institutions. This passage seeks to draw our sight through and beyond such realities, above and past the empirically obvious pangs of this epoch. The passage here summons us to that at which the epistle as a whole aims—namely, a spiritual or heavenly reading of reality. In this case, the pains of this world exceed the bounds of this globe. Any interpretation of 6:12 that fails to catch this wholeheartedly demonic emphasis is not reading the verse in its discrete contribution to hamartiology in Ephesians first, the New Testament second, and Christian theology third. Again, more is found earlier in Ephesians (→2:1–3) and elsewhere in the New Testament (Rom. 1:24–32; 3:9–18, citing Ps. 14:1–3; 5:9; 10:7 [LXX]; 36:1; 53:1–3; Prov. 1:16; Isa. 59:7–8), but the accent of this portion of scripture falls entirely on the need not to rest satisfied with any immanent description of depravity and disorder. Just as much as order finds its roots primarily in something beyond the earthly realm—namely, in the triune God in whom alone we find our rest—so also disorder finds its explanation (inasmuch as chaos, sin, and death are explicable) in forces that are beyond earthly measure.

Ephesians 6:12 stacks various descriptions to identify these true foes: "the rulers" (*tas archas*), "the authorities" (*tas exousias*), "the cosmic powers over this present darkness" (*tous kosmokratoras tou skotous toutou*), and finally "the spiritual forces of evil in the heavenly places" (*ta pneumatika tēs ponērias en tois epouraniois*). While the basic nominal terms in each depiction come from the ordinary terrain of politics ("rulers," "authorities," "powers," and "forces"), in the third and fourth instances they are further described so as to redefine them radically. Lest rulers and authorities be viewed like any old king or tetrarch, these are then noted to be distinctly "cosmic powers over this present darkness" rather than territorial powers over a purportedly enduring or eternal dominion (which was the common bravado of a human claimant to power). Further, they are then pegged as "spiritual forces of evil in the heavenly places"; three crucial claims are made here. They are, first, "spiritual forces" rather than merely military or political forces. Second, their spiritual dominion somehow relates to evil, whether by causation or by source or location (a genitival relationship); they rule in an evil way or manner. Third, this evil tyranny occurs "in the heavenly places" rather than on this terrestrial surface; while the term "heavenly places" does not allude to otherworldly space, it does identify a particular nexus within this created order—namely, the places wherein God's presence is found thickest. These evil spirits combat God's righteous presence in just those places.

While modern Christians might hesitate at the language of warfare, our ancestors did not flinch, and they plainly had scriptural reasons to employ it. The Old Testament speaks of warfare between God's own and their enemies, paradigmatically depicted by the formative work of God in freeing Israel from Egypt. Such language was not left behind in the New Testament either. Yet the presence of warfare language does not mean that it is brought into the Christian lexicon undisturbed. In fact, the way in which Christians think about divine warfare undergoes a remarkable transfiguration in scripture. One such judgment is expressed by Augustine of Hippo: "We have to distinguish between enemies for whom we must pray and enemies against whom we must pray. Human enemies, of whatever kind, are not to be hated. . . . The enemies against whom we need to pray are the devil and his angels" (2000a: 347–48). This claim shapes how we think about imprecatory psalms, and Augustine roots the principle directly in Eph. 6:12. The true enemy is the spiritual foe, who does not possess flesh and blood.

What is the end of bearing this armor? Ephesians 6:11 says the end is "that you may be able to stand against the schemes of the devil." Then 6:13 adds: "that you may be able to withstand in the evil day, and having done all, to stand firm." Standing is the order of the day, though the verses say much about the context for holding that ground. Against whom are we to stand? The scheming devil. When? "In the evil day." How? "Having done all." One might think that a survivalist ethic involves certain moral necessities shorn of other purportedly accidental duties, but the apostle does not make any such suggestion. The one who will stand is the one marked by doing all—that is, by wholeness. Likely the reader is to think back to 4:12–16, where the notion of fullness, wholeness, and maturity was sketched as an end. Not surprisingly, doing all so that one might stand firm jives with that prior text's emphasis on one's stature, that the posture or frame of the Christian fit that of Christ himself (→4:13).

The link between this passage and chapter 4 warrants further consideration. Ephesians 4:1 spoke of the need to walk, and now 6:11 and 6:13 address the call to stand firm. Does this latter passage represent a shift or an interpolation? At first glance, the call to stand firm may seem far more fixed on mere survival over against the earlier summons to be on the march. Yet there are no other signs of interpolation or of tension here. A parallel may prove helpful as we seek to read both calls with full seriousness. The New Testament portrays the exalted and ascended Christ as sitting and standing. Hebrews 1:3 says that "after making purification for sins, he sat down at the right hand of the Majesty on high." Yet Acts 7:55 tells of when Stephen "gazed into heaven and saw the glory of God, and Jesus standing at the right hand of God." Does the ascended Christ occupy a throne, or does he stand? The question presumes a false dichotomy, and each passage conveys something notable of his present activity. As a great high priest and, indeed, as a sacrifice, he has offered the final sacrifice for sin and therefore sits in that capacity. As king and lord of a people, however, he stands attentive to their needs and watchful over not merely the agony but especially the temptation of one such as Stephen. Here in Eph. 4–6, believers are called to walk in a particular way—that is, to employ their agency and moral action in certain habits, rhythms, and practices, even as they must prepare to stand against the onslaught of demonic opposition. Even the front lines of the infantry possess immune systems, so the notion of exertion and that of protection cannot be treated as mutually exclusive.

Because the opposition is spiritual, the weaponry must exceed earthly wits and natural skill. Believers need armor that is designed to fend off and to assault hell's own forces. Again, use of warfare imagery and the affirmation that Christians are engaged in a battle in no way suggests that it is a battle similar to others, whether in the first century or the twenty-first century. While 6:12 noted the strange identification of the enemy, 6:13–17 will now fix on the mysterious weaponry of this sort of skirmish. Readers of the Old Testament will not be surprised that the weapons with which God's own are arrayed often do not fit the wisdom of this world, whether in Moses's outstretched hands (Exod. 17:11–12) or the vocal chords of those conquering Jericho (Josh. 6:1–27) or the smashing of ancient pottery employed by the precious few led by Gideon (Judg. 7:19–23). Time after time, divine victory has crucified the expectations of standard military strategy: "Some trust in chariots and some in horses, but we trust in the name of the LORD our God. They collapse and fall, but we rise and stand upright" (Ps. 20:7–8; see also Isa. 31:3; 36:9).

The weaponry will be described as that which befits one to "stand therefore" (6:14). One can stand in such a way, "having fastened on the belt of truth." If ever truth-telling has seemed obvious, it cannot be taken for granted. Not in ancient Israel, when honest scales had to be legislated (Deut. 25:13–16; Prov. 11:1; 16:11; 20:10, 23). Not in first-century Roman society, as the apostles regularly had to call for sincerity in speech (Titus 2:8). Certainly not today, when spin and deception mark so much of what we hear and what we are inclined to say (or leave unsaid). These moral concerns about truth-telling are summed up in the ninth commandment: "You shall not bear false witness against your neighbor" (Exod. 20:16; Deut. 5:20). Truth may not seem expedient or even strategic, but it is to be worn as a belt so that the Christian is bounded by a commitment to truth. That vow involves a concern to listen truthfully, eschewing spin and subterfuge, and to speak honestly in a way that helps others receive or find the truth. Truth is "fastened" and thus not at all a luxury or a nonessential.

"Having put on the breastplate of righteousness" also marks the way in which the Christian will stand. The term here is otherwise rendered "justice" (*tēs dikaiosynēs*). Ephesians 6:1 introduced the language of justice already in declaring obedience to one's own parents (honoring the fifth commandment) to be right (*dikaion*). Whether in that earlier adjectival form or this later genitival, nominal appearance, the language of justice conveys its snug fit with the moral legislation granted in holy scripture. Not only are particular commands to be honored—say, truth-telling—but there is a formal concern here to be the sort of person who puts on justice as one's own breastplate protecting one's core. In this regard, the apostle speaks of the significance of being guarded by tending to the law that teaches not only "what man is to believe concerning God [but also] what duty God requires of man" (Westminster Shorter Catechism 3).

With "shoes for your feet, having put on the readiness given by the gospel of peace" (6:15), one can stand. In this first-century world, shoes were of greater consequence than in one's modern urban existence. Streets were messy. Byways were rocky and often quite narrow. Not for nothing does the psalmist often acclaim, therefore, being granted a "broad place" (Pss. 18:19; 31:8). The other great gift was to possess comfortable, reliable footwear that protected the feet. What fits these shoes to be reliable? "Readiness" is the key term, and it seems to speak of being equipped (→4:12; see also 2 Tim. 3:16–17). In what way is the Christian equipped with the necessary footwear? "The gospel of peace" provides this "readiness": good news about peace, about God's own peace and the way that God in Christ makes peace by the way of life, death, and life on the far side of that rupture and judgment. Peace is inherently relational, speaking of restoration of a right and good connection between God and humans and, by extension, among humans. The gospel that fits the Christian to be ready for battle with demons will be a gospel that does not settle with the cleansed conscience but looks all the way through Christ's work to its fitting end in restored fellowship.

"In all circumstances take up the shield of faith, with which you can extinguish all the flaming darts of the evil one" (6:16). The "evil one" must be a synonym for the "devil" (6:11); while there are plural enemies ("the rulers," "the authorities," "the cosmic powers," and "the spiritual forces of evil"), there is also a specification of a singular, particular person who is *the* adversary. For all the texture with which Ephesians speaks of evil and sin coming through multifarious conduits (→2:1–3), the text will not allow us to avoid a doctrine of Satan. He lobs "flaming darts" at the Christian, and these need to be "extinguish[ed]." This image seems to suggest that he is trying to burn it all down, and he must be fended off; ignoring him is not a viable option. How shall he be warded off? Here the "shield of faith" is crucial "in all circumstances."

Paul elsewhere speaks of the way in which faith is not an occasional summons to Christian agency but an ongoing duty. When he addresses the feisty debates about dietary law and about festivals in Rom. 14, he offers a substantive response as well as a mandate for how to engage with those with whom one disagrees (hence the "strong" and "weak" as categories here). In addressing that call to live amidst disagreement, he speaks of the danger of being led to action apart from faith. Why?

"For whatever does not proceed from faith is sin" (Rom. 14:23). Faith does not mark merely the inception point of the Christian life but the ongoing posture of children of God, consciously receiving all they have from their Father in heaven (see also Heb. 11:6). Therefore, faith wards off temptation and accusation—the darts of the tempter—"in all circumstances," both in times of plenty and seasons of want. In occasions of strength, faith reorients one humbly to the giver of every good thing; in settings of struggle, faith turns one again in hope to the one who gives life where none might be expected, the God who freed Israel from slavery in Egypt and raised Jesus from the dead.

"And take the helmet of salvation" (6:17). The language of a helmet speaks of that which crowns the head and guards the most significant part of the body. The head exercises executive function and must be guarded—not merely from decapitation but from a debilitating blow that would leave it incapable of right functioning. "Salvation" (*tou sōtēriou*; →2:8 for comment on the *sōtēria* word group) here not only guards the Christian from oblivion—that is, the loss of head and life—but also enables the Christian to live according to created design and to walk the path intended for them to fullness (4:1, 10). That salvation plays such a key role reminds the congregation that the greatest need is not mere knowledge or simply inspiration but ultimately rescue.

"And take . . . the sword of the Spirit, which is the word of God" (6:17). On the one hand, this final piece of armor may seem similar to justice and to the law to which we are meant to conform; in this vein, it speaks of a map or guide to that for which we are designed. On the other hand, rather more is said here in that this is the "sword of the Spirit" and thus does far more than merely map the terrain through which we ought to journey. This word is "living and active, sharper than any two-edged sword, piercing to the division of soul and of spirit, of joints and of marrow, and discerning the thoughts and intentions of the heart" (Heb. 4:12). Texts such as this have prompted theologians to speak of the union of word and Spirit, not merely as a trinitarian reality within the Godhead, but also as an operative agency for our benefit. The Spirit makes the word effective; just as the word comes from and represents God (*theou*, "of God"), so the word also bears the life-giving work of the Spirit (*tou pneumatos*, "of the Spirit").

There are verbal parallels to texts in Isaiah (11:4–5; 52:7; 59:17) that were then developed within later Jewish literature that predates Ephesians. What is their significance? The parallels may suggest a christological focus here, wherein prophetic texts (e.g., Isa. 11:4–5) speak of a branch to come from Jesse and use terms (e.g., "righteousness" and "belt") that later appear among the armor of God here. The connection is complicated, however, by the fact that the pairings do not match; the belts of righteousness and faithfulness in Isaiah become the belt of truth in Eph. 6 (even though righteousness does appear, albeit as a breastplate rather than a belt). Even were a literary connection to be acknowledged, a question would still arise regarding the significance of that connection. Christological reference in Isa. 11, for instance, does not mean that any later allusion must be christological; indeed, the logic of Ephesians ("in him you also" in 1:13; 2:22) may suggest a more participatory alternative.

Finally, 6:18 describes the manner in which these Christians are to possess this armor, employing the participle to summon them to be "praying at all times in the Spirit, with all prayer and supplication." The participle here seems to speak to the mode of exercising or employing these tools. Lest we be tempted to "be strong" in immanent gifts or abilities, the apostle reorients us by calling us to prayer. The verse does not speak of prayer in the general or abstract sense either, but it fixes on "supplication" specifically. Now, it is crucial to catch that this is non-exhaustive, for the verse first mentions "all prayer," but it then goes on to specify "supplication" as its central focus. Prayer has also been tied tightly with the filling of the Spirit earlier in the epistle (→5:18, 20), so this reminder unsurprisingly follows mention of the "sword *of the Spirit.*" This final comment also alerts us, it seems, to the significance that these articles are "the whole armor of God" (*tēn panoplian tou theou*). These items serve their purpose inasmuch as they are related to God; apart from God, if we might imagine such a situation, they would prove feckless and incompetent. A commitment to truth, for instance, proves useful in a world where there is a just and honest judge who will one day bring all darkness to light and right every wrong; apart from such a realm, lies may well be most efficacious in getting ahead. This armor uniquely positions its bearer to receive from God: his strength, his power, his might, deployed for their protection.

Six articles of armor are given and are to be taken up. In this, the Spirit fills or indwells the Christian. Might it be that this provision's numbering hearkens back to the days of God's creative activity in Gen. 1:1–2:4? While the number seven speaks of perfection, it is actually six days of activity (of making and filling) that fit the earth for God's inhabiting presence. Here six pieces of armor equip the Christian for maturity and for military action in the great battle against the evil one. In putting on this armor, "the measure of the stature of the fullness of Christ" (→4:13) proves to come not merely by hearing the word but also by the Spirit so superintending and supervening that hearing that it leads to the formation of character traits.

6:18b–22 To that end, keep alert with all perseverance, making supplication for all the saints, and also for me, that words may be given to me in opening my mouth boldly to proclaim the mystery of the gospel, for which I am an ambassador in chains, that I may declare it boldly, as I ought to speak.

So that you also may know how I am and what I am doing, Tychicus the beloved brother and faithful minister in the Lord will tell you everything. I have sent him to you for this very purpose, that you may know how we are, and that he may encourage your hearts.

Paul's closing words are pointed and direct. He addresses the Christians, and he also gestures toward his own future.

They are to remain alert or attentive. Apparently numbness will be a temptation, yet they can prick their ears to remain engaged and to keep their eyes ever watchful. Further, this alertness—what Oliver O'Donovan calls "wakefulness"—will involve "all perseverance" (6:18).[5] Not only will it not come naturally or automatically, but, it seems, it will receive counter-indications and even opposition. Effort goes into maintaining attentiveness, then, and perseverance involves moral choice (though far more before and besides that, as Ephesians itself has given us eyes to see the spiritual forces of powerful grace behind all change and continued faith, and in so doing Ephesians has given us prompting also to explore social causation in this regard). The final thing said of this alertness is that it manifests in the action of supplicatory prayer on behalf of all Christians and of the apostle specifically; the participial form seems to convey the manner or means of keeping alert here. Perseverance does not involve outgrowing prayer, and alertness does not issue in self-adapted fix-its. The one who sustains a life of watchfulness will be the person who remains on their knees.

As for Paul the apostle, he will also seek to "proclaim the mystery of the gospel," yet in doing so he depends also on the hope that "words may be given to me" (6:19). It is significant here at the end of the epistle to remember that this is Paul *the apostle* writing, in that his future involves nothing other than proclamation because his apostolic summons is a sending with a word to proclaim to the Gentiles. Twice he states that he is to proclaim the gospel mystery "boldly" (two variants of the term *parrēsia* are present here in 6:19 and 6:20). It seems that this is what makes prayer so necessary—namely, that he wishes to proclaim the gospel boldly amidst crosscurrents that would press one away from candid and incessant witness. In the fact of expected opposition—he

---

5. Oliver O'Donovan, *Entering into Rest*, Ethics as Theology 3 (Grand Rapids: Eerdmans, 2017).

writes in chains, after all!—he longs to remain bold, neither to stop nor to squelch his volume.

His apostolic calling is expressed in three further ways here. First, he expects God to open his mouth and to give words (6:19). Second, he refers to himself as an "ambassador" or an emissary-minister, an authorized representative rather than an executive calling his own shots (6:20); even though he uses the verbal description of his apostleship there (*presbeuō*), it is still a passive reality at its roots. Third, he concludes this description of his testimony and God's provision as involving a bold manner with the gospel words at the end of 6:20: "as I ought to speak" (*hōs dei me lalēsai*). These are words of propriety or fittingness; his future testimony should fit or cohere with a particular and given design. The God who has given that design is the very one to whom prayers for help are now offered; "from him and through him and to him are all things" (Rom. 11:36). So Paul begs for aid, first from the Christians and second, through their prayers, from the God of grace. He also reminds them of his apostolic authority and mission, especially of aims not merely to stand but to gain ground. Given the call to withstand attacks in 6:10–17, surely it is a strategic rhetorical move here to remind them that the kingdom is advancing in this epoch; while defensive postures are necessary, they are not sufficient to describe the apostolic and missiological vision of Ephesians.

The two roads of Paul and his audience may well diverge, yet a connection remains between them. This is no mere letter. They are invited to supplicate themselves on his behalf before God, so reading here is a self-involving act because the text beckons a relational echo. And Paul promises future communication as well, not merely directly but through indirect, intentional means. Tychicus will play the role of intermediary in this regard. He does so bearing trustworthy credentials as a "beloved brother and faithful minister in the Lord." Is he "beloved" of Paul or of the Christians? It is not clear here, though the former is more likely; he is commended as faithful or steadfast, suggesting that he is somewhat less familiar to them.

This future reporting will provide for three needs being met. First, "that you also may know how I am . . . [and] how we are" (6:21, 22). It is not clear here whose updates are being passed along, though the apostle is clearly prioritized; who is this "we" that appears in 6:22? The text does not say, and 1:1 only identifies Paul as writing the letter, with no mention of any partners in his gospel work (as in Gal. 1:2; Phil. 1:1; Col. 1:1). Second, "that you also may know . . . what I am doing" (6:21). Clearly his status—presumably in or out of prison—concerns them, but his witness and apostolic action are of similar concern. Third, "that he may encourage your hearts" (6:22). Just as Paul's apostolic testimony does not merely serve instrumentally to get the gospel word to them but also serves in itself as an illustration of gospel power (→3:1–13), so here there is a suggestion that future testimonies of God's faithfulness in and through him will lead to much encouragement. Why? Ephesians 1–3 gives four illustrations of divine power that bolster Christian confidence in this God's capacity to bless them (as in the prayers of 1:17–19 and 3:16–19); the apostle imagines future examples of mighty divine faithfulness serving as similar encouragements.

6:23–24 Peace be to the brothers, and love with faith, from God the Father and the Lord Jesus Christ. Grace be with all who love our Lord Jesus Christ with love incorruptible.

The epistle that began with such a lengthy, unrelenting word of blessing (→1:3–14) returns to the posture of benediction at its close. The enveloping nature of blessing perhaps provides a lens for how the entire epistle can and should be read. Wherever life may turn and whatever events may transpire (even taking on chains and prison), God's powerful presence can be known and trusted in all circumstances. God's eternity is no reserve or hesitation from engaging and aiding his creatures but the very fullness from which the triune God extends his love to them with such might.

Four things are given over in blessing: peace, love, faith, and grace. "Grace and peace" began the letter's offering to its recipients (→1:2). God's gift of favor and of peace marks the conclusion as well. To these blessings are added love and faith. Love was introduced as a major theme in chapters 2–3, grounding the intervention of Christ in the "great love with which he loved us" (2:4) and then expressing the concern that you be "rooted and grounded in love" (3:17) and that you might "know the love of Christ that surpasses all knowledge" (3:19). The term serves as a crucial link between what God does and what action God calls us to share in: "walk in love, as Christ loved us" (→5:2). As for faith, it famously appears in 2:7–8 and recurs in the next chapter: "we have boldness and access with confidence through our faith in him" (3:12). This faith brings unity (4:13) and serves as a shield in the battle (6:16). Love marks action for another that God calls us to participate in, while faith emphasizes that all such moral participation comes by way of dependence and conscious trust; even our love exists only in trust.

This blessing comes in the name of "God the Father and the Lord Jesus Christ." As in 1:2, so here the Father and the Lord are the subjects blessing these Christians. Any spiritual blessing comes from them, though their character as a "spiritual blessing" (→1:3) suggests that the Holy Spirit is also operative in bringing their giving to completion. The blessing suggests that the triune God who has been active in four distinct ways—raising and exalting Jesus (1:20–23), bringing dead sinners to life graciously (2:1–10), reconciling the circumcised and uncircumcised by the cross (2:11–22), and calling the apostle into his kingdom work (3:1–13)—will continue to act to bless. He does so for the "brothers." The term is gender-inclusive here—true for men and women—though it is rendered specifically in the male term because it connects to contemporary inheritance law whereby male heirs tended to receive the whole estate. In speaking of a blessing for the brothers, then, it is identifying all these Christian men and women as those who are in fact heirs and inheritors (→1:14; 3:6).

This blessing falls on "all who love our Lord Jesus Christ with love incorruptible." Why is this love "incorruptible"? Is the term objectively or subjectively true? Here the apostle speaks of an incorruptible action owing to its incorruptible object, the Lord Jesus Christ. These graces or gifts are known only in him, but in him they are secure and inviolable precisely because of his power and might. Not for nothing has "fullness" been such a pivotal term throughout Ephesians, not only inasmuch as it conveys the giving of God to share what is his with his children but also in that it marks the position of secure stability from which God makes such spiritual grants. Those who do love this Lord Jesus Christ will therefore enjoy that inheritance for which we have been sealed by the Holy Spirit until the time of our possession (1:14).

BIBLIOGRAPHY

Allen, Michael. 2013a. "'It Is No Longer I Who Live': Christ's Faith and Christian Faith." *Journal of Reformed Theology* 7 (1): 3–26.

———. 2013b. *Justification and the Gospel: Understanding the Contexts and the Controversies.* Grand Rapids: Baker Academic.

———. 2017. *Sanctification.* New Studies in Dogmatics. Grand Rapids: Zondervan Academic.

Allen, Michael, and Jonathan Linebaugh, eds. 2015. *Reformation Readings of Paul: Explorations in History and Exegesis.* Downers Grove, IL: IVP Academic.

Allen, Michael, and Scott R. Swain. 2015. *Reformed Catholicity: The Promise of Retrieval for Theology and Biblical Interpretation.* Grand Rapids: Baker Academic.

Augustine. 2000a. *Expositions of the Psalms.* Vol. 1, *Expositions 1–32.* Works of Saint Augustine III/15. Edited by John E. Rotelle. Translated by Maria Boulding. Hyde Park, NY: New City Press.

———. 2000b. *Expositions of the Psalms.* Vol. 2, *Expositions 33–50.* Works of Saint Augustine III/16. Edited by John E. Rotelle. Translated by Maria Boulding. Hyde Park, NY: New City Press.

———. 2002. *Expositions of the Psalms.* Vol. 4, *Expositions 73–98.* Works of Saint Augustine III/18. Edited by John E. Rotelle. Translated by Maria Boulding. Hyde Park, NY: New City Press.

———. 2004. *Expositions of the Psalms.* Vol. 6, *Expositions 121–150.* Works of Saint Augustine III/20. Edited by Boniface Ramsey. Translated by Maria Boulding. Hyde Park, NY: New City Press.

Austin, Victor Lee. 2010. *Up with Authority: Why We Need Authority to Flourish as Human Beings.* London: T&T Clark.

Barclay, John M. G. 2011. *Pauline Churches and Diaspora Jews.* Wissenschaftliche Untersuchungen zum Neuen Testament 275. Tübingen: Mohr Siebeck.

———. 2013. "Faith and Self-Detachment from Cultural Norms: A Study in Romans 14–15." *Zeitschrift für die Neutestamentliche Wissenschaft und Kunde der Älteren Kirche* 104 (2): 192–208.

———. 2015. *Paul and the Gift.* Grand Rapids: Eerdmans.

Barth, Karl. 2017. *The Epistle to the Ephesians.* Edited by R. David Nelson. Translated by Ross M. Wright. Grand Rapids: Baker Academic.

Barth, Markus. 1959. *The Broken Wall: A Study of the Epistle to the Ephesians*. Valley Forge, PA: Judson.

———. 1974a. *Ephesians 1–3*. Anchor Bible 34. Garden City, NY: Doubleday.

———. 1974b. *Ephesians 4–6*. Anchor Bible 34a. Garden City, NY: Doubleday.

Bavinck, Herman. 1894. "The Future of Calvinism." *Presbyterian and Reformed Review* 5 (17): 1–24. Available at http://commons.ptsem.edu/id/presbyterianrefo5171warf-dmd002.

Bray, Gerald L., ed. 2011. *Galatians and Ephesians*. Reformation Commentary on Scripture: New Testament 10. Downers Grove, IL: IVP Academic.

Bruce, F. F. 1984. *The Epistles to the Colossians, to Philemon, and to the Ephesians*. New International Commentary on the New Testament. Grand Rapids: Eerdmans.

Byassee, Jason. 2007. *Praise Seeking Understanding: Reading the Psalms with Augustine*. Radical Traditions. Grand Rapids: Eerdmans.

Calvin, John. 1965a. *The Acts of the Apostles 1–13*. Calvin's Commentaries. Edited by David W. Torrance and T. F. Torrance. Translated by John W. Fraser and W. G. J. McDonald. Grand Rapids: Eerdmans.

———. 1965b. "The Epistle to the Ephesians." In *The Epistles of Paul the Apostle to the Galatians, Ephesians, Philippians, and Colossians*, edited by David W. Torrance and Thomas F. Torrance, translated by T. H. L. Parker, 121–224. Calvin's New Testament Commentaries. Grand Rapids: Eerdmans.

———. 2006. *The Institutes of the Christian Religion*. Edited by John T. McNeill. Translated by Ford Lewis Battles. Library of Christian Classics 20–21. Louisville: Westminster John Knox.

Chester, Stephen. 2017. *Reading Paul with the Reformers: Reconciling Old and New Perspectives*. Grand Rapids: Eerdmans.

Childs, Brevard S. 2008. *The Church's Guide for Reading Paul: The Canonical Shaping of the Pauline Corpus*. Grand Rapids: Baker Academic.

Eire, Carlos. 2010. *Learning to Die in Miami: Confessions of a Refugee Boy*. New York: Free Press.

Fowl, Stephen. 1998. *Engaging Scripture: A Model for Theological Interpretation*. Challenges in Contemporary Theology. Oxford: Blackwell.

———. 2012. *Ephesians*. New Testament Library. Louisville: Westminster John Knox.

Gombis, Timothy J. 2010. *The Drama of Ephesians: Participating in the Triumph of God*. Downers Grove, IL: IVP Academic.

Gregory of Nazianzus. 2008. "Oration 39: On the Baptism of Christ." In *Festal Orations*, edited and translated by Nonna Verna Harrison, 79–98. Popular Patristics 36. Crestwood, NY: St. Vladimir's Seminary Press.

Gregory of Nyssa. 1978. *The Life of Moses*. Translated by A. Malherbe and E. Fergusson. New York: Paulist Press.

Hafemann, Scott J. 1995. *Paul, Moses, and the History of Israel: The Letter/Spirit Contrast and the Argument from Scripture in 2 Corinthians 3*. Wissenschaftliche Untersuchungen zum Neuen Testament I/81. Tübingen: Mohr Siebeck.

Hoehner, Harold. 2002. *Ephesians: An Exegetical Commentary*. Grand Rapids: Baker Academic.

Horton, Michael S. 2011. "Ephesians 4:1–16: The Ascension, the Church, and the Spoils of War." In *Theological Commentary: Evangelical Perspectives*, edited by R. Michael Allen, 129–53. London: T&T Clark.

Hütter, Reinhard. 2000. *Suffering Divine Things: Theology as Church Practice*. Translated by Doug Stott. Grand Rapids: Eerdmans.

———. 2004. *Bound to Be Free: Evangelical Catholic Engagements in Ecclesiology, Ethics, and Ecumenism*. Grand Rapids: Eerdmans.

Irenaeus of Lyons. 1997. *On the Apostolic Preaching*. Popular Patristics 17. Translated by John Behr. Crestwood, NY: St. Vladimir's Seminary Press.

Jenson, Robert W. 2002. "Triune Grace." *Dialog* 41 (4): 285–93.

Johnson, Luke Timothy. 1996. *Scripture and Discernment: Decision-Making in the Church*. 2nd ed. Nashville: Abingdon.

Kim, Seyoon. 2008. *Christ and Caesar: The Gospel and the Roman Empire in the Writings of Paul and Luke*. Grand Rapids: Baker Academic.

Leithart, Peter J. 2016. *The End of Protestantism: Pursuing Unity in a Fragmented Church*. Grand Rapids: Brazos.

Lincoln, Andrew T. 1990. *Ephesians*. Word Biblical Commentary 42. Waco: Word.

Linebaugh, Jonathan A. 2013a. *God, Grace, and Righteousness in Wisdom of Solomon and Paul's Letter to the Romans: Texts in Conversation*. Supplements to Novum Testamentum 152. Leiden: Brill.

———. 2013b. "The Christo-Centrism of Faith in Christ: Martin Luther's Reading of Galatians 2:16, 19–20." *New Testament Studies* 59 (4): 535–44.

Luther, Martin. 1957. "Heidelberg Disputation, 1518." In *Career of the Reformer*, vol. 1, edited and translated by Harold J. Grimm, 35–70. Luther's Works 31. Philadelphia: Fortress.

———. 1979. *Lectures on Galatians (1535)*. Translated by Erasmus Middleton. Grand Rapids: Kregel.

Macaskill, Grant. 2018. *The New Testament and Intellectual Humility*. Oxford: Oxford University Press.

McFarland, Ian. 2000. "A Canonical Reading of Ephesians 5:22–33: Theological Gleanings." *Theology Today* 57 (3): 344–56.

Middleton, J. Richard. 2014. *A New Heaven and a New Earth: Reclaiming Biblical Eschatology*. Grand Rapids: Baker Academic.

Pennington, Jonathan. 2017. *The Sermon on the Mount and Human Flourishing*. Grand Rapids: Baker Academic.

Rowe, C. Kavin. 2009. *Early Narrative Christology: The Lord in the Gospel of Luke*. Grand Rapids: Baker Academic.

Sanders, E. P. 1977. *Paul and Palestinian Judaism: A Comparison of Patterns of Religion*. Philadelphia: Fortress.

Seitz, Christopher. 2014. *Colossians*. Brazos Theological Commentary on the Bible. Grand Rapids: Brazos.

Talbert, Charles. 2007. *Ephesians and Colossians*. Paideia Commentary on the New Testament. Grand Rapids: Baker Academic.

Tanner, Kathryn. 2010. *Christ the Key*. Current Issues in Theology. Cambridge: Cambridge University Press.

Thielman, Frank. 2010. *Ephesians*. Baker Exegetical Commentary on the New Testament. Grand Rapids: Baker Academic.

Thiessen, Matthew. 2011. *Contesting Conversion: Genealogy, Circumcision, and Identity in Ancient Judaism and Christianity*. New York: Oxford University Press.

Thomas Aquinas. 1964–80. *Summa Theologiae*. Blackfriars edition. Edited by Thomas Gilby and T. C. O'Brien. New York: McGraw-Hill.

———. 1966. *Commentary on St. Paul's Epistle to the Ephesians*. Aquinas Scripture Commentaries 2. Translated by Matthew Lamb. Albany, NY: Magi.

Treier, Daniel J. 2011. *Proverbs and Ecclesiastes*. Brazos Theological Commentary on the Bible. Grand Rapids: Brazos.

Vanhoozer, Kevin J. 2010. *Remythologizing Theology: Divine Action, Passion, and Authorship*. Cambridge Studies in Christian Doctrine. Cambridge: Cambridge University Press.

Volf, Miroslav, and Matthew Croasmun. 2019. *For the Life of the World: Theology That Makes a Difference*. Grand Rapids: Brazos.

von Rad, Gerhard. 1966. "The Theological Problem of the Old Testament Doctrine of Creation." In *The Problem of the Hexateuch and Other Essays*, 131–43. New York: McGraw-Hill.

Wallis, Ian. 1995. *The Faith of Jesus Christ in Early Christian Traditions*. Cambridge: Cambridge University Press.

Webster, John. 2001. *Word and Church: Essays in Christian Dogmatics*. Edinburgh: T&T Clark.

———. 2003. *Holiness*. Grand Rapids: Eerdmans.

———. 2006. *Confessing God: Essays in Christian Dogmatics II*. London: T&T Clark.

———. 2007. "The Presence of Christ Exalted." Kantzer Lectures at the Henry Center for Theological Understanding, Trinity Evangelical Divinity School, Deerfield, Illinois, September 17, 2007, available at https://henrycenter.tiu.edu/resource/the-presence-of-christ-exalted.

———. 2011. *The Grace of Truth*. Edited by Daniel Jay Bush and Brannon Eugene Ellis. Farmington Hills, MI: Oil Lamp Books.

———. 2015a. *God without Measure: Working Papers in Christian Theology*. Vol. 1, *God and the Works of God*. London: Bloomsbury T&T Clark.

———. 2015b. *God without Measure: Working Papers in Christian Theology*. Vol. 2, *Virtue and Intellect*. London: Bloomsbury T&T Clark.

———. 2017. "'A Relation beyond All Relations': God and Creatures in Barth's Lectures on Ephesians, 1921–22." In Karl Barth, *The Epistle to the Ephesians*, edited by R. David Nelson, translated by Ross M. Wright, 31–49. Grand Rapids: Baker Academic.

Yeago, David. 1993. "Gnosticism, Antinomianism, and Reformation Theology: Reflections on the Costs of a Construal." *Pro Ecclesia* 2 (1): 37–49.

———. 1994. "The New Testament and the Nicene Dogma: A Contribution to the Recovery of Theological Exegesis." *Pro Ecclesia* 3 (2):152–64.

Ziegler, Geoffrey M. 2018. *Free to Be Sons of God*. Phillipsburg, NJ: P&R.

Ziegler, Philip. 2018. *Militant Grace: The Apocalyptic Turn and the Future of Christian Theology*. Grand Rapids: Baker Academic.

SCRIPTURE AND ANCIENT
WRITINGS INDEX

SUBJECT INDEX